JAPANESE PROVERBS AND SAYINGS

JAPANESE PROVERBS AND SAYINGS

Daniel Crump Buchanan

UNIVERSITY OF OKLAHOMA PRESS
NORMAN AND LONDON

BY DANIEL CRUMP BUCHANAN

Inari: Its Origin, Development and Nature (Tokyo, 1935)
Japanese Proverbs and Sayings (Norman, 1965)

TO THE MEMORY OF
MY MOTHER, MINNIE CRUMP BUCHANAN
AND
MY WIFE, KATHARINE BAETJER BUCHANAN
THIS BOOK IS AFFECTIONATELY AND GRATEFULLY
DEDICATED

LIBRARY OF CONGRESS CATALOG CARD NUMBER: 65–24192

ISBN: 0–8061–1082–1

PREFACE

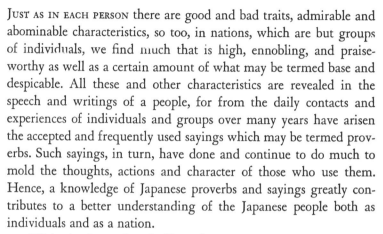

JUST AS IN EACH PERSON there are good and bad traits, admirable and abominable characteristics, so too, in nations, which are but groups of individuals, we find much that is high, ennobling, and praiseworthy as well as a certain amount of what may be termed base and despicable. All these and other characteristics are revealed in the speech and writings of a people, for from the daily contacts and experiences of individuals and groups over many years have arisen the accepted and frequently used sayings which may be termed proverbs. Such sayings, in turn, have done and continue to do much to mold the thoughts, actions and character of those who use them. Hence, a knowledge of Japanese proverbs and sayings greatly contributes to a better understanding of the Japanese people both as individuals and as a nation.

With the increasing facility of communication in the world, there is slowly emerging a better understanding of each other by peoples and nations. Greater borrowing and a wider exchange of ideas, techniques, and experiences is another result. There is gradually evolving—whether good or bad is beside the point—a world culture, a world attitude, and a world procedure.

However, in each nation there are certain pockets of resistance—customs, ideals, and practices which hold out against conformity. This is clearly seen in Japan. On the surface, Japan is in many respects a modern nation, little different from the United States and other advanced Western nations. Nevertheless, beneath these outward similarities the careful observer from abroad will find much that is different and strange. Each morning, for example, millions of Japanese will don Western clothes and spend the day in schools, factories, shops, offices, or other places of employment. On returning home after work, however, these garments are doffed and a relaxing hot bath taken, after which, attired in a comfortable, freshly washed *yukata* or a *kimono,* the evening meal with the family is enjoyed.

This may be followed by a radio or television program in which world events, some phase of ancient Japanese history, or a story of the heroic days of old is presented. Many of the old ways and customs still persist in the homes of the majority of the Japanese, often accompanied by modern technical conveniences and equipment. There is much that is attractive and beneficial in the old ways, which if completely abandoned, would be a great loss both to Japanese and to world culture, for to such culture all nations and especially the Japanese have much to contribute.

DANIEL C. BUCHANAN

Easton, Maryland

ACKNOWLEDGMENTS

I AM DEEPLY INDEBTED to Mr. Andrew Y. Kuroda, Orientalia Division of the Library of Congress, and to my sister Miss Elizabeth O. Buchanan for painstakingly reading the manuscript and making many valuable suggestions. To Mr. Wellington Brink, of Easton, Maryland, go my sincere thanks for his careful proofreading of the English parts of this volume. Errors inevitably will appear in any book, but the three above-named persons have greatly contributed to the removal of many inaccuracies in this study.

My special thanks go to Mr. Takeo Takamatsu, Publishing Department of the Japan Travel Bureau, for permission to use material contained in two small but popular books published by that organization: *Japanese Proverbs,* by Professor Oto-o Fujii, and *Japanese Proverbs and Proverbial Phrases,* by Mr. Rokuo Okada. I am grateful to Mr. Okada for his interesting explanation of the proverbs *"Moto no Mokuami," "Iza Kamakura to iu toki ni wa,"* and *"Ningen banji Saio no uma."* Mr. Masaji Ishihara, editor-in-chief of the Kairyudo Publishing Company, Ltd., has kindly given his consent to the use of certain material contained in *A Collection of Japanese Proverbs and Sayings,* a volume published by his company and compiled in 1940 by the late Professor Hitoshi Midzukami. Numerous Japanese friends, many of whom are no longer living, have earned my profound gratitude for early interesting me in the proverbs of their country, so many of which illustrate the character and personality traits of a great people.

DANIEL C. BUCHANAN

CONTENTS

Japanese Characteristics

PRONUNCIATION OF JAPANESE

a   like *a* in *father*, but slightly shorter.
e   like *e* in *end*.
i   as in *machine*, but a little shorter.
o   as in *more*.
u   as in *put*.

Long marks over the vowels indicate the extension of the sound. Consonants are pronounced as in English, except *r* which has a slight *d* sound before it. Each consonant is pronounced separately but rapidly, even when they come together. Combinations of vowels are also pronounced separately. Accentuation is so hard to distinguish that the beginner in Japanese should endeavor to give the same emphasis to each syllable.

INTRODUCTION

●

THAT THE PROVERBS AND SAYINGS of a people truly reveal their national character and personality traits is so generally acknowledged that it is almost axiomatic. The English philosopher Sir Francis Bacon observed nearly four hundred years ago that "the genius, wit and spirit of a nation are discovered in its proverbs." At about the same time the Spanish writer Miguel de Cervantes remarked that "proverbs are short sentences drawn from long experiences." One hundred years later the English Quaker William Penn commented: "The wisdom of nations lies in their proverbs, which are brief and pithy." Benjamin Disraeli, one of the keenest minds of the nineteenth century, stated that "proverbs were anterior to books and formed the wisdom of the vulgar, and in the earliest ages were the unwritten laws of morality." The foregoing as well as many other excellent authorities agree that the ancient wisdom of a people and the cream of a nation's thought are often found in their proverbs. Such being the case, to study and understand Japanese proverbs is, in the opinion of the writer, an excellent way to appreciate and evaluate the character and personality of the people who produced them.

The Japanese themselves even to this day make wide use of their proverbs and pithy sayings. These proverbs are not regarded as so many trite or hackneyed expressions but are frequently quoted by writers and speakers, as well as by the man on the street, to illustrate a point or clinch an argument. An educational card game that children in Japan love to play is based on the *iroha* syllabary with two sets of forty-eight cards each. In the first set each card has a letter or syllable of the Japanese alphabet which forms the beginning of a well-known proverb, and a picture to illustrate it. Each card of the second set has the corresponding proverb in full. The proverbs are then read aloud, and the one who can identify and pick up the greatest number of picture cards is declared the winner.

While the origin of many proverbs is known, the sources of quite a few are lost in antiquity. Most of the proverbs quoted in this book are indigenous, but many are of Chinese origin and show the influence of Confucian ethics and Buddhist teachings. In addition, with the opening of Japan to the West, quite a few English proverbs and some from other European languages were translated into Japanese and adopted by the people. There are also numerous Japanese and English proverbs that are similar in meaning, but with no evidence of borrowing on the part of either. In this book English parallels to Japanese proverbs are often given where the meaning of the latter would be clarified. Space and printing limitations have precluded setting forth the proverbs in Japanese and Chinese type, though to do so would greatly increase the value of this volume as a book of reference, and be most useful to the serious student of the Japanese language. For the general public, however, the printing of the Japanese proverbs in Latin letters is sufficient to give some idea of their pronunciation.

A number of interesting and readable books have been published in English on Japanese proverbs. As far back as 1928 there appeared a booklet, *Popular Proverbs of Nippon,* by Mr. Aisaburo Akiyama. Seven years later the same author enlarged and revised his work and published in 1935, under the aegis of the Japan Welcome Society of Kyoto, his very readable *Japanese Proverbs and Proverbial Phrases.* In 1940 the Board of Tourist Industry of Japanese Government Railways published a small but well-prepared booklet, *Japanese Proverbs,* by Professor Oto-o Fujii. That same year Professor Hitoshi Midzukami published *A Collection of Japanese Proverbs and Sayings,* in which 1,259 such maxims are given in Japanese and English, and where possible parallel English proverbs are put down. A profusely illustrated and charmingly written book, *Japanese Proverbs,* by Mr. Rokuo Okada first appeared in 1955. Published by the Japan Travel Bureau, it aims to explain Japanese psychology to Western people. Kenkyyusha's *New Japanese-English Dictionary* is a veritable mine of information, in which many well-known Japanese proverbs are quoted and translated into English. Helpful as all these books are to those who seek the appreciation and understanding of Japanese proverbs, the best sources and most complete collections are to be had in various Japanese language publications.

Both *Rigen Dai Jiten* (*Great Dictionary of Proverbs*), compiled by Richihei Nakano and published by the Tōhō Shōin in 1933, and *Gengo Dai Jiten* (*Great Dictionary of Words*), compiled by Professor Oto-o Fujii, the 3rd edition being published in 1954 by *Yūhōdō*, are excellent and comprehensive sources. The spoken language of the people is one of the richest sources; and the long-time Western resident of Japan with a good knowledge of the vernacular can soon gather many proverbs from daily conversation, the theater, public addresses, and radio and television programs.

No claim is made for this study as a definitive description of Japanese character. Many of the characteristics given are not applicable to some Japanese, and certainly not to thousands of *Nisei* who are just as American as countless others who trace their ancestry back to the Pilgrim Fathers or to the first settlers of Virginia. In no sense does this study present a complete list of Japanese proverbs. Of the more than 30,000 extant, some 2,500 proverbs and idiomatic sayings have been selected as illustrative of how many Japanese think and act. No nation or civilization is perfect. Japanese psychology and culture have their shortcomings as well as many excellent characteristics. These are presented in this book in alphabetical sequence. The reader will notice that many of the characteristics and proverbs discussed are common to other peoples. This is to be expected, and is a great help to mutual understanding throughout the world, for as the Japanese proverb has it: *"Ninjō ni kokkyō nashi,"* "There are no barriers to human nature." Parts of thirty years have been spent in gathering material for this study, which is herewith presented in the hope that it will contribute to a better understanding of the Japanese people.

JAPANESE PROVERBS AND SAYINGS

JAPANESE CHARACTERISTICS

●

AESTHETICS

THOUGH WILLIAM CULLEN BRYANT did not have the Japanese in mind when he wrote the opening lines of "Thanatopsis," his description of the lover of nature well applies to them:

> *To him who in the love of Nature holds*
> *Communion with her visible forms, she speaks*
> *A various language.*

A strong aesthetic sense coupled with a deep love of nature is an outstanding trait of the Japanese people. Born and reared in one of the most beautiful of all countries, the Japanese have a sensitive awareness of nature and a marked ability to respond to natural beauty. This characteristic is well expressed in their architecture, gardening, painting, poetry, drama, and various other cultural media. It has been aptly said that the Japanese are artistic to their finger tips; and this aesthetic, nature-observant trait is clearly shown in their proverbs and sayings.

GENERAL:

Kuni horobite sanka ari: "A country may go to ruin but its mountains and streams remain." Probably taken from an ancient Chinese saying which points out that, though the land may be wasted by an unwise ruler, beautiful scenery is still present.

Tsukiyo ni kome no meshi: "Moonlight and boiled rice." That is, one never tires of eating even a simple meal of boiled rice by the light of the moon.

Umi no mono tomo yama (kawa) no mono tomo tsukanu: "It belongs neither to the sea nor to the mountain (river)," i.e., the true nature of the thing is uncertain. English parallel: Neither fish, flesh, nor fowl.

3

ANIMALS AND BIRDS:

Aki takaku uma koyu: "Autumn high, horses fatten." Taken from the writings of the Chinese poet Tu Shen-yen; this proverb is a favorite of the Japanese, who are fond of the autumn, when the sky is clear and high and the farmer's faithful workhorse becomes fat.

Ashimoto kara tori ga tatsu yō: "As though a bird had flown up from under your feet." An expression for an unexpected affair that suddenly takes place. It is often used of any abrupt occurrence.

Fukuro no me wa ōkiku temo nezumi hodo mienu: "Although the owl has large eyes he can't see as well as a mouse." Size does not necessarily denote efficiency.

Tori no naku ne wa izuku mo onaji: "The tone of the bird's song is the same everywhere." Wherever you may be nature can be enjoyed.

Tsuru wa sennen, kame wa mannen: "The crane for a thousand years, the turtle for ten thousand years." This expression gives weight to the common belief in the longevity of these animals.

U no me, taka no me: "The cormorant's eyes, the hawk's eyes." The cormorant is watchful for things in the water, the hawk for things on land and in the air. Hence, the above proverb means to be extremely sharp-eyed, vigilant, and watchful.

Uo to mizu: "Fish and water." A figurative expression to indicate two close friends who constantly help each other. English parallel: To be hand in glove with.

FLOWERS AND TREES:

Azami no hana mo hito-sakari: "Thistle blossoms last but a moment." Though a noxious weed, even the beautiful and fragile thistle flower has its place in the scheme of nature. In time everything has some use. English parallels: Every dog has its day; everything has its time.

Banryokusō-chū kō itten: "A red spot amidst the green grass." (Lit., "Within ten thousand greens, one red spot.") An expression to indicate the only lady in a gathering of gentlemen. English parallels: A rose among thorns. A flower among vegetables.

Hana no atari ni miyama gi: "The intimacy of tree-covered

mountains in the vicinity of blossoming (cherry) trees." The saying is frequently used to describe a scene of great beauty and peace.

Hana wa oritashi, kozue wa takashi: "I would like to break off the flower, but the branch is too high." Often quoted when a man is in love with a high-born lady who is indifferent to his passion.

Hana wa sakari, tsuki wa kumo naki wo nomi miru mono kawa?: "Why only when flowers at their best and the moon at its fullest should they be seen?" Taken from the essays of Kenkō, a literary Buddhist priest, this proverb well expresses the true attitude of Japanese towards art, i.e., true beauty is not to be found in perfection or completion, but just *before* things are perfect or complete.

Hana wo mite eda wo oru: "Look at the flowers and then break off a branch." Observe them well in their natural surroundings, and then make sure that they are worth taking.

Hana wo motaseru: "To cause others to hold the flowers"; because they think they are deserving and their pride is not wounded. The above is said of any thoughtful and polite deed.

Hitome sembon: "One look, a thousand trees!" An expression used to describe places noted for plum or cherry blossoms.

Sakura wa hana no araware nikeri: "The cherry tree is known among others by its flowers." This statement well describes the pre-eminence given by the Japanese to cherry blossoms. It is also used metaphorically to describe a person who stands out among his fellows.

Tōki wa hana no ka: "At a distance enjoy the fragrance of flowers," i.e., don't become too intimate with a worthwhile person. English parallel: Familiarity breeds contempt.

Tsuki ni murakumo hana ni kaze: "As clouds to the moon and winds to the blossoms." Just as clouds and winds change the aspect of things, so prosperity does not last long. Nothing is certain in this world, for even the fairest aspects of nature will some day have their beauty removed. English parallel: Change of fortune is the lot of life.

Ume wa hyakka no sakigake: "The plum is the pioneer of a hundred flowers"; so said because its blossoms open earlier than all other plants and trees, often blooming when snow is still on the ground, thus the Japanese speak of it as "a brave flower."

Yahari no ni oke renge-sō: "Better leave the Chinese milk-vetch where they are in the field." It is sometimes advisable to leave wild flowers and fair girls in their natural surroundings, where they will look to better advantage than at any other place.

Yanagi wa midori, hana wa kurenai: "Willows when green, flowers when red," i.e., beauty and truth are best seen in the state of nature.

Yo no naka wa mikka minu ma no sakura: "Three days not having looked at the world, and lo it is full of cherry blossoms!" Another much-quoted spring proverb that well expresses the great love for nature the Japanese have.

SEASONS AND WEATHER:

Asa kumoreba yū ni hareru: "If cloudy in the morning it clears in the evening." Based on actual weather observation in Japan, this saying may also be interpreted metaphorically. English parallel: Cloudy mornings turn to fair evenings.

Atsui samui mo higan made: "Summer heat or winter cold is only until the equinox." Hence, there is no need to complain about extremes in temperature, for mild weather will come sooner or later. The vernal equinox (March 21) generally marks the end of cold winter winds in Japan; the autumnal equinox (September 23), the end of hot, sultry days.

Ichi-yō ochite tenka no aki wo shiru: "With the fall of one leaf we know that autumn has come to the world." So a single sign is sufficient to foretell the approaching fate of a prosperous man or nation. English parallel: A straw shows which way the wind blows.

Jō hachigatsu ni jō tsukiyo: "Regular August and regular moon-light nights," i.e., ideal weather for the ripening of crops.

Kambatsu ni kikin nashi: "Drought brings no famine." English parallel: Drought brings no dearth.

Undei no sa: "The difference between clouds and mud," i.e., all the difference in the world.

Tsuki to suppon no sa (chigai): "As different as the moon is from the snapping turtle." This expression, too, is commonly used to indicate a very great difference. English parallel: As different as chalk from cheese.

Yoagari no tenki wa nagamochi senu: "The weather that clears up at night never holds long." This is a meteorological fact. So also an evil man who reforms because of hard times or other vicissitudes often does not continue his moral life when prosperity again comes.

FREQUENTLY PAIRED IN ORIENTAL ART AND LITERATURE:

Kōyō ni shika: "The deer in autumnal foliage."

Sasa ni suzume: "The sparrow in the bamboo grass." Notice the alliteration in the Japanese original, and in some of the succeeding expressions.

Shakuyaku ni shishi: "The lion in the peonies."

Takeyabu ni tora: "The tiger in the bamboo-thicket."

Ume ni uguisu: "The nightingale in the plum tree."

Yanagi ni tsubame: "The swallow in the willow."

Uguisu no ume wo mitsuketa yō: "Like the nightingale that has found a plum tree." Since the nightingale generally comes to the plum tree to sing, the two have a literary association. Hence the above proverb is used to describe the condition of a man who has been placed in a suitable and comfortable position.

AMBITION

As a PEOPLE the Japanese are eager to advance their position and excel in all they do. Their strong desire for advancement and for recognition has led them to borrow from other peoples what they felt was superior to their own, though often improving on the original. In cultural matters they are stubbornly conservative and do not easily give up the old. Their desire to surpass others in all things has led them to become the foremost nation in Asia, and one of the most advanced in the world. Their ambition is clearly indicated in the proverbs which follow.

Ai yori idete ai yori mo koshi: "Coming from the indigo plant but a deeper color than the indigo plant." This proverb, borrowed from ancient China, is similar in meaning to the next one.

Kōri wa mizu yori idete mizu yori tsumetashi: "Ice coming from water is colder than water." The above two sayings apply to a person who surpasses his parent, master, or teacher in skill in any profession or trade.

Donshū-no-uo wa sairyū ni sumazu: "Boat-swallowing-fish do not live in brooks." Cramped circumstances do not produce great men.

Taigyo wa shōchi ni sumazu: "Large fish do not live in a small pond." Men who aspire for great advancement in the future will not content themselves with nor long remain in inferior positions. English parallel: A great ship must have deep water.

Gan ga tobeba ishigame mo jidanda: "When wild geese soar overhead even terrapins stamp their feet on the ground." Everyone wishes to fly high. The success of some who have high ideals and talents inspire those of more lowly traits.

Gyūji wo toru: "To take the lead." (Lit., "To hold the bull's ear.") In ancient China princes of different areas would meet and make a peace pact by sucking the blood from the ear of a bull which the butcher had previously cut and held for the purpose. Thus by transference of meaning, the expression "to hold the bull's ear" came to denote "to become a covenanting prince," hence "to take the lead" in any undertaking.

Hashiru uma ni mo muchi: "A whip even to a galloping horse." Even an industrious person may need an incentive.

Hyaku hatsu hyaku chū: "Complete success." (Lit., "One hundred shots, one hundred hits.") English parallel: Every shot hits the mark.

Iwashi no atama to naru yori tai no shippo to nare: "Rather than the head of a sardine, be the tail of a sea bream." Better be the tail of something worthwhile than the head of something worthless. English parallel: Choose rather to be the tail of lions than the head of foxes.

Ushi no shiri yori niwatori no atama: "Better be a chicken's head than an ox's rump." This proverb is antithetical to the one above.

Inu ni naru nara ōdokoro no inu ni nare: "If you become a dog, turn into a dog of a wealthy family," i.e., be careful to choose and serve a rich master, thus assuring your happiness and success.

Tachiyora-ba taiboku no kage: "If you stop at a place, get in the shade of a big tree," i.e., if you cannot live independently, attach yourself to a successful man or house. English parallel: It is good sheltering under an old hedge.

Kōryō kui ari: "Too great ambition brings failure." (Lit., "A high-crawling dragon repents.") English parallels: Pride goeth before a fall. He that climbs high falls heavily.

Kuchi mo hatchō te mo hatchō, or *Te-hatchō kuchi-hatchō:* "A person of great eloquence and dexterity." (Lit., "His mouth and hands go eight *chō.*") A *chō* is a Japanese unit of length of about 120 yards; thus 8 *chō* is about 960 yards or approximately three-fourths of a mile. This proverb gives force and meaning to the long distance to which a man's eloquence and talents may reach.

Sakinzureba hito mo seisu: "Take the initiative and you will win." (Lit., "The person who goes ahead controls others.") English parallel: First come, first served.

Sanshō wa kotsubu demo hiriri-to karai: "Even a small grain of Japanese pepper is hot," i.e., a clever and ambitious man even though little has a strong personality which will influence those who come in contact with him.

Suki koso mono no jōzu nare: "The very thing one likes, one does well." This is similar in meaning to the final advice of an American university president to a graduating class: "Young men, the secret of success is to fall in love with your job." English parallel: Fondness gives skill.

Tama migakasareba hikari nashi: "Potential abilities must be developed." (Lit., "A jewel unless polished will not sparkle.") A man if untaught cannot become useful no matter what latent abilities he may have. English parallel: A diamond in the rough.

Tombi ga taka wo umu: "A kite begets a hawk." This expression is used half admiringly and half derisively when a plain woman gives birth to a handsome child, or when the son of a man in an inferior position attains superior rank. English parallel: A black hen lays a white egg.

Tomu ie ni yase inu nashi: "In a wealthy man's house there is no lean dog." English parallel: Like master, like servant.

Tsuki hi ni sekimori nashi: "Time flies." (Lit., "For months and days there is no barrier-keeper.") Since there is nothing to hold back the passage of time, make the best use of it. During the military dictatorship of the Tokugawa family in the seventeenth and eighteenth centuries, barriers were maintained at strategic points on the principal traffic routes throughout the country, where a close check was kept on the goings and comings of all travelers. The scrutiny of passports, persons, and baggage by the barrier-keeper often caused considerable delay. English parallel: Time and tide wait for no man.

Waga mono to omoeba karushi kasa no yuki: "When considered as my own, lightly weighs the snow of my bamboo-hat."

Waga yuki to omoeba karushi kasa no ue: "When I remember it as my snow, how light it is on my sedge hat." The above two proverbs are well-known *haiku* (seventeen-syllable poems). Note that the English translation of each is also in seventeen syllables. *Kasa* is a broad-brimmed umbrella-like hat made of bamboo or sedge grass. Pronounced the same but written with a different Chinese ideograph, *kasa* is also an umbrella. English parallel: A voluntary burden is no burden.

AMOROUSNESS

As a people the Japanese are quite amorous, though often much effort is made to conceal this. Here are some proverbs which indicate that they are not lacking in tender feelings between the two sexes.

Abata mo ekubo: "Even pockmarks look like dimples." This is an abbreviation of the following proverb:

Horeta yoku-me ni ya abata mo ekubo: "To the partial eyes of a lover, pockmarks seem like dimples," i.e., in the eyes of lovers even an ugly feature is beautiful. English parallels: Love is blind; Love sees no faults.

Koi wa shian no hoka: "Love is beyond reflection (consideration.)" In other words, love and reason do not go together. The Japanese word used here is *"koi,"* love between the sexes. It is physical love or desire, the Greek "eros." *"Ai"* is the general Japanese word for love, attachment or affection. English parallel: Love is blind.

Ai okujō no karasu ni oyobu: "Love extends even to the crow on the roof." A person in love will love even such an unlovely thing as a crow on the roof of the beloved's house. English parallels: Love me, love my dog. He who loves Bertrand loves his dog.

Ai wa kyūden ni mo waraya ni mo sumu: "Love lives in palaces as well as in thatched cottages." Love makes no class distinctions.

Ai-ai kasa no nure tsubame: "Two lovers walking in the rain under the same umbrella." (Lit., "Two wet swallows under one umbrella.")

Aibetsu-riku wa yo-no-narai: "The grief of parting and the agony of separation is the way of the world." Because of social customs and practices in pre-World War II Japan, and to a certain extent today, lovers were often separated and prevented from marrying each other.

Aki no shika wa fue ni yoru: "Deer of autumn come at the blowing of a flute." Autumn is the mating time, and male deer of that season are often compared to love-sick men and taken as themes of poetry.

Akujo no fukanasake: "An ugly woman's persistent attentions." These are generally disliked by men. Hence, when an ill-favored woman becomes intimate with a man, she is deeply in love with him.

Atama hagete mo uwaki wa yamanu: "Though bald he does not stop his wanton ways." This is said of a man who though unattractive and old is still interested in amours. English parallel: The wolf loses his teeth but not his inclination.

Atsui koi wa same-yasui: "Hot passion cools easily." English parallel: Hot love is soon cool.

Awaneba itoshisa iya masaru: "Not to meet makes one's loving grow stronger (Lit., 'exceed by far')." English parallel: Absence makes the heart grow fonder.

Bikachō or *Hana no shita wa nagai:* "An easy prey to women." (Lit., "Long under the nose.") This expression is said of:
(1) a man who is infatuated with women (*Onna ni noroi otoko*)
(2) an uxorious husband (*Nyōbō ni noroi otto*)
(3) a hen-pecked husband (*Nihombō no otto*).

Danjo shichisai no shite seki wo onajū sezu: "Boys and girls from the time they are seven years old should not sit together." This Confucian proverb teaches that it is unwise for the sexes to be closely associated even early in life. It was often quoted as an argument against coeducation.

Fumi wa yaritashi, kaku-te wa motazu: "Desiring to send a letter but having no writing hand." This saying describes a person who is in love but has not learned to write well enough to communicate with the loved one.

Horeta yamai ni kusuri nashi: "For love-sickness there is no medicine." English parallel: No herb will cure love.

Koi no yamai ni kusuri nashi: "There is no medicine for sexual passion." The only remedy is marriage.

Horete kayoeba senri mo ichiri: "To a lover going to and fro, a thousand *ri* is but one." A *ri,* the Japanese unit of distance, is a little less than two and one-half miles. English parallels: Baghdad is not remote to a lover. He that hath love in his breast hath spurs at his heels.

Iba-shin-en: "The horse's feelings and the monkey's heart." An expression for uncontrollable fleshy desires. It is often applied to a person who is frantically in love.

Ichi oshi, ni kane, san sugata: "First authority (influence), second money, third a good figure." To win a woman's heart a suitor must be bold, next have money, and finally a good appearance. English parallel: Faint heart never won fair lady.

Ichiren-takushō: "Sinking together." (Lit., "One open lotus, grasp life.") A Buddhist expression with the meaning "to die together," for in the Buddhist paradise (*Gokuraku*) the characteristic flower is the lotus. To sit together on one lotus in paradise is a lover's dream. With this end in view frustrated lovers will often commit double suicide.

Iro to yoku to no futasuji michi: "The two roads of passion and avarice." The man or woman who plans to marry his or her sweetheart from passion, or from the baser motive of getting possession of the other's fortune, is described as using the two roads of passion and money.

Iro wo omō mo moto wa yoku: "Even in thinking of sexual desire the origin is avarice."

Iroke yori kuike: "Eating is preferable to amorousness." This proverb indicates that there are some who prefer eating to sexual activity. English parallel: Without bread and wine even love will pine.

Iso no awabi: "An abalone on the beach." Since the abalone is a univalve mollusk it is taken as a symbol of "one-sidedness." Thus the above proverb denotes an unrequited love.

Keisei ni makoto nashi: "A harlot has no faithfulness." This maxim warns men of such women.

Koi ni dōhan wa jama: "In sexual love company is a nuisance." Another person is a hindrance when two persons wish to engage in love play. English parallels: Two is company, three's a crowd. Love likes no fellowship.

Koi ni jōge no hedate nashi: "In sexual love there are no distinctions between high and low." English parallel: Love lives in a cottage as well as at court.

Koi no shigoku wa shinobugoi: "The extreme form of passionate love is secret love," i.e., a clandestine love affair is most enjoyable. English parallel: Stolen sweets are best.

Koi sureba don suru: "When passionately in love, one becomes stupid," i.e., a person engaged in sexual love-making is less apt to use his reason.

Koi to ikusa wa shudan wo erabazu: "In sexual love and war means are not selected." English parallel: All is fair in love and war.

Koi to seki to wa kakusarenu: "Passionate love and a cough cannot be concealed."

Koi wa hyakka no moto: "Passionate love is the origin of a hundred fruits." These are sometimes good and sometimes evil.

Mejiri no sagatta mono wa tain: "A person with eyes inclining downward at the outer corners is very lewd." This is a well-known saying based on physiognomy. *Mejiri wo sageru:* lit., "to turn down the outer corners of the eyes" is the Japanese idiomatic expression corresponding to the English "to make eyes at" or "to give an amorous glance at" a person.

Mei-mei no Yōki-hi: "Each has his Yang Chi." Every man thinks that in his wife or sweetheart he has a woman as beautiful as Yang Chi, the lovely princess of ancient China.

Nakute zo hito wa koishigari-keru: "When no more the person is longed after." The word *"koishigari"* translated "long for" or "yearn after" has as its base the word *koi,* which as has been explained previously is love between the sexes—the Greek "eros."

Oni mo jūhachi, bancha mo debana: "As even an ogress at eighteen is desirable, so coarse tea at its first infusion is delicious." English parallel: Everything is good in its season.

Oni mo jūhachi, ja mo hatachi: "Even an ogress at eighteen and a serpent at twenty." Women are thought fairest at eighteen or twenty. English parallel: Sweet seventeen!

Rinki wa koi no inochi: "Jealousy is the life of sexual love."

Saya ate: "Scabbard against scabbard." In the feudal period when a man's scabbard touched another's a duel was often fought. Hence, "scabbard against scabbard" came to mean antagonism or rivalry in love affairs.

Sode ni suru: "To jilt, to give a cold shoulder to a person." (Lit., "to do the sleeve.")

Sode wo hiku: "To woo." (Lit., "to pull or pluck the sleeves.")

Ta mo yarō aze mo yarō: "I'll give away rice fields and footpaths." Said by a man who, infatuated with a woman, will give everything to get her.

Tōkute chikai wa danjo (nannyo) no naka: "Far but near are relations between man and woman." The Japanese observe that when a man and a woman are thrown together alone, they first assume indifference, but all too soon get into familiarity.

Ukiyo wa iro to saké: "This fleeting world is but sexual passion and wine." English parallel: Who loves not woman, wine, and song remains a fool his whole life long.

Uta wa danjo no naka wo yawaragu: "Poetry softens the relationship between men and women." In the pre-modern Japan, courtship among the upper classes was largely in the form of delicately couched love poems.

Yake-bokkui ni hi ga tsuki-yasui: "A charred stake easily takes fire," i.e., lovers who have been separated by agreement or by force may easily renew their connection. English parallel: Old pottage is sooner heated than made new.

Yoi naka no isakai: "Little quarrels between lovers." In Japan, as in any other country of the world, lovers are apt to quarrel over little matters.

AWARENESS OF DIFFICULTY

PERSONAL AND NATIONAL CHARACTERISTICS are often revealed in the things that are held to be rare, difficult, or impossible. That the Japanese are well aware of such is indicated in the proverbs which follow.

Akegata no hoshi: "A star at peep of dawn."

Amayo no hoshi: "Stars on a rainy night." The above two sayings are metaphors for things that rarely happen.

Ari no ikari wo hiku yō: "Like an ant dragging an anchor." Said of a person who attempts more than he is capable of doing.

Haita tsuba wo nomikomenu: "Expectorated spittle cannot again be swallowed." English parallel: What is done cannot be undone.

Hasuito de ō-ishi wo tsuru: "To do the impossible." (Lit., "To hang a large stone from a lotus thread.") English parallel: To sweep the sea with a broom.

Hatake kara hamaguri torenu: "Clams cannot be taken in a field." English parallel: To draw blood out of a stone.

Hebi wo takezutsu ni irete mo massugu ni naranu: "A snake though placed in a bamboo tube, cannot become perfectly straight." So a man who is morally crooked cannot be reformed by discipline.

Hi ga nishi kara dete higashi ni iru toki: "When the sun rises in the west and sets in the east." This saying is used to denote something that is impossible or absurd.

Ten ga chi ni naru toki: "When heaven becomes earth." A proverb, similar in meaning to the above one.

Hyōtan namazu: "Gourd catfish," a contraction of *Hyōtan de namazu wo osaeru:* "To pin down a catfish with a gourd." This example of Edo wit states how impossible it is to pin down a non-committal statement, or catch an oily person. English parallel: As slippery as an eel.

Ichido ni ryōji wa dekinu: "Two things cannot be done at one time." English parallel: You can't run and sit at the same time.

Nisoku no waraji wa hakenu: "One cannot wear two pairs of

straw sandals at the same time," i.e., One cannot attend to two things simultaneously. English parallel: A man cannot both ring the bell (in the church) and walk in the (funeral) procession.

Ippatsu senkin wo hiku ga gotoshi: "As if pulling a thousand pounds by a single hair," i.e., to be suspended precariously like the sword of Damocles.

Irimame ni hana: "Flowers from parched peas," i.e., something that very rarely happens.

Ishi ni hana saku: "Flowers bloom from a stone." English parallel: Grapes on thorns and figs on thistles.

Ishi ga nagarete konoha ga shizumu: "The stone floats off and the tree leaf sinks," i.e., something that is entirely unnatural and unexpected.

Ishi kara wata wo toru yō: "Like getting cotton from a stone." Another metaphor for something that is impossible. It is interesting to note here that the Japanese word for asbestos, a mineral, is *ishiwata* or *sekimen.* Both words are written with the Chinese ideographs for "stone" and "cotton." English parallel: No man can flay a stone.

Kareki ni hana no saita yō: "As though a withered tree had burst forth into bloom." English parallel: Planting pebbles and getting potatoes.

Kago de mizu wo kumu yō: "Like dipping up water with a basket."

Kaigara de umi wo hakaru: "To measure the volume of the sea with a shell."

Kaigara de umi wo hosu: "To drain away the sea with a shell." English parallels: To empty the ocean with a sieve. To wipe up the sea with a sponge.

Ki ni take wo tsugu: "To graft a bamboo to a tree." To do something that is both useless and unharmonious. English parallel: To sew a fox's skin to a lion's.

Ki ni yotte uo wo motomeru ga gotoshi: "Like approaching a tree and looking for fish." This expression, from the Chinese classics, indicates something that is hopeless and impossible.

Kumo ni kake-hashi: "To lean a ladder against the clouds." An impractical enterprise is thus described. English parallel: He is building a bridge over the sea.

Kumo wo tsukamu yō na hanashi: "Talking as though he would grasp the clouds." An absurd or wild story is thus described. English parallel: A cock-and-bull story.

Minasoko no hari wo sagasu: "To search for a needle at the bottom of the water." English parallel: To look for a needle in a haystack.

Mizu no ue ni kazu kaku: "To write a number on water." A figure of speech for a useless thing to do. On the grave of the poet John Keats is the epitaph: "Here lies one whose name is writ on water . . ."

Nito wo ou mono wa itto wo mo ezu: "He who chases two hares will not catch even one." This indicates that it is impossible to face two ways at the same time, and is the Japanese version of the English proverb: He who pursues two hares will catch neither. Another English parallel: A donkey between two haystacks starves.

Ryūsha ni mukō tōrō no gotoshi: "Like a mantis turning upon the Imperial carriage." This saying is applied to a person who tries to fight or attack an enemy of far superior strength who will be sure to overpower him. English parallel: The fly trying to bite the tortoise.

Tōrō no ono wo motte ryūsha ni mukō gotoshi: "Like the mantis with an ax attacking an Imperial chariot." This is another version of the above proverb.

Sajō ni rōkaku wo chiku: "To built a castle on sand." Like the English parallel, "To build a house on sand," the proverb indicates a foolish and useless undertaking.

Sakana ni ki nobori: "Fish climbing trees," i.e., something that is absurd or impossible is thus described.

Senaka ni me nashi: "In the back there are no eyes." Indicating the absurdity of trying to observe everything and especially what is behind.

Shakushi wa mimi-kaki no kawari ni naranu: "A dipper can't be used for an ear-pick." A larger object, though similar in form, does not serve the purpose of a smaller one.

Shijimi-kai de idogae wo suru yō: "Like well-cleaning with a corbicula." Since the corbicula is a very small shell, the above proverb describes an almost impossible undertaking.

Taizan wo wakibasande Hokkai wo koyu: "To pass over the North Sea with a large mountain under one's arm." This figure is used to characterize an impossibility.

Takane no hana: "A flower on an inaccessible height," i.e., something beyond one's ability to gain, an unattainable prize. English parallel: Wishing for the moon.

Tare ka karasu no shi-yū wo shiran?: "Who can tell the sex of a crow?" This expression, borrowed from ancient Chinese literature, is used when it is impossible to say which of two villains is more wicked.

Umoregi ni hana ga saku: "Fossil wood (lignite) will sometimes bear flowers," i.e., people who are living in oblivion will sometimes produce something worthwhile. Though an almost impossible contingency, it is considered very auspicious.

Unagi ni nigura: "A packsaddle on an eel." This expression which indicates something difficult to fasten, is used to describe the equivocal and ambiguous manner of speaking some men have.

BODY CONSCIOUSNESS

THE JAPANESE, who are very conscious of the body and all of its functions, have many proverbs and idiomatic sayings dealing with various parts of the human physique. A very clean people, who bathe more often than other races, they see nothing shocking in nudity when occasions warrant it. The undraped human form is often seen but not observed at hot-springs resorts, rural areas, and public bathhouses. The washing of parts of the body, especially the mouth and hands, at lavers provided with running water, are preliminary procedures for entry into shrines, temples, and similar sacred enclosures. Ideas of purity, however, are largely external and ritualistic, for frequently next to famous shrines and popular temples will be found *geisha* quarters, prostitute districts, and other houses of assignation. The following are some of the more widely used idioms and proverbial sayings that deal with parts of the body.

Asнı (Feet):
Namben mo ashi wo hakobu: "To visit a person repeatedly." (Lit., "To transport one's feet many times.")
Ashi ni kizu: "To have a guilty conscience." (Lit., "To have a foot wound.")
Ashi wo dasu: "To reveal a secret." (Lit., "To put forth the feet.") English parallel: To let the cat out of the bag.
Ashi wo arau: "To go straight; become decent." (Lit., "To wash the feet.")
Ageashi wo toru: "To catch a person on the slip of his tongue." (Lit., "To catch another's raised leg.") This wrestling term means to take advantage of the weak points in your opponent's argument; to trip him up.

ATAMA (Head):
Atama wo motageru: "To rise into prominence." (Lit., "To lift up the head.")
Atama wo osaeru: "To keep in restraint." (Lit., "To press down the head.") English parallel: To keep under one's thumb.
Atama wo haneru: "To take money on the side." (Lit., "To reject the head.") English parallel: To take a squeeze.
Atama wo karu: "To cut the hair of the head." (Lit., "To clip the head.")
Atama ni oku: "To take under consideration." (Lit., "To place into the head.")
Atama-kabu: "A chief, leader, or executive." (Lit., "The head stump.")
Atama kazu: "The number of persons." (Lit., "The number of heads.")
Atama wari: "Sharing expenses." (Lit., "Head allotment.")
Atama no kyūyō me no shōgatsu: "Very interesting." (Lit., "Recreation for the head, New Year's feast for the eyes.")
Mazu waga atama no hai wo harae: "Mind your own business." This rude expression translated literally is: "First drive off the flies from your own head."

CHI (Blood):

Chi wo waketa naka ni kagiru: "Blood is thicker than water." (Lit., "Blood-shared relationships are the best.")

Chi no deru yō na kane: "Money raised by desperate means." (Lit., "Blood-coming-out money.")

Chi mo namida mo nai: "Cold blooded; inconsiderate." (Lit., "Having neither blood nor tears.")

Chi ari namida aru: "Sympathetic; considerate." (Lit., "Having blood and tears.")

Chi no meguri ga warui: "Dull, slow-witted." (Lit., "The blood circulates badly.")

HA (Tooth):

Ha ga kiku: "To be of use." (Lit., "The teeth take effect.")

Ha ga tatsu: "To be able to do; to cause to understand." (Lit., "The teeth stand.")

Ha ni awanai: "To be unsuitable." (Lit., "Does not match the teeth.")

Hagayui: "Irritated; impatient." (Lit., "Itching teeth.")

Ha wo muku: "To become angry." (Lit., "To bare the teeth.")

Ha wo narasu: "To be angry; be sorry." (Lit., "To clash the teeth.")

Ha wo misenai: "To remain serious." (Lit., "Not to show the teeth.")

Shiroi ha wo miseru: "To smile; be complaisant." (Lit., "To show white teeth.")

Ha-gotae ga suru: "It is tough; there is opposition." (Lit., "There is opposition to the teeth.")

Ha ga tatanu: "Beyond my power." (Lit., "The teeth will not stand up to it.")

Ha ni kinu kisenai: "To speak frankly." (Lit., "Not to clothe the teeth with silk.")

HANA (Nose; Self):

Hana ga takai: "To be proud." (Lit., "The nose is high.")

Hana ga aku: "To be amazed." (Lit., "The nose opens.")

Hana wo oru: "To humiliate." (Lit., "To break the nose.")
Hana ni tsuku: "To be disgusted with." (Lit., "To adhere to the nose.") English parallel: It stinks.
Hana no saki de ashirau: "To treat in a haughty manner; to turn up one's nose." (Lit., "To receive before the end of one's nose.")
Hana wo takameru: "To be proud; be boastful." (Lit., "To elevate one's nose.")
Hana-saki no shian: "Short-sighted thought." (Lit., "Nose-end consideration.")
Hana no shita: "The mouth." (Lit., "Below the nose.")
Hana no shita ga nagai: "He is infatuated with a woman." (Lit., "He is long under the nose.") This has been explained under AMOROUSNESS.
Hanagusuri: "A bribe." (Lit., "Nose medicine.")

HARA (Belly, Abdomen, Heart, Mind, Spirit):
Hara ga ōkii: "To be pregnant; to have a potbelly; to be bighearted." (Lit., "The abdomen is large.")
Hara wo kakaete warau: "To hold one's sides with laughter." (Lit., "To laugh embracing one's abdomen.")
Hara no naka de warau: "To laugh in one's sleeve." (Lit., "To laugh in one's belly.")
Jibun no hara wo koyasu: "To feather one's own nest." (Lit., "To fatten one's own belly.")
Hara mo mi no uchi: "Be temperate in eating and drinking." (Lit., "The belly, too, is part of me.") English parallel: He that eats till he is sick must fast till he is well.
Hara hachi-gō isha irazu: "Temperance calls no doctor." (Lit., "The belly eight-tenths full needs no physician.") English parallel: "Temperance is the best physic."
Hara-guroi: "Wicked; evil hearted." (Lit., "Black bellied.")
Hara wo watte iwaseba: "To be frank with you." (Lit., "If I spoke with split-open belly.")
Hara ga tatsu: "To get angry; be furious." (Lit., "The belly stands.")
Haradachi: "Anger." (Lit., "Belly-standing.")

Hito no hara wo yomu: "To read another's thoughts." (Lit., "To read a person's belly, or mind.")

Man-ichi sō de nakattara hara wo kirō: "I'll be hanged if it is not so." (Lit., "Ten thousand to one if it is not so I'll cut my belly.")

Jū nin tō hara: "Ten men, ten minds." (Lit., "Ten men, ten bellies.")

HIFU (The skin or complexions of humans) :
Hifu ga kirei: " She has a fair complexion." (Lit., "She has a beautiful skin.")

HIZA (Knee, Lap):
Hiza wo susumeru: "To come nearer; draw closer." (Lit., "To advance the knees.")

Hiza wo majiete kataru: "To have a heart-to-heart talk." (Lit., "To talk with mutually drawn-together knees.")

Hiza tomo dango: "Take counsel of your pillow." (Lit., "Consult, even if it be with your knees.") English parallel: Two hearts are better than one.

Hiza-kurige: "A hike; a walking trip." (Lit., "Knee chestnut-haired horse.") English parallel: Shank's mare.

HONE (Bone; Frame; Spirit; Backbone):
Hone ni naru: "To die." (Lit., "To become bones.")

Hone no aru otoko: "A man of spirit." (Lit., "A man of bones.")

Hone-nashi otoko: "A spineless fellow." (Lit., "A boneless man.")

Honeori: "Labor; exertion; service." (Lit., "Bone breaking.")

Hone-oshimi: "Lazy; indolent." (Lit., "Bone sparing.")

Hone yasumi: "Relaxation; well-earned rest." (Lit., "Bone-rest.")

KAO (Face; standing or status expression) :
Kao wo dasu: "To visit; put in an appearance; make a call." (Lit., "To expose the face.")

Kao ga tatsu: "To keep face; to maintain one's status." (Lit., "The face stands.")

Kao ga tachimasen: "I have lost face." (Lit., "The face does not stand.")

Kao ga tsubureru: "My status is gone." (Lit., "The face is smashed.")

Kao ga yogoreru: "To become ashamed." (Lit., "The face is soiled.")

Kao wo yogosu: "To bring shame upon another." (Lit., "To soil the face.")

Kao ni doro wo nuru: "To put to shame." (Lit., "To smear dirt upon a person's face.")

Kao-awase: "Introduction; presentation." (Lit., "Putting faces together.")

Kao ga ii: "His status is good; his reputation is fine." (Lit., "His face is good.")

Kao wo uru: "To gain popularity; acquire influence; work for fame." (Lit., "To sell face.")

Kao wo ureta hito: "A well-known person." (Lit., "A person who has sold face.")

Kao no hiroi hito: "A person of many acquaintances." (Lit., "A person whose face is broad.")

Kao kara hi ga deru: "To be exceedingly ashamed; to blush with embarrassment." (Lit., "Fire comes from the face.")

Kao wo kasu: "To assist a person to gain standing." (Lit., "To lend the face.") This has the same meaning as *"Namae wo kasu."* (Lit., "To lend the name.")

Nigai kao wo suru: "To frown; make a wry face." (Lit., "To make a bitter face.")

Shiran-kao wo suru: "To appear not to see; avoid; have no relations with." (Lit., "To make a not-knowing face.") This idiom is somewhat similar in meaning to *Tanuki-ne wo suru:* "To pretend not to see or know." (Lit., "To act the sleeping badger.") English parallels: poker face; play 'possum.

KARADA (Body: Health):

Jiyū na karada de aru: "To be one's own master." (Lit., "It's a free body.")

Karada ga tsuzukimasu ka?: "Can you stand the strain?" (Lit., "Can the body hold out?")

Undō wa karada wo jōbu ni suru: "Exercise promotes health."
(Lit., "Exercise makes the body robust.")
Nani-yori mo karada go taisetsu desu yo: "Health is everything,
you know." (Lit., "Above everything the body is most important.")

KATA (Shoulder):
Kata de kaze wo kitte aruku: "To strut along; swagger." (Lit.,
"To walk cutting the wind with your shoulders.") The proud *samurai*
often walked in that manner.
Hito no kata wo motsu: "To support or side with a person." (Lit.,
"To hold a person's shoulder.")
Kata ga karuku naru: "To be relieved of responsibility." (Lit.,
"The shoulders become light.")
Kata wo narabete hashiru: "To run neck and neck." (Lit., "To
run with shoulders side by side.")

KAWA (The Skin; the Hide):
Kare wa ningen no kawa wo shita kemono da: "He is a brute
in human shape." (Lit., "He is an animal in human skin.") English
parallel: A wolf in sheep's clothing.
Bijin to iu mo kawa ichimai: "Beauty is but skin deep." (Lit.,
"Though she may be a beauty, it is but one layer of skin.")

KE (Hair):
Ke wo fuete kizu wo motomeru: "To bring misfortune upon
oneself through too much scrutiny into another's faults." (Lit., "To
blow the hair and get a wound.")
Mi ni ke ga yodatsu: "To be frightened." (Lit., "The body's hairs
stand on end.")

KIMO (The Liver; Courage, Nerve):
Kimo no futoi: "Daring; bold; courageous." (Lit., "Thick liv-
ered.")
Kimo no chiisai: "Timid; cowardly." (Lit., "Small livered.")
English parallel: White livered.
Kimo wo hiyasu: "To be scared; be terrified." (Lit., "To cool the
liver.")

Kimo ga yotte iru: "To have nerves of steel." (Lit., "The liver is relied upon.")

Kimo wo tsubusu: "To be amazed; be astounded." (Lit., "The liver is smashed.")

KOKORO (Mind; Heart; Spirit; Intention):
Kokoro no ōkii: "Liberal; generous." (Lit., "Big hearted.")
Kokoro-bosoi: "Helpless; discouraging." (Lit., "Slender heart.")
Hito no kokoro wo ubau: "To charm or captivate a person." (Lit., "To snatch away a person's heart.")
Kokoro ni kakaru: "To be anxious about." (Lit., "To be suspended from the heart.")
Kokoro-zukai: "Anxiety; worry." (Lit., "Heart messenger.")
Kokorozuke: "A gratuity; tip." (Lit., "Heart addition.")
Kokoro-danomi: "Dependence; hope; reliance." (Lit., "Heart request.")
Kokoro futatsu ni mi wa hitotsu: "One cannot be in two places at once." (Lit., "To two hearts, one body.")

KOSHI (The Waist, Loins, Hips):
Koshikake: "A seat." (Lit., "Hip suspending.")
Hito no hanashi no koshi wo oru: "To interrupt a person." (Lit., "To break the loins of a person's speech.")
Koshi ga yowai: "To be cowardly." (Lit., "The loins are weak.")
English parallel: To be weak-kneed.
Koshi ga tsuyoi: "To be firm; brave." (Lit., "The loins are strong.")
Koshi wo sageru: "To condescend." (Lit., "To lower one's loins or hips.")
Koshi-nuke: "A coward." (Lit., "Removed loins.")

KUBI (Neck; Head):
Kubi wo sukumeru: "To duck one's head; to shrug the shoulders." (Lit., "To make the neck crouch.")
Kubi wo hineru: "To think hard; to put one's head on one side." (Lit., "To twist one's neck.")

Kubi wo nagaku shite matsu: "To look forward to with impatience; to be on tiptoe of expectancy." (Lit., "To make the neck long and wait.") English parallel: To wait with craned neck.

Kubi wo kiru: "To behead; to dismiss, discharge (from a position)." (Lit., "To cut the neck.")

Kubi-nashi: "Headless; beheaded." (Lit., "Without a neck.")

Sō de nakattara kubi wo yaru: "I'll be hanged if it is not so." (Lit., "If it is not so, I'll give you my head.") Notice that in the Japanese language the word *"kubi"* is used for "neck" and also for "head."

KUCHI: "Mouth" is the original meaning, but some of the important derivative meanings are "lips," "speech," "word," "taste," "mouthpiece," "an opening," or "vacancy," "a call," "an engagement," "a share," "a lot," "kind, item or brand."

Kuchi ga oi: "A good talker; many people; many entrances; many positions." (Lit., "Mouths are many.")

Kuchi ga sukunai: "A poor talker; few people; few entrances; few positions." (Lit., "Mouths are few.")

Kuchi ga karui: "To speak without thinking." (Lit., "The mouth is light.")

Kuchi ga omoi: "To talk little or reluctantly." (Lit., "The mouth is heavy.")

Karuguchi wo tataku: "To speak unthinkingly." (Lit., "To strike a light mouth.")

Kuchi ga urusai: "To say something that need not be said." (Lit., "His mouth is annoying.")

Kuchi ga warui: "To have a sharp (caustic) tongue." (Lit., "His mouth is bad," or "His words are bad.")

Kuchiwaru mono: "A foul-mouthed or abusive person." (Lit., "A bad-mouthed person.")

Uso wo ieba kuchi ga magaru: "If you tell lies your mouth will become crooked," is a well-known saying frequently quoted to children to encourage truthfulness.

Kuchi-hiroi: "Boastful." (Lit., "Wide mouthed.") English parallel: Big mouthed.

Kuchisugi: "Potboiling; livelihood." (Lit., "Mouth excessive.")

Kuchi ga aḳu: "There is a vacant position." (Lit., "The mouth opens.")

Kuchi wo sagasu: "To look for a position." (Lit., "To look for a mouth.")

Kuchi-dashi: "Obtruding remarks; interference." (Lit., "Putting forward the mouth.")

Kuchi-dome: "Muzzling; bribing to secrecy." (Lit., "Mouth stopping.")

Kuchi-dome-ḳin: "A bribe; hush money." (Lit., "Mouth-stopping money.")

Kuchi wo fuḳu: "To pretend." (Lit., "To wipe one's mouth.")

Kuchi ni au: "To suit one's taste." (Lit., "To agree with one's mouth.")

Kuchi-guruma: "Wheedling, cajolery." (Lit., "Mouth wheel.")

Kuchi-guruma ni noseru: "To wheedle, coax, take a person in by glib talk." (Lit., "To place a person on a mouth wheel.") This is somewhat similar to the American slang expression: "To take a person for a ride."

Kuchi ḳara umareta: "To be a chatterbox." (Lit., "To be born from the mouth.")

Kuchi-gatai: "A discreet person." (Lit., "Hard mouthed.")

Kuchi-yaḳamashii: "Nagging, critical." (Lit., "Mouth-noisy.")

Kuchi-hatchō: "A skillful speaker or debater." Under AMBI-TION an interesting explanation of *chō* is given as a unit of length. Using the same word pronunciation but a different Chinese ideograph for writing it, *chō* may have the meaning of "merit" or "strength." In Japanese idiom the number "8" pronounced *hachi* or *yatsu* is often a symbol of perfection and is a mystic number. Hence, *hachi chō*, contracted to *hatchō*, literally "eight strengths" or "eight merits," means skilled or versatile. Thus *ashi-hatchō* is one skilled in the use of his feet; *te-hatchō,* one skilled in the use of his hands. A good pastor of a church is punningly referred to as *Boḳushi nijū-yon-chō* ("Pastor twenty-four merits") because he is very versatile in speech, gestures, and movement.

Kuchi-buchōhō: "An unskillful speaker." Lit., ("Mouth clumsy.") A sure way to gain the attention of your audience in making a speech in Japanese is to start with the following sentence: *"Watakushi wa nihongo wa kuchi-buchōhō de gozaimasu kara, dōmo o-kiki-gurushii desu ga, sukoshi no aida go-shimbō wo negaimasu."* ("I am such a clumsy fellow in speaking Japanese that it must indeed be painful for you to listen, but please be patient for a little while.")

Kuchi wo yogosu: "To eat." (Lit., "To soil the mouth.")

Kuchi-ire: "Recommendation; acting as an agency." (Lit., "Mouth putting in.")

Kuchi-guchi ni: "Here and there; in various quarters; severally, mutually, unanimously." (Lit., "From mouth to mouth.")

KUCHIBIRU (The Lips):

Kuchibiru wo kaesu: "To speak ill of; to abuse a person." (Lit., "To turn the lips.")

Kuchibiru no usui: "Talkative or glib." (Lit., "Thin-lipped.")

Usui kuchibiru ni ben ōshi: "A thin-lipped person has much eloquence."

Kuchibiru no usui mono wa yoku shaberu: "A thin-lipped person talks a lot." The two above proverbs are physiological observations by the Japanese and often prove true.

ME: "Eye" is the original meaning, but important derivative meanings are "sight," "notice," "viewpoint," "discrimination," and "to meet."

Me utsuri suru: "To be embarrassed or confused in choice." (Lit., "To shift the eyes.")

Me ga chiru: "The glance is distracted." (Lit., "The eyes are scattered.")

Me ga tsubureru: "To become blind." (Lit., "The eyes are crushed.")

Me ga suwaru: "The eyes are fixed." (Lit., "The eyes are seated.")

Me wo tsuburu: "To sleep; die; shut the eyes."

Me ga tomaru: "To pay heed." (Lit., "The eyes stop.")

Me ni tomeru: "To observe with care." (Lit., "To fasten to the eyes.")

Me wo yaru: "To look towards." (Lit., "To give the eyes.")

Me wo nusumu: "To do by stealth." (Lit., "To steal the eyes.")

Me wo tōsu: "To scan or read rapidly." (Lit., "To pass through the eyes.")

Me ga tsuku: "To look at carefully." (Lit., "The eyes adhere.")

Me ga hayui: "To understand quickly." (Lit., "The eyes are rapid.")

Me ga osoi: "To be slow to understand." (Lit., "The eyes are slow.")

Me ga takai: "The views are advanced; the ideas are lofty." (Lit., "The eyes are high.")

Me ga chikai: "To be short-sighted." (Lit., "The eyes are near.")

Me ga tōi: "To be farsighted; to have grand ideas." (Lit., "The eyes are distant.")

Me ga ōi: "Many people are looking." (Lit., "The eyes are numerous.")

Me ga sukunai: "There are few people." (Lit., "The eyes are few.")

Me ga fueru: "The number of persons increases." (Lit., "The eyes increase.")

Me wo kakeru: "To be kind to." (Lit., "To suspend the eyes.")

O me ni kakeru: "To show; to give; to meet." (Lit., "To hang to the eyes.")

Me ga todoku: "To be careful or attentive." (Lit., "The eyes reach.")

Me ga aru: "To understand well." (Lit., "To have eyes.")

Me ga koeru: "To have a trained eye." (Lit., "The eyes grow fat.")

Me wo samasu: "To awaken." (Lit., "To waken the eyes.")

Me wo mawasu: "To be very busy; to lose consciousness." (Lit., "To revolve the eyes.")

Me wo ubau: "Too beautiful to look at." (Lit., "To snatch the eyes.")

Me ga nai: "Inability to judge." (Lit., "Has no eyes.")

Me wo sankaku ni suru: "To be angry." (Lit., "To make triangles of the eyes.")

Me ni kado wo tateru: "To be angry." (Lit., "To set up angles in the eyes.")

Me wa kuchi hodo mono wo iu: "The eyes speak as much as the mouth."

Me ni nokoru: "To remain in memory." (Lit., "To remain in the eyes.")

Me ni ukabu: "To remember (especially the dead)." (Lit., "To float in one's eyes.")

Me ni sawaru: "To be a nuisance; to be in the way." (Lit., "To hinder the eyes.")

Me no shōgatsu: "A feast for the eyes." (Lit., "New Year for the eyes." So said because New Year's Day in Japan is a time of great feasting and rejoicing.)

Mesaki: "Before one's eyes; under one's nose." This Japanese word also has the secondary meaning of "foresight," "acumen," and "appearance."

Mesaki no kawatta: "New, novel, or out of the ordinary." (Lit., "Changed appearance.")

Mesaki wo kaeru: "To do something new; to make a departure." (Lit., "To change the appearance.")

Meshita: "An inferior or subordinate." (Lit., "Below the eyes.")

Meue: "A superior; a senior; one's betters." (Lit., "Above the eyes.")

Me no kusuri: "Only a little." (Lit., "Eye medicine.").

Me no doku: "Something that should not be seen." (Lit., "Eye poison.")

Me no ue no kobu (tankobu): "An eyesore; something in the way." It also has the meaning of "a person who obstructs the advancement of another." (Lit., "A wen above the eye.")

Me kara hana e nukeru: "To do something quickly and cleverly." (Lit., "To remove from the eye to the nose.") This phrase is used to describe a person quick in deeds and decisions.

Mejirushi: "A sign or landmark." (Lit., "Eye emblem.")

Me to hana no aida: "Very close." (Lit., "Between the eyes and nose.")

Me wo maruku suru: "To be greatly astonished or very angry." (Lit., "To make the eyes round.")

O me dama chōdai: "To be scolded." (Lit., "To receive one's eyeballs.")

Yowari-me ni tatari-me: "Misfortunes never come singly." (Lit., "To weak eyes cursed eyes.")

MEMBOKU (Countenance, face; honor; reputation; dignity; prestige): This is to the Japanese one of their most important words. (Lit., "Face and eyes.")

Shinshi no memboku: "A gentleman's honor (reputation)." (Lit., The face and eyes of a gentleman.")

Memboku wo hodokosu: "To gain honor; to do honor to oneself." (Lit., "To give alms to the face and eyes.")

Memboku wo ushinau: "To suffer a let-down; to lose face; to disgrace oneself." (Lit., "To lose face and eyes.")

Memboku nai: "To be ashamed." (Lit., "To have no face and eyes.")

Ikka no memboku to naru: "To be a credit to one's family; to bring honor to the house." (Lit., "To become the face and eyes of the family.")

MI (The Body, Person, Self): This word has important secondary meanings of "one's station in life"; "heart"; "mind"; "soul"; "power, ability"; "flesh, meat."

Mi no uchi no takara wa kuchiru koto nashi: "Treasures laid up in the mind do not decay."

Mi kara deta sabi: "To have no one to blame but oneself; a man must take the consequences of his own deeds." (Lit., "It is rust from the person himself.")

Mi ga iru: "To be interested in." (Lit., "The self enters.")

Mi ni naru: "To do a person good; to be beneficial." (Lit., "It comes to a person.")

MIMI (Ears, Hearing):

Mimi ga chikai: "To hear well." (Lit., "The ears are near.")

Mimi ga tōi: "To be deaf; to hear poorly." (Lit., "The ears are distant.")

Mimi ga hayai: "To hear well." (Lit., "The ears are quick.")

Mimi ga koeru: "To have a trained or cultivated ear." (Lit., "The ears grow fat.")

Mimi ga itai: "To hear something bad about oneself." (Lit., "The ears are painful.") English parallel: The ears burn.

Mimi wo katamukeru: "To listen attentively." (Lit., "To tilt or incline the ears.")

Mimi wo kasu: "To listen." (Lit., "To lend the ears.")

Mimi ga yoko ni tsuku: "To listen well." (Lit., "The ears stick to the side.")

Chotto mimi wo haishaku sasete kudasai: "Please listen." (Lit., "Please make me the loan of your ears.") An English parallel is Mark Anthony's speech from Julius Caesar: "Friends, Roman, countrymen, lend me your ears."

Mimi ni tako ga dekiru hodo kiku: "I am sick of listening." (Lit., "I have heard it so much a corn has developed in my ears.")

Mimi ni juku suru: "To hear and understand well." (Lit., "To ripen in the ears.")

Mimi ni sakarau: "To oppose; be distasteful." (Lit., "To be contrary to the ears.")

Mimi-yori: "Pleasing; encouraging." (Lit., "Ear-approach.")

Mimi-atarashii: "News." (Lit., "New to the ears.")

Chūgen mimi ni sakarau: "Honest advice is distasteful." (Lit., "Faithful words are contrary to the ears.")

Mimi-gakumon wo suru: "To have learning because of things heard." (Lit., "To be ear-learned.") To have a wide variety of knowledge acquired through hearing discourses made by persons more learned than oneself. This is often said of people who have not gone to school, or who have read or traveled extensively.

Mimi tōkereba inochi nagashi: "A deaf person lives long." (Lit., "If the ears are distant the life is long.") Since one sense is gone the others are perhaps more developed and the deaf person becomes more careful. However, the above proverb does not necessarily hold true in these days of modern speeding vehicles.

Mimi no itai koto wo iu: "To say something unpleasant." (Lit., "To say something that hurts the ears.") English parallel: To put a flea into one's ear.

Mimi no ana wo hotte yoku kike: "Listen attentively." (Lit., "Dig out your earholes and listen well.")

MUNE ('The Bosom, the Chest; the Heart, Mind, Feeling):

Mune ga hiroi: "To be large hearted, magnanimous." (Lit., "The bosom is wide.")

Mune wo uchi-akeru: "To unbosom oneself, to open one's mind." (Lit., "To strike open the bosom.")

Mune ni ichimotsu aru: "To have one's own ax to grind." (Lit., "To have one thing in the bosom.")

NIKU (Flesh, Meat):

Nikuteki na: "Voluptuous, fleshy. (Lit., "Fleshlike.")

Niku no yūwaku: "Temptations of the flesh."

Niku no manzoku: "Sensual gratification." (Lit., "Satisfaction of the flesh.")

Niku no kairaku: "Pleasures of the flesh."

Nikutai: "The flesh, the body, the outer man." (Lit., "Flesh body.")

Nikuyoku: "Animal passions; carnal desires." (Lit., "Flesh appetites.")

Nikugan: "The naked eye." (Lit., "The flesh eye.")

Nikuhitsu: "One's own handwriting, autograph." (Lit., "Flesh brush.")

SHIRI (The Buttocks, the Hips):

Shiri no karui onna or *shirigarui onna:* "A woman of easy virtue." (Lit., "A light-buttocks woman.")

Shiri ga nagai: "To stay long." (Lit., "The buttocks are long.")

Shiri ga omoi: "To be lazy or inactive." (Lit., "The buttocks are heavy.")

Shiri wa motte yuku: "To complain to a person." (Lit., "To go taking along his buttocks.")

Shiri-nugui wo suru: "To repair another's blunder; to wipe up the mess." (Lit., "To wipe the buttocks.")

Onna no shiri ni shikarete iru: "To be tied to a woman's apron strings." (Lit., "To be spread on a woman's buttocks.")

Shiri ni hi ga tsuku: "To be pressed by urgent business." (Lit., "The buttocks are in contact with fire.")

Hito no shiri ni tsuku: "To play second fiddle." (Lit., "To be attached to a person's buttocks.")

Tsumetai mono wa neko no hana to onna no shiri: "Cold things are a cat's nose and a woman's buttocks." English parallel: A cat's nose and a maiden's knees are always cold.

SHITA (The Tongue):

Shita no nagai wa dorobo: "A long-tongued person is a robber." Note that this is quite different from the English phrase "long-tongued," which means to be talkative.

Issun no shita ni go shaku no mi wo son su: "The tongue is mightier than the sword." (Lit., "To one inch of tongue five feet of blade loses.")

Naishō de shita wo dasu: "To laugh in one's sleeve." (Lit., "To stick out the tongue in secret.")

Nimai-jita wo tsukau: "To tell a lie; be double faced." (Lit., "To use a double tongue.")

SUNE (The Leg, Shank):

Oya no sune wo kajiru: "To live on one's parents." (Lit., "To chew on the legs of one's parents.")

Sune ni kizu: "To have a guilty conscience." (Lit., "To have a wound on one's shank.") See *Ashi ni kizu:* "To have a guilty conscience." (Lit., "To have a wound on one's foot.")

Sune ni kizu moteba sasahara hashiru: "A man with a guilty conscience will seek cover." (Lit., "A man with a wound on his leg will run to a plain of dwarf bambo.")

Sune ippon, ude ippon: "To be entirely on one's own." (Lit., "One shank, one arm.")

Te (Hand, Arm). Other secondary and important meanings are: "man"; "handwriting"; "skill, performance"; "direction"; "trouble"; "control, management"; and "possessions."

Te no kireru yō na fuda (satsu): "A crisp note." (Lit., "A hand-cutting letter.")

Te ga taranai: "To be shorthanded." (Lit., "Not enough hands.")

Te mo ashi mo denai: "To be at wit's end." (Lit., "Neither the hands nor the feet will go out.") *Sono ne de wa, te mo ashi mo denai:* "The price is quite prohibitive; I can't touch it at that price." (Lit., "At that price neither the hands nor the feet will go out.")

Te wo wakeru: "To form parties; divide into groups." (Lit., "To divide the hands.")

Te ga yoi: "To write a good hand." (Lit., "The hand is good.")

Te ga aite iru: "To be free (disengaged)." (Lit., "The hands are open.")

Hyaku-man te wo tsukau: "To try all possible means." (Lit., "To use a million hands.") English parallel: To leave no stone unturned.

Te mo ashi mo fumu tokoro shirazu: "To be in a rapture or ecstasy of joy." (Lit., "Knowing not how the hands dance, and the place the feet tread.")

Te ni haitta mono da: "To be at home; to be an adept." (Lit., "It's a thing in hand.")

O te no mono: "One's forte; one's strong point." (Lit., "The thing in hand.")

Te ni awanu: "To get out of hand." (Lit., "Not to agree with the hands.")

Te ga nagai: "To be a kleptomaniac." (Lit., "The hands are long.")

Te wo utsu: "To strike a bargain." (Lit., "To strike hands.")

Te irazu: "Untouched; requiring little trouble." (Lit., "No need for hands.")

Te ga akeba kuchi ga aku: "If a person will not work he may not eat." (Lit., "If the hands are empty the mouth is empty.") English parallel: Work not, eat not.

Ikkyoshu ittōsoku: "A slight effort; a small amount of labor." (Lit., "To raise one hand and throw out one leg.")

Te wo nurasazu ni toru: "To obtain something without using any special effort." (Lit., "To take without wetting one's hand.") This saying is derived from fishing.

TSUME (Claw, Talons, Nail, Hoof):

Tsume no aka hodo nai: "Not the slightest dishonesty in one's conduct." (Lit., "Not the slightest dirt in the nails.")

Tsume ni tomoshibi wo tomosu: "To lead a niggardly or stingy life." (Lit., "To make a light with fingernail parings.")

Tsume de hirotte mi de kobosu: "Little gain, much expense." (Lit., "Picking up with the fingernails, spilling with a winnowing fan.")

UDE (Arm): Secondary meanings are "ability," "skill," and "talent."

Ude wo kumu: "To fold one's arms." (Lit., "To braid the arms.")

Ude makuri suru: "To roll up the sleeves." (Lit., "To roll up the arms.")

Ude ga nageku: "To be itching for action." (Lit., "The arm grieves.")

Ude ippon de yo wo wataru: "To be fully self-supporting." (Lit., "To cross over the world with a single arm.") English parallel: To paddle one's own canoe.

Ude no aru: "Able, capable." (Lit., "Has an arm.")

Ude no hito: "A man of ability." (Lit., "A man of arm.")

Ude ni hineru wo kakeru: "To strain every nerve." (Lit., "To put a twist in the arm.")

Chikara-kobu: "Muscular development of the biceps."

Chikara-kobu wo ireru: "To take great interest in; to show a zeal for." (Lit., "To put your biceps into it.")

YUBI (Finger; Toe):

Yubi wo sasu: "To point to or at." (Lit., "To point a finger.")

Yubi wo someru: "To have a finger in; to make an attempt; to try." (Lit., "To dye the finger.")

Yubiori: "A man or talent of the highest order." (Lit., "Finger-breaking.")

Yubi-ato: "A fingerprint." (Lit., "Finger remainder.")

Yubi-jirushi: "An index." (Lit., "Finger sign.")

CAUTION

NEARLY THREE CENTURIES of living under a totalitarian, police-controlled type of government, where every act was watched and every word reported to the authorities, have made the Japanese more cautious and timid than the people of other countries. The strict control of the people by the authorities during the Tokugawa era, and the complete domination of all residents by the "thought-control police" in the period prior to and during World War II, have left a scar on Japanese characters, a scar that will take many generations to erase, despite the freedoms guaranteed in the new consitution. One of the first acts of General MacArthur and his staff after landing in Japan was to break the hold of the police on the people.

Bara ni toge ari: "Even beautiful things have disadvantages and must be used with caution." (Lit., "Roses have thorns.") English parallel: No rose without a thorn.

Deru kui (kugi) wa utareru: "A protruding stake (nail) will be hammered in." It is at times wiser to lie low than to be forward, for the latter will certainly cause trouble.

Fugu wa kuitashi, inochi wa oshishi: "I desire to eat globefish but I value my life." The flesh of Japanese globefish is most delightful in flavor, but if not properly prepared, it is so poisonous that it proves fatal to the eater. So this proverb is used when a person hesitates to take any chance at a great risk, or when there is a conflict between the dictates of heart and head. English parallel: Honey is sweet but the bee stings.

Fugu-jiru kuu baka, kuwanu baka: "He who eats globefish soup is a fool; so is he who does not." Since the flesh of globefish is poisonous, the eater may be reckoned a fool. However, the flesh of the fish is so delicious that anybody who would not taste it may also be counted a fool.

Futaba ni shite karazareba, ono wo mochiyuru ni ataru: "Take necessary measures early." (Lit., "If you don't crop it while it is a bud, it will grow into something that will require an ax.") English parallel: Nip the briar in the bud.

Hadaka de mono wo otosu tameshi nashi: "Destitute people are not likely to lose anything." (Lit., "There is no instance of a nude man dropping anything.") If you have anything at all, you must exercise caution lest you lose it.

Nete ite koronda tameshi nashi: "Be careful before starting something new." (Lit., "There is no instance of a person falling down while sleeping.") Since Japanese sleep on the floor on thick quilts, they would not injure themselves if they rolled out of bed while sleeping.

Hajime wa shojo no gotoku, owari wa datto no gotoshi: "First go cautiously but finally boldly." (Lit., "At first shy as a maiden, at last swift as an escaping hare.")

Haya karō, waru karō: "The faster the worse." Things that are done very quickly, that is without due reflection, often turn out badly. English parallels: Haste makes waste; good and quickly seldom meet.

Hito wa hisshō wo kisu-bekarazu: "Man cannot count on certain victory." Since it is not in man to command success he must be cautious.

Ii mono ni yasui mono nashi: "Beware of cheap products." (Lit., "Good articles are not cheap.") English parallel: The lion's skin is never cheap.

Yasu karō, waru karō: "What is cheap may also be bad." English parallel: Cheapest is dearest.

Inu no ha ni nomi: "A flea between a dog's teeth." What is small is sometimes difficult to catch or hold. Hence, be cautious lest small things escape you.

Ippō kiite geji wo tatazu (suru na): "Don't give an order after listening only to one side." Be sure to look on both sides before making decisions. English parallel: Look on both sides of the shield.

Ishibashi wo tataite wataru: "To cross a stone bridge by tapping on it." This describes the caution of a blind man tapping with his stick as he walks across a stone bridge. The proverb is used metaphorically to describe an over-cautious person.

Isogoba maware: "When in a hurry make a detour." English parallels: The more haste the worse speed. Haste makes waste. Slow but sure. The long way around is the shortest way home.

Kakusu koto wa senu ga yoi: "It is better not to do something that you would hide."

Kakusu yori arawaruru wa nashi: "No secret but will come to light." (Lit., "As much as you try to hide it, the matter will be revealed.") English parallel: Murder will out.

Katte kabuto no o wo shimeyo: "Having conquered, tighten the thongs of your helmet." This well-known advice, though attributed to Tokugawa Ieyasu, the founder of the Tokugawa dynasty of war lords, is found in ancient Chinese writings. English parallel: In the time of mirth take heed.

Keikai wa keibi: This literally means "A warning is a defence," and is taken from the English proverb, "Forewarned is forearmed."

Kido katakereba inu irazu: "When the entrance is carefully shut a dog does not come in." English opposite: At open doors dogs come in.

Kichigai (kyōjin) ni hamono: "An edged tool to an insane person." The greatest caution should be taken not to let madmen or irresponsible people get hold of tools or weapons with which they may injure themselves or others. English parallel: Don't give a sword to a child.

Kō no kusuri wa otsu no doku: "What is *A*'s medicine is *B*'s poison." English parallel: One man's meat is another's poison.

Korobanu saki no tsue: "Take all necessary precautions." (Lit., "Before you fall take a staff.")

Nurenu saki no kasa: "Take an umbrella before you get wet," i.e., be prepared for anything. English parallel: Prevention is better than cure.

Kunshi wa ayauki ni chikayorazu: "A man of honor does not come near to danger," i.e., a gentleman of high moral character is discreet in his dealings with people and things. A wise man does not court danger.

Kuragari kara ushi wo hikidasu na: "Don't lead an ox out of darkness." Because you may be gored or injured in some other way.

Hence it is well that you see and understand the whole situation before you make a move.

Kusare nawa ni uma wo tsunagu yō: "Like hitching a horse with a rotten rope." A warning against attempting to attain one's end through insecure ways.

Kyō wa hito no mi, asu wa waga mi: "What today is the circumstance of another person, on the morrow will be mine." This saying warns against congratulating oneself on the good fortune one enjoys at present. English parallel: What's my turn today may be thine tomorrow.

Mado kara yari: "A sudden danger." (Lit., "A spear from the window.")

Yabu kara bō: "A cudgel from a bamboo bush." Both the above proverbs are metaphors for an abrupt word or deed. Such unexpected attacks necessitate extreme caution.

Mi no hodo wo shire: "Attempt nothing you cannot do." (Lit., "Know your limits.")

Minato-guchi de nansen: "Shipwreck at the harbor entrance," i.e., the importance of vigilance. English parallel: There's many a slip 'twixt cup and lip.

Nanatabi tazunete hito wo utagae: "Inquire seven times then doubt a person." In both Near and Far Eastern numerology seven is used to indicate "quite a number." For example in Japan on January 7 "the seven herbs" *("nanakusa")* are eaten to insure good health throughout the year.

Nen ni wa nen wo ire: "One cannot be too careful." (Lit., "To caution put in caution.") English parallel: Hear twice before you speak once.

Neko ni katsuobushi wo azukeru yō: "Like setting a cat to guard dried bonito." Dried bonito *("katsuobushi")* is something that a cat likes very much and given the opportunity will always eat. Hence, temptations should not be put in the way of people, especially men and women in their mutual relations. English parallels: To set a wolf to guard the sheep. To set a fox to watch the geese.

Ni-no-ashi wo fumu: "To hesitate, balk, or demur." (Lit., "To step on the second foot.")

Oni no rusu ni sentaku: "Make use of your opportunities." (Lit., "Wash your clothes when the devil is away.") This proverb originated in the eleventh century when a bandit chieftain known as "the devil" *("Oni")* lived near the capital city, Kyoto, and frequently attacked the inhabitants. It was only when he was away that the women of the city felt safe enough to go out of their homes to wash their clothes in the streams of the city. English parallel: When the cat's away the mice will play.

Sennichi no katta kaya wo ichinichi ni horobosu: "Miscanthus which took a thousand days to reap is destroyed in one day." The miscanthus is a reed used in Japan, especially in rural areas, for roofing, since it keeps the house warm in winter and cool in summer. Its chief drawback is that it is easily set on fire by sparks or flame from a neighbor's house. The moral of the above saying is that carelessness or ill luck can destroy in one day the result of many days' hard labor. English parallel: An hour may destroy what it took an age to build.

Shin-tai kiwamaru: "To be in a dilemma." (Lit., "To advance or retreat—that's the extremity.") English parallel: To be between the devil and the deep blue sea.

Tori wo nakazuba utaremaji: "Silence keeps one safe." (Lit., "If the bird had not sung it wouldn't have been shot.") I.e., people will not get into trouble if they keep quiet.

U no mane wo suru karasu mizu ni oboru: "Keep within your limitations." (Lit., "The crow that mimics a cormorant gets drowned.") This is a warning to men who are not content to do well what they can do, but insist on going beyond their ability and skill. English parallel: The frog burst when it tried to make itself as big as a bull.

Yamiyo ni teppō: "An aimless attempt." (Lit., "Shooting a gun on a dark night.") A business or journey started without due preparation or consideration will surely meet with failure. English parallel: A shot in the dark.

Yōjin ni aki wa nai: "One cannot be too cautious." (Lit., "There is no being bored with precautions.")

Yōjin wa mae ni ari: "Precaution must be taken in advance."

English parallels: A stitch in time saves nine. An ounce of prevention is worth a pound of cure.

Yōjin ni shiro horobizu: "The castle is not overthrown by precaution."

Yudan taiteki: "Carelessness is a great enemy." The Japanese word *"yudan"* translated "carelessness" or "incaution," literally means "without oil." Hence, it can be appropriately applied to the five foolish virgins in the New Testament narrative. See Matthew 25:1-13.

Kappa no kawa nagare: "The *Kappa* drowns in the river." The *Kappa* is an imaginary river goblin that drowns people. Though credited with great skill in swimming, even he sometimes drowns. This and the three proverbs which follow point to the danger of overconfidence and the need for exercising caution at all times.

Kawadachi wa kawa de hatsuru: "The river-bred person comes to an end in the river."

Mizu wo shiru mono mizu ni oboru: "The person who knows water drowns in the water."

Yoku oyogu mono wa yoku oboru: "The person who swims well drowns." English parallel: The best swimmer often drowns.

CLASS CONSCIOUSNESS

JAPAN IS A CASTE SOCIETY. Every Japanese has a place in its hierarchal system—a hereditary place. In the feudal period the most exploited and poorest class, the farmers, were not the lowest class. They had a place of honor just below the warrior class and above the artisan and merchant classes. In the two hundred and fifty years of totalitarian government by military dictators prior to the emergence of Japan into the modern world, the five classes beginning at the top were: nobles, warriors, farmers, artisans, and merchants. The capstone was the Emperor. The lowest unrecognized class were the untouchables, known as *Eta.* They were the makers of sandals, clogs, and leatherware. Legally this caste system is no longer recognized, but socially the ideas still carry great weight. Many Japanese were aghast when some years ago their Crown Prince chose as his bride a girl whose father was a merchant! In spite of the great advance of democratic ideas and ideals, status means much to the average Japanese. The older people are especially class conscious.

Baka hodo kowai mono wa nai: "There is nothing more fearful than a fool." That is because there is no telling what dangerous mischief he may do. One of the worse insults you can hurl at a Japanese is to call him *"baka"* (a fool). The word is written with the Chinese ideographs for "horse" *("Ba")* and "deer" *("Ka")*, although there is no scientific evidence that the two have ever mated or produced any offspring. It is interesting to note here that the mating of a male ass with a female horse results in the mule; a word which in our Western culture has a derogatory connotation when applied to humans. However, it is a far greater insult to call a Japanese a *"baka"* than to apply the epithet "mule" to an American or Englishman.

Baka mo areba koso, rikō mo hikitatsu. "Just because there are fools wise men look to advantage." English parallel: Were there no fools there would be no wise men.

Baka mo ichi gei: "Even a fool has one accomplishment." Hence, he can prove useful, but it takes a wise man to find out what that accomplishment is.

Baka ni tsukeru kusuri nashi: "There is no medicine to apply to a fool." This proverb is frequently used in describing unreasonable people. English parallel: He who is born a fool is never cured.

Baka no atojie: "The after-wit of a fool." Even a fool can think of brilliant things to say when the need has passed. English parallel: After-wit is everybody's wit.

Baka no hitotsu oboe: "A fool's memory of one thing only." This derisive expression is used to describe a person who cannot make an apt answer to each different question, but repeats only the same answer.

Baka no ō-ashi: "The big feet of a fool." Often a person in order to tease a companion or friend, will use this saying.

Baka no ō-gui: "The big appetite of a fool." Japanese, who pride themselves on their self-control, apply the above epithet to one who is intemperate in eating.

Baka no taka-warai: "The loud laughter of a fool." A disdainful description of a man's boisterous laughter. Most Japanese are not given to a public display of their emotions. Hence the loud laughter of foreigners made them objects of contempt in the early years of contact with the West.

Baka to hasami wa tsukai yō: "Fools and scissors may be put to use," i.e., they will work according to how you use them. English parallel: Praise a fool and you will make him useful.

Baka to kichigai wo yokete tōre: "Avoid and pass by a fool and a madman." Because they are both dangerous it is well not to interfere with them. English parallel: Make way for a madman and a bull.

Baka to kichigai hodo kowai mono wa nai: "There is nothing more fearful than a fool and a madman."

Baka wa baka ja: "A fool is a fool," and therefore can only do a fool's work.

Baka wa sugu ni kane wo nakusu: "A fool will soon use up his money." English parallel: A fool and his money are soon parted.

Dōroku heiroku: "A crowd of fools." Since the foregoing two names are supposed to be the personification of ignorance, the two taken together represent a crowd of fools.

Ebi odore domo kawa wo idezu: "Although shrimps may dance around they do not leave the river." Hence, a man should not leave his own special occupation. He must work according to his own calling. In the feudal period it was very difficult for a man to change his occupation because strict laws prevented him. English parallel: Let the cobbler stick to his last.

Geta mo Amida (Hotoke) mo onaji ki no hashi: "The clog and Amida (Buddha) are both from the same piece of wood." Though equally of wood, one is a commonplace thing while the other is an object of worship. So men, though born equal, are of different degrees of ability and greatness.

Gesu no ato-jie: "The after-wit of a low fellow." The vulgar fellow's wit that comes after the event is of no value.

Hamo mo ichigo, ebi mo ichigo: "The conger eel has one span of life, the lobster also one span of life," i.e., each has its span of life, as have all living creatures. English parallel: Life is but a span.

Kaeru no ko wa kaeru: "The young of frogs are frogs." Hence, they should not attempt to be anything else. This proverb was used and interpreted metaphorically to discourage people from attempting to rise above their station in life. English parallel: Like begets like.

Kago-kaki kago ni norazu: "Sedan bearers do not ride in a sedan." People who have a certain occupation or profession are often so busy making a living that they do not avail themselves of the opportunities of that occupation. English parallels: The shoemaker's children go barefoot. The tailor's wife is worst clad.

Kago ni noru hito, katsugu hito, sono mata waraji wo tsukuru hito: "There are those who ride sedans, those who carry sedans, and those who make straw sandals for the sedan bearers." The latter were the "untouchables" *("Eta"),* and below the social scale. So in life there are the wealthy who are able to take vehicles whenever they go out, while others barely eke out a living by carrying on more lowly work.

Kanemochi kurō ōshi: "Wealthy people have many worries." English parallel: Much coin, much care.

Kanemochi to tanhiki wa tamaru hodo kitanai: "Wealthy persons and spittoons become filthier as accumulation takes place." English parallel: Muck and money go together.

Kawara wa migaitemo tama no naranu: "A tile even though it be polished does not become a jewel." Hence, however polished a person may be, you cannot make him superior to the class in which he was born. Despite this proverb, Japanese history has instances of men like Toyotomo Hideyoshi, who rose from lowly origins to places of great prominence and power. English parallels: You can't make a silk purse out of a sow's ear. Crows are never whiter for washing themselves.

Kei tarigataku, tei tarigatashi: "There is little to choose between them." (Lit., "To be neither elder brother nor younger brother.") This phrase is used to describe two men as being of equal worth, or equal worthlessness. Though not true now in all Japanese homes, the elder brother has a position of greater authority and responsibility than the younger.

Kuwazu hinraku: "Though not eating (much), the poor are at ease." English parallel: Riches breed care, poverty is safe.

Mi wa mi de tōru: "Live according to your station in life."

Otamajakushi wa kaeru ni naru: "Tadpoles will become frogs." There is no hope that they will develop into something better. So people will not usually rise above their breeding and environment.

Sakaya e san ri, tōfuya e ni ri: "To a wineshop three *ri*, to a bean-curd maker two *ri*." The Japanese unit of distance the *"ri"* is a little less than two and one-half miles. The above saying describes a solitary and lonely village. In the thickly-populated Japan of today, there are few communities so inconveniently located.

Saru ni ebōshi: "A nobleman's headgear on a monkey." The *ebōshi* was the hat of nobles in court dress. The monkey remains a monkey though attired in the dress of a nobleman. The moral is, don't attempt to be or do what is beyond your station in life if you don't want to make a monkey of yourself.

Sei wa bannin wo dōretsu ni shi, shi wa yūshō wo akiraka ni su: "Life places all men on the same level, death clearly reveals the champion." This and some other proverbs indicate that certainly some Japanese believed in equality, though here again, it was probably equality of opportunity in the same economic or social strata.

Seikaku wa kawaranu: "Character does not change." The word *seikaku* has the combined meaning of "character," "personality," and "individuality." English parallel: The leopard cannot change its spots.

Shita ni wa shita ga aru: "Inferiors have others below them." Hence, inferiority or superiority are relative, not absolute, terms.

Ue ni wa ue ga aru: "Superiors have others above them." The Japanese are an extremely class-conscious and status-minded people. Each person is aware of his rank and standing in society and acts accordingly.

Ue wo mireba kagiri nashi: "If you look up there are no limits." Therefore it is useless to yearn after what is unobtainable.

Ue wo mireba kiri ga nai: "There is no end if you look up." This proverb is similar in meaning to the preceding one. However, in these days of modern Japan it may also be interpreted, "There are no limits to the heights to which a man of talent and determination can rise."

Ue wo miru na, shita wo miyo: "Don't look above you, rather look below you." This advice is given with the purpose of making a person contented with his station in life. Since it lacks a higher incentive it does not satisfy the Japanese youth of today.

Uri no tsuru ni nasubi wa naranu: "Egg plants do not grow on melon vines," i.e., generally speaking, ordinary parents will not produce wonder children. English parallel: The onion will not produce a rose.

Ushi wa ushi-zure, uma wa uma-zure: "Oxen go with oxen, horses with horses." So people are more contented and do better work if they do not go out of the class to which they belong.

COARSENESS

ALTHOUGH THE JAPANESE are very sensitive and delicate in their appreciation of nature, art, and other aspects of beauty, they can be and frequently are extremely coarse in speech and deed. This is a fact of which many Westerners are quite unaware. As with other civilized people, this indelicacy is more apparent among men than among women. However, among the lower classes and frequently in rural areas even women in community gatherings and parties participate in obscene jokes, dances, and gestures.

Hajime no kachi wa kuso-gachi: "The first victory is no victory." (Lit., "The first victory is a feces victory.") This is a common expression used by the loser of the first match of a game, thus consoling and excusing himself. English parallel: He laughs best who laughs last.

He wo hitte shiri tsubome: "To assume a look of innocence after committing an indiscretion." (Lit., "To close the anus after breaking wind.")

Heso ga yadogae suru: "To be convulsed with laughter." (Lit., "The navel changes its lodgings.")

Heso de cha wo wakasu: "To laugh till one's sides split (ache)." (Lit., "To boil tea on one's navel.") The phrase *heso-cha* (Lit., "navel tea") means "a huge joke."

Heso wo kamu tomo oyobanu: "It is too late to repent." (Lit., "It won't do to bite your navel.")

Hito no shiri wo nuguu: "To accept the result of another's folly or wrongdoing." (Lit., "To wipe the anus of another person.")

Hyaku nichi no seppō he hitotsu: "The preaching of a hundred days gone like one rectal windbreak." The efforts of many days to reform the manners of a person will come to nothing when the teacher himself makes a gross social error.

Inu no kuso de kataki wo toru: "To express anger and contempt." (Lit., "To take revenge by using dog's dung.") During the height of anti-American feeling prior to World War II, I often found dog and sometimes human feces deposited at the front gate of my home in the city of Kyoto. When reported to the city police, they took a serious view of the situation but did not find the culprit. Evidently some "patriotic" Japanese was taking revenge on the enemy of his country!

Itachi no saigo-be: "A last resort." (Lit., "The final windbreak of a weasel.") So said because the weasel when cornered makes a final attempt to get away by using the offensive gas of his rectal windbreak.

Jinkō mo takazu he mo hirazu: "He neither does any distinguished service, nor does he any evil." (Lit., "He neither burns incense nor makes a windbreak.") This proverb from Chinese sources is descriptive of a person who leads a very commonplace life.

Me-kuso hana-kuso wo warō: "Laughing at the faults of others and ignoring your own." (Lit., "The eye mucous laughs at the nose mucous.") English parallel: The pot calls the kettle black.

Setchin (setsuin) da manjū: "Eating a bean-jam bun in a privy." This describes a pleasant experience in very unpleasant surroundings, since most privies in Japan are exceedingly malodorous.

Setsuin de yari wa tsukau yō: "Like wielding a spear in a privy." Since, in such a confined space it is difficult to use a long spear, the above expression describes the difficulty of doing anything in a narrow space.

Shippo wo tsukamaeru: "To find another's faults; or to catch a person tripping." (Lit., "To seize the tail.")

Shiri no ke made nukareru: "To be fleeced of everything." (Lit., "To have even the hairs of the anus pulled out.")

Shiri kui, Kannon: "An insolent statement to Kannon." (Lit., "Chew your anus, Kannon.") Such a remark would be a great insult to Kannon, the goddess of mercy and one of the most popular and beloved of the Buddhist deities.

Shiri-oshi: "Backing or support." (Lit., "Pushing the buttocks.")

Ushi no shōben no yō: "Tardy; long and drawn out." (Lit., "Like an ox's urination.") The above saying is used in describing something that takes a long time to complete.

COURAGE

HISTORY IS REPLETE with instances of Japanese courage. The capture of a 203 meter hill in the siege of Port Arthur during the Russo-Japanese War, the charge of the "three human bombs" when in 1938 the Japanese attacked a strong Chinese position near Shanghai, the repeated refusal of Japanese soldiers and sailors to surrender in spite of overwhelming odds in World War II battles, and many other examples attest to their physical courage. While not so common, their moral courage is apparent when feelings of sorrow or pain are hidden by a smile rather than cause distress to others by a woeful or tearful face. Though I knew that her heart was torn with anguish, I have had a mother tell me, with a little laugh, that her child died a few days ago. Under a mask of stoicism the emotions are concealed, although sorrow, joy, fear, anger, and other feelings are just as strong in the breast of a Japanese as in any American or European. Their capacity to bear pain has led some foreign observers to remark that the Japanese nervous system must be different from that of Europeans, but such a statement has no scientific basis. As a teen-age boy I often accompanied my mother to Red Cross hospitals in Tokyo to visit the wounded brought back from the battlefields of the Russo-Japanese War of 1904–1905. There on every hand could be seen instances of incredible courage; amputations and other operations performed with no anesthetic, for early in the war the supply ran out. While the surgeons sawed off his leg or worked on ugly wounds in the abdominal cavity, the soldier or sailor would joke with doctors and nurses or sing "Kimi-ga-yo," the national anthem. Courage is indeed an outstanding trait of the Japanese.

Ashita michi wo kiite, yūbe ni shisu tomo kanari: "If I hear the way in the morning, even though I die in the evening it will be tolerable." This saying, attributed to Confucius who eagerly sought after the right way of life, is widely quoted and admired in Japan as an example of moral courage.

Atatte kudakero: "Dash against it and be smashed!" The *banzai* or suicide charges of Japanese troops against impregnable positions or withering gunfire carry out the exhortation of this saying. English parallel: Sink or swim.

Gi wo mite sezaru wa yū naki nari: "He who sees righteousness and does not do it is not brave." In this well-known proverb is an exhortation to moral courage.

Haisui no jin: "To draw up in battle array before the water." This saying, derived from an ancient Chinese classic, signifies the desperate determination of an army to fight at all costs. English parallel: To burn the bridges after them.

Ippon-yari: "One supreme effort." (Lit., "One-single-spear!") Just before the surrender of Japan in World War II, bamboo spears were prepared in every village and town, and the populace was instructed to use them in opposing the landing of American troops. There was a great shortage of modern weapons and fighting men, especially in rural areas, and so the order from the authorities was *"ippon-yari!"*—"Forward even with only a spear!" When I was in Japan the fall and winter of 1945–46 with the Strategic Bombing Survey, I talked to many villagers who told me that even old men and women were instructed in the use of the sharpened bamboo poles, great piles of which still lay in accessible places. It was only the Imperial broadcast to surrender that prevented the populace from using such primitive weapons.

Itago ichimai shita jigoku: "One thickness of plank, below hell." This expression is commonly used to explain the hazardous nature of a fisherman's or a sailor's life in his frail craft on the sea. Only the bottom board of his boat keeps him from death. English parallel: Those who go to sea are only four inches from death.

Ja wa sun ni shite hito wo nomu: "Even an inch-long snake will indignantly attempt to swallow a man," i.e., the characteristics of a great hero are displayed even in early childhood.

Koketsu ni irazareba koji wo ezu: "Unless you enter the tiger's den you cannot take the cubs." This is a much-quoted proverb from Chinese sources. English parallel: Nothing ventured, nothing gained.

Kyūso neko wo kamu: "A cornered rat will bite a cat." English parallel: Even the weak when at bay may defeat the strong.

Taorete nochi yamu: "Fight to the last." (Lit., "After you have been struck down, stop.") I.e., "Don't stop fighting until you are incapable of battling further."

Un wa yūsha wo tasuku: "Fate assists the courageous." English parallel: Fortune favors the brave.

COURTESY

TRAVELERS RETURNING FROM JAPAN are always impressed by the punctilious politeness and great courtesy of the people. Their manners to guests and friends are charming. The average well-bred Japanese will go far out of this way to be considerate and helpful. Their excessive regard for etiquette, however, often makes their politeness too formal and gives rise to the following drawbacks: (1) Excessive politeness verging on obsequiousness towards people they know or consider to be their superiors, but almost callous indifference to the needs of those they do not know. (2) Flattery, as the result of overstressing politeness. (3) Rudeness towards inferiors. Often a Japanese will try to show his own importance by being rude to those whom he considers to be in lower status. (4) Deceitfulness. This is shown in the extreme use of self-deprecatory language, and saying "Yes" rather than hurt feelings with a "No." Sometimes the extravagant use of polite language indicates hatred and contempt rather than friendship and good will. It has been correctly observed that the test of Japanese courtesy is ego centered ("Have I acted correctly?"), while the test of American or European courtesy is alter centered ("Is the other person better off because of what has occurred?"). I have often watched with interest and amusement two Japanese meeting each other for the first time when neither knows the status of the other.

Their bows at the beginning will be of equal depth. When it becomes evident that one person is the superior he will bow less deeply while the genuflection of the other becomes more profound.

Arosoi ni wa kowadaka no mono ga katsu: "In a quarrel the higher voiced person will win." So said because a reasonable, gentle, and scrupulous person will not raise his voice as high in a quarrel as his ill-bred and unmannerly opponent.

Ishoku tatte reisetsu wo shiru: "Sufficient food and clothing will produce good manners." Taken from Chinese sources, this proverb is a keen observation of human nature. English parallels: Well fed, well bred. Sharp stomachs make short graces.

Me-hachibu ni motsu: "To hold a thing respectfully." (Lit., "To hold eight-tenths of an inch above the eyes.") This is generally done in receiving a present or carrying an object respectfully. Such a beautiful and gracious custom is more largely observed by women than by men.

Rei sugureba hetsurai to naru: "When politeness is overdone it becomes flattery." One should be moderate in showing courtesy. In fact, anger and disdain are frequently shown by the extreme use of polite terms. Such sarcasm is not lost on the other person.

Shitashii naka ni mo kaki tsukure: "Build a fence even between intimate friends." That is, the fence of courtesy must always be there. English parallel: Familiarity breeds contempt.

Shitashii naka ni mo reigi ari: "Even among intimate friends there should be courtesy." Because of the constant and insistent emphasis on ceremonial politeness dictated by long-established custom, it is almost impossible for Japanese friends to become as intimate with each other as their European or American counterparts.

Uri-kotoba ni kai-kotoba: "Tit for tat; or exchange of compliments in an angry way." (Lit., "To selling-word add buying-word.") As has been pointed out above, when Japanese quarrel they often become exceedingly formal and painfully polite.

Yaiba ni tsuyoki mono wa rei ni suguru: "The man skillful in swordsmanship surpasses in decorum." In feudal Japan, where all men of good breeding wore swords, politeness was considered as important as, and a concomitant of, good swordsmanship.

CRITICALNESS

As a people the Japanese delight in finding and exposing the weaknesses of others. This tendency frequently results in slanderous utterances. Often in the press and in public speeches defamatory statements are made which if given in the United States or many European countries, would result in the originator being sued for slander or libel. Because they are keenly observant and quick to criticize each other and conditions around them, it follows that there is much mutual distrust among the Japanese and high sensitivity to criticism. Is it any wonder, then, that they have few if any close friends to whom they feel they can safely open their heart? As a people they are highly suspicious. This latter trait will be discussed elsewhere in this volume.

Asase ni adanami: "Restless waves in shallows." (Lit., "Enemy waves in shoals.") Shallow waves make the most din and are more dangerous for landing boats. In like manner shallow-minded persons are the most talkative and dangerous. English parallel: Empty vessels give the greatest sound.

Chōchin-mochi ashimoto kurai: "It is dark before the feet of the lantern bearer." That is, one must go abroad for news at home.

Edo wa hito no hakidame: "Edo (the ancient name for Tokyo) is the rubbish heap of men," i.e., all sorts of people from all parts of the country flock there.

Donshū-no-uo wo morasu: "To let go a boat-swallowing fish." *Donshū-no-uo* ("boat-swallowing fish") is the slang term for a notorious criminal. The greatest rascals are often not caught by the law. English parallel: Laws catch flies but let hornets go free.

Heta no naga-dangi: "The unskillful talk long." Poor speakers hold forth a long time. English parallel: Brevity is the soul of wit.

Hito no kuchi ni wa to wa taterarenu: "You can't stop people from talking." ("To people's mouths you cannot put doors.")

Hito no shichinan wa miyuredomo, waga jū-nan wa miezu: "Though you see the seven defects of others, we do not see our own ten defects."

Hito no senaka wa mietemo, jibun no senaka wa mienu: "Though you see the back of another you cannot see your own." A man can easily notice the faults of others but not his own. See Matthew 7:3–5. English parallel: The eye that sees all things sees not itself.

Homare takaku shite soshiri okoru: "As a man's reputation is high so there will arise censure." English parallel: The brighter the moon the more the dog howls.

Ichido yukanu baka, nido yuku baka: "He who never goes is a fool, he who goes twice is also a fool." This saying is used in relation to visiting places in Japan famous for beauty or historical interest. Probably, because there are so many beautiful and noted places, one should not waste his time visiting the same place again until all have been seen and enjoyed.

Ichi wo shitte ni wo shirazu: "He knows the first thing but not the second." (Lit., "Knowing one thing he knows not two.") This expression is applied to a person who knows only half of any matter. English parallel: To look on only one side of the shield.

Iki no kusaki wa nushi shirazu: "The person with a foul breath does not know it." One is often unaware of his own defects.

Jibun de jibun no omomi wa wakaranu: "One does not know one's own weight." This can be interpreted positively, i.e., a person cannot know his own importance; or negatively, i.e., one is not aware of one's faults. The latter interpretation is more often used. English parallel: One cannot see the beam in one's own eye. See Matthew 7:3–5.

Kusai mono mi shirazu: "A stinking person does not know his own foul odor." This can be interpreted literally but is more often taken metaphorically.

Waga kuso kusaku nashi: "I see not my own faults." (Lit., "My own feces do not stink.") That is, a person is not aware of his own defects until they are brought to his attention by other people.

Imo no nieta mo gozonji nai: "He lacks common sense." (Lit., "He doesn't even know whether the potatoes are boiled or not."). A disparaging statement about a person who is not aware of what is taking place under his very nose.

Inaka no gakumon, Kyō no hirune: "Scholarship in rural areas is equivalent to taking a siesta in the metropolis." All that may be learned in the country does not amount to more than a midday nap in the capital. As in other nations, the city man in Japan has from old looked with scorn on the country man, despite the fact that many outstanding leaders have come from rural areas.

Jōzu no te kara mizu ga moru: "An expert sometimes makes a slip." (Lit., "From the fingers of a skillful hand, water may leak.") English parallel: Even Homer nods.

Kaizoku ga sanzoku no tsumi wo ageru: "The pirates recite the crimes of the brigands." He who has faults should not be critical of the faults of others. English parallel: The pot calls the kettle black.

Kanae no keichō wo tō: "To be weighed in the balance and found wanting," or "to have one's ability called in question." (Lit., "To question the relative weight of the tripod kettle.") The Chinese classics relate that in ancient times, King Wu caused metal contributed by the entire country to be made into a tripod kettle, which he transmittted to his descendants as a sign of royalty. Hence, the expression "To question the weight or worth of the tripod kettle" came to mean "to question a man's or a ruler's competency with a view to supplanting him."

Kattai no kusa urami: "Even the leper thinks ill of the syphilitic." English parallel: Every man thinks his own burden the heaviest.

Kinsen wa tanin: "Money matters make strangers." Where money is involved people who are friends often show an inimical attitude and act coldly towards each other. English parallels: Business is business. A ready way to lose your friend is to lend him money.

Kōji ma ōshi: "Good luck invites many mishaps." (Lit., "Good things, demons many.") Sometimes when an individual or family is in fortunate circumstances, many unpleasant happenings take place to make life difficult or unhappy. The above proverb is frequently quoted to remind a person or family enjoying an easy life not to become overconfident. English parallel: Lights are usually followed by shadows.

Koppu no arashi: "A big to-do about a small matter." (Lit., "In a tumbler, a storm.") English parallels: Much ado about nothing. A tempest in a teacup. This last English parallel is so close to the Japanese proverb, it is more than likely that the Japanese is a direct translation.

Kusuri ku-sōbai: "The high cost of medicine." (Lit., "Medicine priced up nine times.") This proverb expresses the common belief that druggists and doctors charge nine times the actual cost. Physicians are included because in Japan many of them produce in their own laboratories the medicines they prescribe to their patients.

Kutsu wo hedatete kayuki wo kaku: "To fail to get at the seat of the trouble." (Lit., "To scratch an itching place through the shoe.") To scratch your shoe when your foot itches is most unsatisfactory.

Kyō ni inaka ari: "In the capital there are rural elements." Even in a metropolis we may find backward people and conditions. Latin parallel: *Rus in urbe.*

Kyō no ki-daore, Ōsaka no kui-daore, Sakai no tate-daore: "Kyōto people ruin themselves in dress extravagence, Ōsaka people in food, and Sakai people in housing." This proverb originating during the feudal period, describes the chief shortcoming of the people living in the three most populous districts.

Kyōboku kaze no netamaru: "Great trees are envied by the wind." This proverb is often quoted when men prominent in political, business, or intellectual life are attacked by their lessers. English parallel: High regions are never without storms.

Kyōboku kaze ōshi: "Tall trees, much wind." The Japanese version of the English proverb: "Tall trees catch much wind."

Kyōboku wa kaze ni nikumareru: "Big trees are hated by the wind." This proverb and the two preceding ones teach that people who are outstanding or prominent receive much criticism. In fact, they are more often subject to attack than the average person.

Meibutsu ni umai mono nashi: "The reality often belies the fame." (Lit., "Among celebrated products there are none delicious.") Much advertised articles are often disappointing, so beware of highly recommended products of famous places. In Japan every city and town has its *"meibutsu"* (lit., "name-thing") or famous product which is sold in great quantities to travelers and tourists.

Mekura no kaki nozoki: "To do something that is unavailing; to pretend." (Lit., "The peeping through the fence by a blind man.") This saying is frequently applied to a person who dares to criticize something of which he knows nothing.

Mekura no magure-atari: "The accidental hit of a blind man." People with no ability may make a lucky guess. English parallel: A blind man may sometimes shoot a crow.

Miso wo tsukeru: "To put bean paste on food." This proverb has the more widely used secondary meaning of "to make a mess of things" or "to make a failure of a project."

Mugei taishoku: "A lazy glutton." (Lit., "No accomplishments, great eater.") This is a scornful description of a good-for-nothing glutton who is unfit for any work.

Nusubito ni kane no ban: "To have a robber watch the money," i.e., to give a position of financial responsibility to a notoriously dishonest person. English parallel: To set the wolf to guard the sheep.

O ni o wo tsukeru: "An exaggerated statement." (Lit., "To add tail to tail.")

Ō-otoko sōmi ni chie ga mawari-kane: "In the entire body of a big man wisdom cannot circulate." Unusually large men are believed to be lacking in mental ability. For example, professional wrestlers, who are often more than six feet tall and weigh over three hundred pounds, are said to be wanting intellectual acuteness. English parallel: Big head, little wit.

Saru no shiri warai: "Monkeys laugh at the buttocks (generally bright red) of other monkeys." This proverb is directed against those who ridicule a trait or habit which they themselves have. English parallel: An ass nicknames another "long ears."

Shijū no baka wa hontō no baka: "A fool at forty is a true fool." Because at that age a man should have acquired some wisdom and discretion.

Shijū baka wa shijū baka: "A fool at forty is always a fool." Note the pun on the word *"shijū,"* which, depending on the Chinese ideograph used, may mean either "forty" or "always."

Shimobe no me ni wa eiyū nashi: "There is no hero in the eyes of his servant." Perhaps because intimate and constant association revealed too many faults. English parallel: No man is a hero to his valet.

Shiro ḳuro no sa: "As different as white from black."

Sora to tsuchi no sa: "As different as the sky from the ground." The two proverbs above are much used to describe extreme differences.

Shōbai-gataḳi: "Trade or professional rivals." (Lit., "Trade enemies.") That is, two or more of the same trade or profession have difficulty in getting along together.

Shōnin ada-gataḳi: "Merchants regard each other as foes." They are always trying to undercut each other.

Shūḳō wa ḳane wo toḳasu: "Criticism (slanders) by many people can melt metal." (Lit., "Many mouths can melt metal.") as previously stated, the Japanese are very sensitive to criticism, especially when it comes from a large group.

Suriḳogi bōzu: "A wooden-pestle priest." This is a contemptuous description of a Buddhist priest whose religious life is waning, just as the wooden pestle from much use is decreasing in size.

Tane ga naḳereba tejina mo deḳinu: "Without some source (seed) sleight of hand cannot be done." There is always some source for everything. English parallel: Without bait fish are not caught.

Tenseḳi koḳe wo shōsezu: "Moss does not grow on a rolling stone." This is probably taken directly from the English proverb, "A rolling stone gathers no moss," and has the same connotation.

Teppō-dama no tsuḳai: "A messenger who does not come back at all"; or one who tarries too long before returning from his errand. (Lit., "A bullet messenger.")

Unomi ni suru: "To swallow whole; to bolt." (Lit., "To swallow like a cormorant.") Hence to accept a matter or statement without careful scrutiny or critical examination.

Uwasa wo sureba ḳage: "Gossip about a person, and his shadow will appear." English parallels: Talk about the devil and he will appear. Talk of an angel and you'll hear his wings.

Waga ḳoto wa tana ni agete oḳu: "My affairs I place up on the shelf." This describes the attitude of a selfish man who, unmindful of what he does, finds fault with what others do.

Yokoyari wo ireru: "A spear thrust from the side." This striking phrase describes an interruption by a third person in a conversation or discussion.

Yoippari no asane-bō: "To keep late hours." (Lit., "Late hours at night and morning sleeper.") One who is late to bed and late to rise is not greatly admired in Japan. English opposite: Early to bed and early to rise, makes a man healthy, wealthy, and wise.

CRUELTY

THERE IS A STREAK OF CRUELTY in Japanese character, which though carefully concealed, comes to the surface in times of national stress such as war or natural calamity. The terrible atrocities committed by Japanese troops in Hankow and Nanking in 1938, the bayonetting of women and children by Japanese soldiers in the sack of Manila, the treatment accorded American prisoners in Bataan, Corregidor, and in prison camps generally, attest to the cruelty latent in Japanese character. From ancient times revenge was held to be a virtue, and the true and dramatic story of the forty-seven *Rōnin* ("lordless samurai") who took vengeance on the high official who insulted their lord forcing the latter to commit suicide, is still today the most popular play in Japan, drawing huge crowds wherever and whenever shown. This emphasis on retribution probably stems back to the days of blood feuds among primitive tribes, but even in these modern times many Japanese consider it a virtuous thing to assist cosmic retribution (karma) to catch up with his enemy.

Akago no te wo nejiru yō: "An easy thing to do." (Lit., "Like twisting the arm of an infant.") This and even worse things were done by Japanese soldiers in China, the Philippine Islands, and other occupied countries.

Bōzu niku-kerya kesa made nikui: "He who hates a Buddhist priest hates even his stole." This is often said of the unforgiving person who hates not only his enemy but also the whole family and friends of the latter. English parallel: He who hates Peter harms his dog.

Chi de chi wo arau: "To wash blood with blood." This strong phrase suggest violent quarrels between *samurai,* or between relatives over matters of inheritance or succession.

Edo no kataki wo Nagasaki de utsu: "To avenge in Nagasaki the wrong suffered in Edo." This is a popular saying to indicate that a man wronged by somebody may take vengeance afterwards by an indirect method.

Hito no itai no wa sannen demo shimbō (gaman) suru: "We can endure the pain of others for even three years." This statement of a person's usual unconcern about the sufferings of others is quite characteristic of many Japanese. My father was one day returning from a trip to a certain village when he saw a large crowd on a bridge laughing, talking, and peering down into the flood-swollen waters below. Dismounting from his bicycle he inquired into the nature of the excitement, and was told that a short while before a woman with her baby on her back had fallen in and drowned. No one, it seemed, felt the need to help them!

Kawamukō no kaji: "A matter of indifference." (Lit., "A fire on the opposite side of the river.") Something that one can look at with indifference.

Hito ware ni tsurakereba, ware mata hito ni tsurashi: "If a man acts bitter to me, I shall be bitter to him." That is, do evil to others as others have done to me.

Hito wo norowaba ana futatsu: "If you curse a man there will be two graves." He who invokes evil upon another person will himself receive evil. English parallel: Curses like chickens come home to roost.

Itai ue no hari: "Pins to pains." Misfortunes come one after the other. This phrase may come from the old Chinese treatment for pain by acupuncture, or the puncturing of bodily tissue with sharp needles. The following six proverbs all have the general meaning that misfortunes seldom come alone.

Itaki kizu ni shio wo sosogu: "To pour salt on a painful wound." This is a quotation from Yamanoue-no Okura's poem, "Dialogue on Poverty," in the *Manyōshū,* a collection of famous poems produced more than twelve centuries ago.

Korogeta ue wo fumareru: "To be trampled on after you fall down."

Mijikai mono wo hashi kiru: "Cutting off the end of a thing which is (already) too short." This is also a well-known quotation from the poems of Yamanoue-no Okura, who was not only famous as a man of letters, but in A.D. 701 was sent as an ambassador to China.

Naki-tsura ni hachi: "To make matters worse." (Lit., "A wasp stings the crying face.") English parallel: Misfortunes seldom come singly.

Omoki uma no uwani utsu: "To slap an upper load on a heavy-laden horse." This saying, too, is taken from the "Dialogue on Poverty," by Yamanoue-no Okura.

Tsunagi uma ni muchi utsu: "To whip a tethered horse." This is metaphorically interpreted "to add to a person's pain and distress." English parallel: To add insult to injury.

Jihi no sesshō: "A merciful killing." This phrase is used to describe cases where it seems more merciful to execute a man rather than let him suffer further.

Kaji-ba dorobō: "A thief at the scene of a fire." The contemptible act of taking unfair advantage of any affliction or misfortune at the cost of the sufferers.

Kawaisa amatte nikusa ga hyakubai: "Excessive tenderness (love) turns to hundred-fold hatred (when betrayed)." English parallel: Who loves too much hates in like extreme.

Shine-gana me kujiro: "Death to thee, your eyes will I pluck out!" An instance of extreme cruelty.

Yowai-mono ijime: "A bully, a blusterer." (Lit., "Oppressing the weak.")

CURIOSITY

As A RACE and as individuals the Japanese are exceedingly curious. A common question when you meet a friend or an acquaintance on the street is, "Where are you going?" To this the usual reply is, "Just over there." Actually your friend does not expect you to state explicitly where you are going. It is a polite gesture showing interest in your movements and welfare. On meeting people for the first time the courteous questions that are usually asked and answered are: "How old are you?" "What part of Japan are you from?" "How many members are in your family?" "Where did you go to school?" "What is your business or occupation?" "Where do you live?" Nor should one be surprised when asked about this or that article, "How much did you pay for it?"

Chajin no monozuki: "A very curious person." (Lit., "The curiosity of a tea votary.") Those who participate in the tea ceremonial ask and reply to many questions dealing with the age, place of manufacture, maker, dealer, material, price, etc., of the various articles used in the rite. In fact, such questions and answers form a very important part of the ceremonial. The host would be highly incensed and keenly disappointed if his guests did not show their interest by such inquiry.

Choito namegata mi ni tsumari: "Small dishonesties and lies lead to big ones and final disaster." (Lit., "Just a little bit of licking is the end of me.") Impelled by curiosity a person may taste a forbidden article or attempt a prohibited procedure. Finding the experiment interesting and pleasant, he goes on to final discovery and punishment. English parallel: From short pleasure, long repentence.

Gumon hyaku shutsu: "The hundred questions of a fool." So said when too many are asked and the interrogated person wishes to stop the interrogator.

Kowai mono mitasa: "What one dreads one must see." (Lit., "The fearful thing I must see.") Though dreading the result, curiosity overcomes the person's fear.

Kowashi mitashi: "What is fearful I wish to see." A slightly different version of the preceding proverb. English parallel: Forbidden fruit is sweet.

Me no yoru tokoro e tama ga yoru: "Where the eyes approach, the eyeballs do too." English parallels: Like draws like. Birds of a feather flock together.

DECEIT

IN GENERAL, one may say that there is no great regard for truth in the exact sense of that term, in Japanese society. What Americans or

Europeans may regard as lies are not so according to Japanese standards. Since the end justifies the means in their way of thinking, lies are justifiable in order to "save face," or to keep from hurting another's feelings. Lies are also frequently spoken in jest and understood in that way. Lies may, again, rise from overpoliteness. The extreme use of words depreciating or humbling oneself—such terms are abundant in the Japanese language—naturally lead to deceit, but the average Japanese quite understands and sees through it all. The feudal system of espionage and reporting, encouraged lying and dishonesty. Philosophic integrity, that is, truth for truth's sake, is rare among the Japanese and does not interest them.

Baka shōjiki: "To be foolishly honest." A person who is completely honest to his own loss is not admired.

Goma wo suru: "To flatter or curry favor with a person." (Lit., "To grind sesame seeds.") This colloquial expression is applied to a person who plays the sycophant or who fawns upon another. English parallel: Apple polishing.

Geta wo haku: "To wear clogs; to get by graft; to take a squeeze." To the original meaning the secondary ones have been added and are in common use.

Gyūtō wo kakagete ba-niku wo uru: "To hang up a cow's head at the shop front, and sell horseflesh."

Yōtō wo kakagete ku-niku wo uru: "To hang up a sheep's head at the shopfront and sell dog meat." The crafty butcher's trick resulted in the above two proverbs of Chinese origin. They were used to describe the inconsistent proceedings of a king, who issues a decree prohibiting certain fashions or customs while permitting them in his own household. English parallel: To cry wine and sell vinegar.

Hana ō kereba mi sukunashi: "Where there are many flowers the fruits are few." This is said of persons who make many promises but fail to keep them. English parallel: Much cry, little wool.

Hari hodo no koto wo bō hodo ni iu: "To exaggerate." (Lit., "To speak of a needle as if it were a club.") English parallel: To make a mountain out of a molehill.

Ikken kyo ni hoete banken jitsu wo tsutō: "When one dog barks for nothing all other dogs bark in earnest." (Lit., "One dog barks an inanity, ten thousand dogs assert its truth.") When one person starts a false rumor, all other people will spread it as truth. English parallel: One barking dog sets all the street to barking.

Kamban ni itsuwari nashi: "Signboards do not lie." This saying was probably originated by tradesmen to encourage people to have faith in their signs. The statement in itself is not wholly true, for we know that many shop signs and advertisements are quite misleading.

Kane areba baka mo danna: "If you have money even a fool is master." A wealthy man, though a fool, will have many bowing to and agreeing with him. English parallel: Money makes the man.

Kangen wo gujin wo yorokobashimu: "Sweet words please fools." Only those who are intellectually deficient are misled by the honeyed words of flatterers and sycophants. The Japanese are quick to see this even though there is much of it in their language and customs. English parallel: Fair words please fools.

Kuchi ni mitsu ari, hara ni ken ari: "He has honey in his mouth but a sword in his belly (heart)." This describes a false and dangerous person who has evil designs on others, but outwardly is very pleasant and sweet speaking. English parallel: Mouth of honey, heart of gall.

Magaraneba yo ga watarenu: "Unless you are crooked you can't get along in the world." What a commentary this is on the dishonesty and deceit in the world! The proverb may also be interpreted: "Unless you conform to the notions and customs of others you can't go through this world."

Mawata ni hari wo tsutsumu yō: "Like a needle concealed in a mass of floss silk." This figurative expression means to simulate kindness though harboring dangerous plans, and warns us against persons who conceal evil designs under fair looks.

Mizu kiyokereba uo sumazu: "Fish do not live in clear water." Here again the implication is that deceit and dishonesty is a necessary part of the environment of people who wish to succeed in the world. In other words, strict integrity would leave a person isolated.

Neko wo kaburu: "To play the hypocrite; to feign innocence." (Lit., "To put on a cat show.") In Japanese lore the cat is said to have the power to bewitch people and has been known to dance. Hence, a young and beautiful geisha is often called "a cat" *("neko")* because she bewitches men into thinking that she loves them, though actually she is after their money or the trade or political secrets they possess. English parallel: He is only shamming.

Nusubito takedakeshii: "The brazen-faced airs of a thief." This phrase is descriptive of a wicked man's impudence in attempting to pass off his evil deeds as though they were good ones.

On wo ada: "Evil for kindness." To return an obligation with injury. There are some people who return a kind deed with evil, but such are much despised by most Japanese, who are very conscious of repaying their obligations with kindness.

Oni no nembutsu: "The Buddhist prayers of a devil." This saying is used when a cruel and wicked man feigns kindness and sympathy. A person will go to the temple and chant a Buddhist sutra at the funeral of his departed friend. Another man who has been on bad terms with the deceased will also attend the funeral service for appearance's sake and chant a sutra, when actually he has no sympathy with the sorrowing family. The deed of the second man is spoken of as "the sutra-chanting of a devil" and is despised because of its deceit.

Oni no me ni mo namida: "Tears even in a devil's eyes." This proverb has a double meaning: (1) Even the most heartless man is sometimes moved to tears by a very sad affair, and (2) False sympathy. English parallel: Crocodile tears.

Kariudo mo wana ni kakaru: "Even a hunter is sometimes caught in a trap." That is, the man who plots to ruin another will often be ruined himself by the very means he employs on the other man. English parallel: Harm watch, harm catch.

Hito wo toru kame hito ni torareru: "The tortoise that catches a man is caught by a man." This has the same meaning as the proverb given above.

Rakkyō kūte kuchi wo nugū: "Feigning innocence." (Lit., "Wiping the mouth after eating leeks.")

Shimo to uso to wa nochi ga warui; "Frost and falsehood both become evil afterwards." This is probably taken directly from the English proverb: Frost and fraud both end in foul.

Shishi shinchū no mushi: "The worm in the lion's body." This describes a traitor who plays false to the master or country that gives him subsistence and protection. English parallel: A snake in one's bosom.

Shōbai to byōbu wa magaranu to tatanu: "Business and folding screens must be crooked to stand," i.e., dishonesty is necessary for success in business. No wonder that in the feudal period in Japan the merchant was in the lowest class, just above the outcaste. This cannot be said of merchants in modern Japan, most of whom are honest and truthful.

Tamago to chikai wa kudake-yasui: "Eggs and vows are easily broken."

Torō, torō de torowareru: "Let's catch, let's catch (we say) and we are caught." He who tries to catch others by shady business deals often ends up by getting caught himself.

Usotsuki wa dorobō no hajimari: "A liar is the beginning of a thief."

Uso wa nusubito no hajimari: "A lie is the beginning of a thief." English parallel: Show me a liar and I'll show you a thief.

Uso wa ato kara hageru: "Lies are afterwards disclosed." (Lit., "Lies afterward fade.") That is, they soon lose their gloss. They may succeed but for a short time. English parallel: Lies melt like snow.

Uso kara deta makoto: "The truth that comes out of a lie." Sometimes truth is revealed by a lie. Many a true word is spoken in jest. English parallel: Crooked logs make straight fires.

Uso no yō na makoto (hontō): "A truth that looks like a lie." English parallel: Truth is stranger than fiction.

Uso mo hōben: "A lie, also, is an expedient." That is lying may be resorted to for the sake of convenience. English parallel: A necessary lie is harmless.

Uwamae wo haneru: "To take a commission." (Lit., "To cut off above and before.")

Yamai ni wa katarenu: "Illness cannot be defeated." Since there is no way to contend against it successfully, politicians, business men, and the public in general make sickness a convenient excuse. When they get into a difficult situation, they will often plead "illness" and withdraw or resign until matters have cleared up. Westerners feel it is a cowardly thing to do, for it is a refusal to meet the issue fairly and squarely. However, in the East a direct approach is generally not done, for a roundabout way is considered better.

DETAIL

As a race the Japanese are exceedingly neat in their persons and homes. Great emphasis is placed on details in planning and execution. "A place for everything and everything in its place" would appear to be one of their mottoes. To see or live in disorder gives the Japanese pain. They are perfectionists who constantly strive to improve conditions and their surroundings. This zeal for detail is found not only in Japanese art and literature but also in their scientific studies and achievement.

Ari no ana kara tsutsumi ga kuzureru: "An ant hole may collapse an embankment," i.e., be careful of small mistakes or omissions.

Senjō no tsutsumi mo ari no ana yori kuzuru: "Even a ten-thousand-foot embankment may give way because of an ant hole." This proverb, taken from ancient Chinese wisdom, points out that a small oversight may lead to a great disaster. English parallel: A little leak will sink a great ship.

Daiji wa shōji kara: "Serious disasters come from small causes."

Hotarubi wo motte shumisan wo yaku: "To burn Mount Sumeru with the glow of a firefly." Sumeru is an imaginary great mountain in Buddhist lore. This proverb indicates that a trifle may often cause a great disaster, so extreme care should be taken at all times. English parallel: A small spark makes a great fire.

Bentō wa yōi kara: "The lunch is from previous preparations." English parallel: Make hay while the sun shines.

Chiisaku tomo hari wa nomarenu: "Even small things are to be used with care." (Lit., "Though small a needle is not to be swallowed.")

Daichi ni tsuchi: "To strike the ground with a hammer." (Lit., "Against the solid earth, a hammer.") When we try to hit a small thing we often miss, but never fail when we strike the ground. Thus the above phrase means "Not to fail in one's intentions."

Hajime wa daiji: "The beginning is most important." A good beginning is most likely to insure success. English parallel: Well begun is half done.

Hotoke tsukutte manako wo irezu: "It lacks the finishing touch." (Lit., "Buddha's image is made but the eyes have not been put in.")

Hotoke tsukutte tamashii irezu: "You do not give the finishing touch to your work." (Lit., "Buddha's image is made but the spirit has not been put in.") English parallel: Plowing the field and forgetting the seed. The reference to putting in the soul harks back to the special Buddhist service when that is done after the craftsman has made the image, and before it can become an object of worship.

Ichi-bu hachi ken: "Be careful not to make even little mistakes." (Lit., "One-tenth of an inch, forty-eight feet.") In aiming, the difference between aim and result may be very great when mistakes are made, as we soon find out whether we shoot an arrow, bullet, or any other projectile.

Kareki mo yama no nigiwai: "Even withered trees give prosperity to the mountain." Things of small worth will be of value when in numbers. English parallel: Anything is better than nothing.

Keshi no naka ni Shumisan ari: "The small beginning of great things." (Lit., "In a poppy seed is Mount Sumeru.") English parallels: A forest in an acorn. Great oaks from little acorns grow.

Kuruma no ryōrin ni okeru ga gotoshi: "Inseparably related things." (Lit., "It is like both wheels of a cart.")

Me-hachibu ni motsu: "To hold a thing most respectfully." (Lit., "To hold it eight-tenths of an inch above the eyes.") This is done as a matter of ceremony when making a presentation to or receiving something from a superior.

Nama-byōhō wa ō-kega no moto: "A little learning is dangerous." (Lit., "Raw military tactics are the cause of great injuries.") English parallel: A little knowledge is a dangerous thing.

Nozomu nara mazu sonae yo: "If you desire it, first prepare for it."

Nusubito no hirune mo ate ga aru: "Make careful plans then rest in preparation." (Lit., "Even in the thief's siesta there is a purpose.")

I.e., everyone has his own objects in view for doing something. English parallel: A fox sleeps but counts hens in his dreams.

Omoni ni kozuke: "An increase in troubles." (Lit., "To a heavy load a small addition.") English parallel: The last straw that breaks the camel's back.

Ō-zukai yori ko-zukai: "Rather than big expenses, take care of little expenses." English parallel: Take care of the pence and the pounds will take care of themselves.

Seite wa koto wo shisonzuru: "The hasty hand will do things wrong." English parallel: Haste makes waste.

Sukima no kaze wa samui: "The wind that comes in through a crack is cold." For such a draft may bring on some illness. Likewise, if you do not take care of small trifles you may later have to deal with big consequences.

Taikō wa saikin wo kaerimizu: "In undertaking a great work one must not have regard for minor defects."

Taijin wa shōji ni kō sezu: "A great man does not stick at trifles." (Lit., "A great man does not seize small things.")

Taiko wo uteba kane ga hazureru: "While beating the drum the bell fails." While carrying on one duty the other is neglected. In many Buddhist services both the beating of the drum and the ringing of the bell is the responsibility of one priest or acolyte.

Tekizai tekisho: "The right man in the right place." (Lit., "Suitable ability in the suitable place.") English parallel: Everything is good in its place.

Tōki omonbakari-naki mono wa kanarazu chikaki urei: "Prudence and careful forethought are needful in the conduct of life." (Lit., "One who attaches no importance to far off things will certainly have near troubles.")

Usagi no hirune: "Inattention is fatal." (Lit., "The hare's midday nap.") This proverb is based on the hare and tortoise story in Aesop's fables, many of which are given in Japanese elementary school readers, in which the hare lost the race because he took a nap on the way. Thus, failure to exercise due attention resulted in the discomforting defeat of the hare.

Yori-gonomi suru mono wa kasu wo tsukamu: "If you are over fastidious you will fare worse." (Lit., "The person who is too choosy will grasp refuse.")

DISCIPLINE

IN MANY WAYS the Japanese are amongst the world's most disciplined people. During his early years the child has little restrictions or prohibitions, but these increase as he grows older so that by the time he enters school he is aware of many things he must or must not do. When he has reached adulthood his obligations and restrictions are truly formidable. From early childhood Japanese are taught to conceal emotions and to bear pain and sorrow without flinching. This concealment of feelings is carried out even in the case of the loss of loved ones. A stoical indifference to food, warmth and other bodily comforts is deliberately cultivated. For example, for three weeks during the coldest part of winter, all the boys in a high school will arise at 4:30 A.M. and frequently, without breakfast, hasten to school and for two hours engage in martial exercises, *jūdō* and *kendō* (fencing) after which regular classes are held in unheated rooms. This is done to harden them and inure them to bodily discomfort and pain. Much emphasis, also, is placed on self-discipline *(shūyō)*, which is regarded as a means "to build up personality, increase efficiency, and to train for full and complete action in the world." This is realized by attaining *"muga,"* which is variously translated "annihilation of self," "ecstasy with no sense that I am doing it," "effortlessness," "oneness with the Universe," and "to live as already dead." It will be seen that the teachings of Zen Buddhism have played and still do play a prominent part in attaining the above ideals.

Awateru kani wa ana e hairanu: "Confused crabs miss their holes." People who get too excited or agitated are like hasty crabs rushing for their holes at the sign of danger. Lacking discipline, they are unable to behave correctly and composedly.

Urotae kani ana ni irazu: "A bewildered crab does not enter its hole." That is, the confused or demoralized person is in great danger. English parallel: The hasty angler loses the fish.

Bankon-sakusetsu ni aite riki wo miru: "A hero is revealed by misfortune." (Lit., "Superior ability is seen in meeting hardship and adversity.") English parallel: The school of adversity is the best school.

Kannan nanji wo tama ni su: "Hardships will make a jewel of you," i.e., Privations will wear off all unnecessary softness of character, leaving only a hard and polished jewel. English parallel: Sweet are the uses of adversity.

Konku ni masaru kyōiku nashi: "There is no education that can surpass privations." Forced marches in summer heat or winter snow for twenty-four hours without food or water were part of the regular training of the Japanese soldier. Is it to be wondered then that their military authorities felt that he was more than a match for the "soft" American, brought up in the lap of luxury?

Konnan wa toku no motoi: "Adversity is the foundation of virtue." English parallel: Adversity is the parent of virtue.

Bushi wa kuwanedo taka-yōji: "A warrior, though he has not eaten, will hold his toothpick high." That is, he pretends that he has had a hearty meal, for it is beneath his dignity to beg for food. English parallel: The warrior lives an honorable life even in poverty.

Chimmoku wa kin nari: "Silence is gold." Evidently a direct translation of the English proverb. The Chinese ideograph used can be read either *"kin"* or *"kane"* and is translated "gold," "money," or "metal."

Damari mushi wa kabe wo horu (tōsu): "Silent worms dig holes in (pierce) the walls." English parallel: Silent men, like still waters, are deep and dangerous.

Damaru mono ni yudan suna: "Don't be heedless of silent people." We should beware of silent people, for there is no knowing what dangerous thoughts they may be having or what mischief to others they may be planning.

Enryo hidarui shi, date samushi: "To be reserved makes one faint with hunger; to be dandyish makes one cold," i.e. To be abstemious and disciplined is not comfortable. English parallel: A bashful dog never fattens.

Gen izureba shiba mo oyobazu: "A statement once let loose cannot be caught by four (galloping) horses." Hence, the great need of discipline in speech. English parallel: A word or a stone once let go cannot be recalled.

Ichigon wo izureba shiba mo oi-gatashi: "One word let slip and four horses would fail to catch it." This proverb is a slightly different version of the one above.

Kuchi kara dereba seken: "As soon as it goes out of your mouth it goes to the world." Hence, the need for great self-control in speech.

Shi mo shita ni oyobazu: "A four-horse team cannot overtake the tongue." This saying is from the Analects of Confucius. The word *"shi"* is written as the double Chinese ideograph for "horse" and "four."

Gusha no yūben wa chimmoku nari: "An idiot's eloquence is silence." Since he is a fool and has nothing worthwhile to say, he must practice much restraint and not say anything.

Haigun no shō wa hei wo katarazu: "A general of a defeated army should not talk of tactics." This saying is both a self warning and a friendly counsel not to make critical and proud remarks on the lost chances after failing in any undertaking.

Hara no kawa ga hareba me no kawa ga tarumu: "When the skin of the belly swells, the eyelids sag." When a person has eaten too much he gets sleepy and careless and an enemy can easily attack and overcome him. Here the danger of intemperance in eating and the need for self-discipline is clearly shown.

Heike wo horobosu mono wa Heike: "It was the Heike who overthrew the Heike." "Heike" is the Japanese-Chinese pronunciation of "Taira," a famous clan that ruled Japan for many years. However, instead of keeping their early simple and martial way of life, the clan adopted frivolous and luxurious habits, thus sapping their strength and morale. This gave their more vigorous and warlike rivals, the Genji (Minamoto), an opportunity to attack. After a long and hard-fought war the Heike (Taira) were decisively defeated and the control of Japan passed into the hands of the Genji (Minamoto) clan. English parallel: As you sow so shall you reap.

Jigō-jitoku: "The natural consequences of one's own deeds." (Lit., "Self-occupation, self-complacency.") As explained above, because of their self-occupation in luxurious ways and their self-complacency the Taira family fell before the onslaught of the Minamoto. English parallel: "As you sow so shall you reap.

Mi kara deta sabi: "A fault of one's own making." (Lit., "Rust that comes from the article itself.") English parallel: It is all your own doing.

Hikigaeru ga ka wo nonda yō: "Like a toad that has swallowed a mosquito." This saying describes a person who is so self-disciplined that he always acts in a cool, disinterested way. English parallel: Like a cat that has swallowed the canary.

Hito no senki wo zutsū ni yamu na: "Mind your own business." (Lit., "Don't suffer headache for the lumbago of another.")

Hoeru inu wa kamanu: "A barking dog does not bite." There is little to fear from a talking, unrestrained person. Although such are despised they do not cause concern. English parallel: Barking dogs don't bite.

Hoeru inu wa yowai: "A barking dog is weak." So undisciplined people who give vent to their feelings by talk alone are not feared.

Hotoke no kao mo sando: "There are limits to one's endurance." (Lit., "Even Buddha's face does not wear a benign look the third time.") Even a Buddha-like long-suffering person will be aroused if you strike his face three times. English parallel: Too much familiarity breeds contempt.

Jizō no kao mo sando made: "There are limits to insults one can accept." (Lit., "Even the face of Jizō, three times"). Jizō, a popular Buddhist deity, is the patient and loving guardian of little children and travelers.

Ichi ni tora wo hanatsu yō: "Like letting a tiger loose into the market." This points out the folly of leaving at large an undisciplined and dangerous person who is likely to do great harm to many people.

Isha no fu-yōjō: "The physician is careless of his own health." (Lit., "The intemperance of doctors.") The physician is busy healing the diseases of others but often neglects his own well-being. People often meddle in the affairs of others while disregarding their own. English parallel: It is a good doctor who follows his own directions.

Konya (kōya) no shira-hakama: "The white skirt of the dyer."
A *hakama* is a divided skirt. Since a dyer is very busy in his trade,
he dyes the clothing of other people rather than his own. English
parallels: The tailor's wife is worst clad. The shoemaker's children
go barefoot. The ass that carrieth wine drinketh water.

On-yōshi minoue shirazu: "The fortuneteller cannot tell his own
fortune." This proverb is similar in meaning to the two preceding
ones.

Ishibotoke mo mono wo iu: "Even a stone Buddha will say things
on occasion." A disciplined man, no matter how taciturn or modest
he may be, will speak his mind when the right time comes.

Ishibotoke ni mono wo iwaseru: "To cause a stone Buddha to
speak." This refers to various stratagems to get an unsociable or very
modest person to join in the general conversation.

Ishi-jizō ni hachi: "A person insensible to pain." (Lit., "A wasp
to a stone Jizō.") This saying characterizes a man who is insensible
to either moral or physical pain.

Iu wa yasuku, okonō wa katashi: This is a literal Japanese trans-
lation of the English proverb: "Easy to say, hard to do."

Iwanu ga hana: "Better leave it unsaid." (Lit., "Not to speak is
the flower of wisdom.") The person who knows when not to speak
has true self-discipline. English parallel: Silence is golden.

Kanshaku-mochi no koto yaburi: "A hot-tempered person does
much harm." (Lit., "A short-tempered man destroys things.") So
the well-disciplined person keeps control of his temper.

Kao ga kokoro no kagami: "The face is the mirror of the heart."
Hence, the average Japanese strives to make his face as inscrutable
as possible, lest an enemy or rival divine his thoughts.

Kaze fuke domo yama wa ugokazu: "Though the wind blows,
the mountain does not move." This proverb explains the state of
mind of a person who is so self-controlled that he is indifferent to
any tumult or disturbance.

Kerai to naraneba kerai wo tsukaenu: "By obeying we learn to
command." (Lit., "Unless you have been a retainer you cannot use
a retainer.")

Ki no mata kara umareta yō: "Like one born from the fork of a tree." That is, with no more feelings than wood.

Kiji mo nakazuba utaremai: "Had the pheasant not screamed it would not have been shot." A person would not have found himself in trouble had he kept quiet and refrained from unwise remarks.

Kingin hoshikaranu kao suru: "To appear not to care for money." (Lit., "To make a face as though he did not wish for gold and silver.") The ideal *samurai* in the feudal period despised money and would not touch it. Either his wife or a retainer handled the filthy lucre for him.

Kokoro ni jō wo orose: "Put your mind under lock and key." This is an exhortation to be wide awake to any situation but at the same time self-controlled.

Kuchi ni amaki mono kanarazu-shimo hara wo yashinawazu: "Things sweet to the mouth do not necessarily nourish the belly." What at first seems good and desirable is not always best for the person. English parallel: That is not always good in the maw that is sweet.

Kuchi ni zei wa kakaranu: "To be free to speak." (Lit., "No tax is placed on the mouth.") English parallel: Talking pays no toll.

Kuchi no owari wa te no hajime: "When the mouth ceases (to speak) the hands begin (to strike)." When quarreling words are ineffective fists will begin to fly, but the man who is fully disciplined will refrain from using either.

Kuchi to fundoshi wa kataku shimeyo: "Shut tightly your mouth and your loincloth." The meaning is: refuse to be drawn into an argument, but be prepared for physical encounter or exertion.

Kuchi wa wazawai no mon (kado): "The mouth is the gate of misfortune and evil." Indiscreet words result in much harm and bring untold suffering. English parallel: Let not your tongue cut your throat.

Kuchi wa toji, me wo ake: "Shut the mouth and open the eyes." This injunction is taken directly from the English hortatory proverb: "Mouth shut and eyes open."

Kuchi wo tozaseba arasoi okorazu: "If the mouth is fastened shut no quarrel arises." A popular proverb, but not observed by many people. English parallel: A shut mouth keeps one out of strife.

Kusuri mo sugureba doku: "Even medicine when exceeded becomes poison." This has been scientifically proven and is especially true in these days of modern drugs. English parallel: Too much wax burns the church.

Mi wo sutete koso ukabu se mo aru: "Only when you throw yourself away will you find shallows on which you may float to safety." This proverb teaches the importance of complete relaxation. The man who is truly disciplined and self-controlled can relax and float through dangers to safety. This proverb may also be taken to mean: "Only when you make such a supreme effort as to forget self, will you attain success." English parallels: He that loseth his life shall find it. Nothing ventured nothing gained.

Mizaru, kikazaru, iwazaru: Lit., "Not to see, not to hear, not to speak." That is, not to see other's faults, not to hear other's scandals, and not to talk of other's failures. The Japanese word for "not," *"zaru,"* has a sound almost similar to *"saru"* or "monkey." Hence, the above proverb is portrayed in Japanese painting and sculpture as three monkeys sitting side by side: the first with his hands to his eyes ("see no evil"), the second with his hands to his ears ("hear no evil"), and the third with his hands to his mouth ("speak no evil"). These mark the well-bred and well-disciplined person. Note that the emphasis is negative—not what one should do, but what one should *not* do. Another good example of negative injunction is the Confucian form of the Golden Rule: "What you do not wish others to do to you, do not to them."

Nakanu neko wa nezumi wo toru: "The cat that does not mew catches rats," i.e., the truly efficient person goes about his business quietly.

Naranu kannin suru ga kannin: "To endure what is unendurable is true endurance." True forbearance lies in bearing what is unbearable. This well-known proverb exhorts us to bear with patience an insult or wrong done to us, in the hope of winning over the wrongdoer and getting him to make amends peacefully. The saying was quoted by the Emperor of Japan when on August 15, 1945, he broad-casted to the people his order to surrender to the Allied Powers.

Narau yori nare yo: "Practice makes perfect." (Lit., "Better than to be taught is to become experienced.")

Nō naki inu no takaboe: "The dog that has no understanding barks loudly." (Lit. "The loud bark of the brainless dog.") People who are inefficient do much talking, but the truly capable person is quiet.

Nō naki no kuchitataki: "The incessant and loud jabber of incapable persons."

Nukanu tachi no kōmyō: "To perform a glorious exploit with undrawn sword." This proverb originally applied to warriors on the battlefield but it is now used in referring to a man who attains his object without going to extremes.

Nō aru taka tsume wo kakusu: "The wise hawk conceals his talons." That is, a truly wise person does not make show of his resources and ability. English parallels: Who knows most says least. Still waters run deep. Cats hide their claws.

Ryō-ko wa fukaku zōshite munashiki ga gotoshi: "A skilled merchant keeps his goods deeply hid and acts as if he had none." So, a wise person conceals his talents and pretends that he hasn't any.

Nukegake no kōmyō: "A splendid exploit by stealing a march on others." This expression is applied to a man who scores a brilliant success in advance of others. English parallel: Making "a scoop."

Nusubito ga inu ni kuwawareta: "The thief is eaten by the dogs." He was so silent and had such self-control that even when the dogs were chewing him up he made no outcry. Such a person is greatly admired by the Japanese, as did the Spartans of ancient Greece praise the boy who made no sound when under his garment the stolen fox ate into his vitals.

Ō-dori suru yori ko-dori seyo: "Make a small gain rather than a big one." It is good business to get many small profits rather than a few big ones. English parallel: Little and often fills the purse.

Okuba ni mono ga hasamatta yō: "Extreme reserve." (Lit., "As if something had stuck between one's back teeth.") When a Japanese, asked to make a speech, wishes to appear reserved or has no desire to commit himself, he will talk slowly with appropriate pauses and hisses between words, but actually says little that is meaningful.

Sanchū no zoku tairageru koto yasuku, shinchū no zoku tairageru koto katashi: "The bandits in the mountain are easily subjected, but it is difficult to subject the bandits in my heart." English parallel: The greatest victory is victory over self.

Saya-bashira yori kuchibashira: "The tongue is more to be feared than the sword." (Lit., "Rather than a fast scabbard a fast mouth is more fearful.")

Seite wa koto wo shisonjiru: "Hasty ones make blunders." (Lit., "The hasty hand bungles things.") English parallel: Haste makes waste.

Shiina no sakibashiri: "An immature ear of corn appears first." A forward person is often unworthy and useless. A person too quick to speak and act may not be as useful as one who is more thoughtful and slow.

Shiru mono iwazu, iu mono shirazu: "Those who know do not speak, those who speak do not know." A wise man is silent while an ignorant man chatters. English parallel: Who knows most says least.

Shōjin ikari yasushi: "Little men get angry easily." A man who can control his anger under trying circumstances is a "big man," for he has learned self-discipline.

Shu ni majiwareba akaku naru: "He who mixes with vermillion becomes red," i.e., it is important to keep away from corrupting influences. English parallel: He who touches pitch defiles himself.

Suku michi yori yaburu: "The road that is preferred leads to destruction." That is, the easy, delightful road may often lead to ruin. The man who refuses the steep and narrow path of life but takes instead the broad and easy road will end life as a failure. See Matthew 7:13–14.

Tai-in wa ichi ni kakuru: "A great sage lives in a town." (Lit., "A great retired person lives hid in the market.") Though a hermit may lead a pious life in a desert or a lonely mountain, a truly great person lives in crowded streets and is not affected by his surroundings. He can have a disciplined life in spite of his surroundings.

Taru koto wo shiru mono wa kōfuku nari: "He who knows when he has enough is fortunate." He is blessed who knows how to be satisfied. English parallels: Contentment is natural wealth. Enough is as good as a feast.

Taru wo shirazaru mono wa mazushii: "He is poor who does not feel content." (Lit., "He who knows not when he has enough is poor.") English parallel: He is not rich who is not satisfied.

Ukedachi ni naru: "To be on the defensive." (Lit., "To be parrying.") The odds are generally against the person who is on the defensive, whether physically or metaphorically.

Urei uchi ni areba iro soto in arawaru: "If there is sadness within it will be revealed externally by the color of the face." Hence, strive to control your facial expression so as not to cause embarrassment or sorrow to others.

Ushi no tsuno wo hachi ga sashita yō: "As if an ox's horn were stung by a wasp." A description of a person who is utterly indifferent to the criticisms of others. English parallel: An elephant does not feel a fleabite.

Wazawai wa kuchi yori kitaru: "Misfortune comes from the mouth." Consequently, better keep it shut.

Wazawai wa kuchi yori ide, yamai wa kuchi yori iru: "Misfortune comes out of your mouth, disease goes in at your mouth." One often gets into trouble through thoughtless words, and illnesses often come from intemperance in eating and drinking, or from certain viruses that enter through the mouth.

DRINK

THE JAPANESE NATIONAL DRINK is *"saké,"* a rice wine with varying alcoholic content. It is used to help the drinker relax and put aside the excessive demands of punctilious ceremony in all of life's relationships. Though they are great admirers of heavy drinkers, the Japanese recognize the dangers of excessive indulgence. It is remarkable how much emotional release a Japanese can get from a relatively small amount of *saké.* Among the foreign drinks now obtainable in Japan, beer is the most popular, large amounts of which are brewed in different parts of the country.

Chidori ashi de aruku: "To walk like a plover." This expression is used to indicate the zigzag reel of a drunken man.

Dorobō-zake no dekinu mono: "There are people who cannot drink stolen *saké*." Because they have conscientious scruples.

Futsuka yoi ni wa mukae-zaké: "For a two-day intoxication take another drink." English parallel: Let us take a hair of the dog that bit us.

Geko no tatetaru kura wa nashi: "There is no warehouse built by a teetotaler." This saying, which is a fling at the abstemious by the alcoholists, asserts that no nondrinker has even been known to have become rich enough to build a warehouse for storing his wealth.

Hana wa hankai, saké wa bisui: "As to flowers, when half open; as to *saké*, when a person is half tipsy." Just as flowers are at their best when half open, so wine is most enjoyed when a person is slightly drunk.

Ippai wa hito saké wo nomi, nihai wa saké saké wo nomi, sambai wa saké hito wo nomu: "The first cup, the man drinks wine; the second cup, wine drinks wine; the third cup, wine drinks up the man." English parallel: Wine is a turncoat; first a friend, then an enemy.

Jōgo wa doku wo shirazu, geko wa kusuri wo shirazu: "The tippler does not know the poison, the teetotaler the medicine (contained in *saké*)."

Jōgo wa honshō wo arawasu: "The tippler discloses his true character." Because all his inhibitions are removed through alcohol.

Jūmonji ni fumu: "To walk like the figure ten." The Japanese figure ten is shaped like the Latin cross. Hence, to walk with one's footsteps making a cross on the ground is to walk in a drunken manner.

Kane wa hi de kokoromi, hito wa saké de kokoromu: "Metal is tested by fire, man by wine.

Kintoki no kaji mimai: "Kintoki going to the scene of a fire (to express his sympathy for the sufferers)." Kintoki, a hero of old Japan, was reputed to have had an extremely red face. Hence, the above saying is used to describe the red face of a drunken man.

Namayoi honshō tagawazu: "The half tipsy man does not depart from his true character." That is, he never loses his self-consciousness, for he knows what he says and does. English parallel: Wine shows the true character.

Nomanu saké ni wa yowanu: "You don't get drunk on wine which you do not drink."

Okame ga amazaké ni yotta yō: "Something extremely funny." (Lit., "As if Okame had gotten drunk on sweet rice wine.") Okame is the popular deity of rollicking fun. When he gets drunk on *"amazaké* (sweet rice wine), much merriment is likely to take place.

Ryōshu wa kamban wo yō sezu: "Good liquor needs no signboard." This is the Japanese translation of the English proverb: Good wine needs no bush.

Sakazuki wa tatami no moyō de wa nai: "Wine cups are not a pattern for the floor mats." That is, they should not be so numerous as to be used for a pattern.

Saké to asane wa bimbō no chikamichi: "Wine and late-rising are short cuts to poverty." *"Asane,"* here translated "late-rising," is literally "morning sleep."

Saké nakute nan no onore ga sakura kana: This proverb is also a much quoted *haiku* or seventeen-syllable poem and may be roughly translated: "Without wine, even beautiful cherry blossoms have small attraction!" Note that the English translation is also in seventeen syllables.

Saké no seki ni wa chin, neko, baba: "When you sit down with wine, (you dislike) dogs, cats, and old women."

Saké wa honshin wo arawasu: "Wine reveals a person's true heart." English parallel: The true man comes out in drink.

Saké wa hyaku yaku no chō, hyaku doku no chō: "Wine is the best of all (lit., 'one hundred') medicines and the worst of all poisons." In Japan, rice wine *(saké)* is held to be healthful when taken moderately but harmful when imbibed in large quantities.

Saké wa hyaku yaku no moto: "Wine is the source of all (lit., 'one hundred') medicines." That is, it is the best of all medicines.

Saké wa kan, shaku wa tabo: "The wine should be warm, the pourer should have a chignon." This saying describes ideal conditions for drinking—warm wine poured by an attractively dressed young woman! The *tabo* (chignon) was used in Japan for the hair arrangement of young unmarried women.

Saké wa kyōsui: "Wine is lunatic water." English parallel: When wine is in, the wit is out.

Saké wa nomu tomo, saké ni nomareru na: "Though you drink wine, do not be drunk by wine." Good advice to be moderate in drinking.

Saké wa rei ni hajimatte ran ni owaru: "Wine begins with formalities and ends in a riot."

Saké wa urei wo harau tama-hōki: "Wine is a jewel-broom to sweep away sorrow." English parallel: Wine makes glad the heart of man.

Sasa no tsuyu ni mo yō hodo: "(So weak at drinking) that he even becomes tipsy on the dew of the bamboo grass." This saying is a derogatory expression to describe a poor drinker.

Seinen to saké wa tobi-uma ni muchi: "Youth and wine are like a whip to a galloping horse."

Shita no mawarenu hodo: "Dead drunk." (Lit., "So drunk that the tongue no longer turns.")

Sokonuke jōgo: "An insatiable drinker." (Lit., "A bottoms-removed heavy drinker.") English parallel: "Bottoms up!"

Yoite wa honshō wo arawasu: "When drunk a man reveals his true self."

Yoizame (Eizame) no mizu geko shirazu: "The first drink of cold water after intoxication is unknown to the teetotaler." That is, a nondrinker has no experience of the delicious taste of a glass of cold water after waking up from a drunken spree.

Yoizame (Eizame) no mizu wa kanro no aji: "To the heavy drinker on awakening, water tastes like nectar."

EMOTION

BASICALLY the Japanese are a highly emotional people. Much faith is put in intuition. This statement may surprise many Westerners who have always regarded the Japanese as "deadpan" stoics. Though easily moved to tears or anger, social conformity dictates that the feelings be hidden. Sometimes these pent-up emotions explode with disastrous results. As a people, the Japanese are much given to fads and enthusiasms, but the fervent admiration of today may easily change on the morrow to coolness or even repugnance. Loving change for the sake of change, the younger generation will often take up ideas or practices which may startle their elders or those in authority. However, such are not long retained for they are soon dropped for something else new or interesting. Hence, the Japanese have been accused of being exceedingly fickle, volatile, and unpredictable. Inazo Nitobe, a very wise and observant man, wrote some years ago of his own people: "The emotions of the Japanese are shallow . . . their sympathy, too, has no depth and appears to have no content." To the writer, this criticism seems overly harsh, but it cannot be denied that numerous instances can be cited to sustain Nitobe's judgment. All people have contradictory characteristics, and the Japanese are no exception. Accordingly, it need not be thought strange when the statement is made that the Japanese are both a disciplined and an emotional people. Over their original and basic emotionalism there has been superimposed the strong discipline of self-control and the concealment of the feelings. Thus emotional instability is hidden under the mask of stoicism.

Aki no sora wa nanatabi han kawaru: "The sky in autumn changes seven and a half times." This is because fall weather is very changeable.

Otoko-gokoro to aki no sora: "A man's heart is as changeable as the skies in autumn." (Lit., "A man's heart and the autumnal sky.") This is what women say about the fickleness of men in amorous affairs. To this the men reply with the following much-quoted proverb:

Onna no kokoro to haru-biyori: "A woman's heart is as changeable as the weather in spring." (Lit., "A woman's heart and spring weather.") English parallel: Woman is as fickle as April weather.

Ame harete kasa wasuru: "When the rain stops the rain hat is forgotten." When the need is past the useful article is left behind. Two other proverbs of similar meaning are:

Nodo-moto sugureba atsusa wo wasureru: "After it has passed the throat the hotness of it is forgotten." That is, after the danger is passed it is no longer remembered. English parallel: Vows made in storms are forgotten in calms.

Atsusa wasurete kage wasuru: "The heat forgotten, the shade forgotten." English parallel: The peril past, the saint mocked.

Ato wa no to nare yama to nare: "After I'm gone, let the place become a wild moor or a mountain." Said of an irresponsible person who leaves the work assigned to him only partially finished or in great confusion when he has to go. English parallel: After me the deluge.

Bun sō-ō ni kaze ga fuku: "The wind blows to suit our condition." In proportion to a man's fitness or station in life the winds (of adversity) will blow on him.

Edokko wa ki ga hayai: "Edo people are quick tempered." The old name for Tokyo was Edo. Its people are proverbially short tempered and easily come to blows when offended.

Edokko wa satsuki no koi no fukinagashi: "The Edoite is like the May carp streamers." That is, swelled with air but quite useless except to announce the number of sons in the family. The reference is to the Boys' Festival of May 5, when a large paper or cloth carp is flown from a tall pole for each son in the family.

Edokko wa yoigoshi no zeni wo tsukawanai: "The Edoite will not keep overnight his earnings." He uses up his money as he goes along. In contrast to the Kyotoite, who is more thrifty, the Edoite is somewhat of a spendthrift.

Eshi to daigen-nin no te ni kakareba, shiroi mono wa kuroku naru: "At the hands of painters and lawyers white things become black." This is probably a translation of the English proverb: Lawyers and painters can soon change white to black.

Gyofu no ri wo shimeru: "To get a fisherman's profit." That is, to play off one person against another.

Hachi no su wo tsutsuita yō: "Just as if one has poked a wasp's nest." This metaphor describes great turmoil and confusion caused by some sudden occurrence.

Hito no senaka wa mietemo jibun no senaka wa mienu: "Though you may see another's back you cannot see your own." A man can take notice of the faults of others but cannot see his own. English parallel: The eye that sees all things else sees not itself.

Inu to saru no naka: "To be on bad terms." (Lit., "The terms of a dog and a monkey.") The quarrelsome relationship between people is often so described.

Inu to neko no naka: "To be on bad terms." (Lit., "The relationships of a dog and a cat.") The antagonistic terms between two people is sometimes so described. English parallel: They agree like cats and dogs.

Itteki senkin: "To throw away money in one big fling." (Lit., "One fling, a thousand gold pieces.")

Jinshin wa sono men no gotoshi: "Men's hearts (minds) are as different as their faces." (Lit., "Men's minds are like their faces.") That is, they are different. You will as soon find two faces alike as find two minds alike.

Kariru toki no Jizō-gao, kaesu toki no Emma gao: "Jizō's face when borrowing, Emma's face when repaying." Jizō, the guardian diety of children, is depicted with a smiling face, but Emma, the king of hell, has a ferocious expression. So a man will have a very meek look when requesting a loan, but shows an angry visage when asked for payment. English parallel: When I lent I was a friend, when I asked I was unkind.

Yō aru toki no Jizō-gao, yō naki toki no Emma-gao: "When you have business the man shows you the face of Jizō (i.e., smiling), when you have no business he shows the face of Emma (i.e., scowling)." The same man will show you two entirely different expressions depending on whether he will profit by you or not.

Kenka ni kaburu kasa wa nai: "In a fight no broad hat can be put on." In fighting you must except rough handling, so an umbrella-hat would be in the way.

Kichigai ga hachi ni sasareta yō: "Like a madman stung by a hornet." This expression describes the tremendous uproar of a person in wild excitement.

Kitsune wo uma ni noseta yō: "Like a fox placed on the back of a horse." An expression used to describe a person who talks very rapidly and absurdly.

Kiyomizu no butai kara tobi-orareta yō: "It's very risky." (Lit., "Like leaping down from the stage—or porch—of *Kiyomizu* temple.") Since the temple is built on the edge of a very high cliff, the above expression is used to describe doing something desperate, or taking a big risk.

Kokoro futatsu ni mi wa hitotsu: "Two hearts for one body." The Japanese word *"kokoro"* has the meaning not only of "heart" but also "mind," "will," "spirit," "interest," and "inclination." Hence, the above proverb not only emphasizes the impossibility of being in two places at the same time, but also the danger of having a divided mind or will.

Kumo no ko wo chirasu yō: "Like the scattering of young spiders." This figure of speech is often used to describe the confusion of a leaderless and defeated army, or the dispersal of a mob when police order the people to stop their demonstration.

Kurushii toki no kamidanomi: "To invoke the gods in time of distress." When one is suffering physically or mentally, one is apt to call upon the gods, whereas in a happy, contented life little attention is paid to them. This proverb is also quoted when a person in trouble calls for help on another person whom otherwise he would ignore. English parallel: Danger past, God forgotten.

Mikka bōzu: "A three-day priest." This disparaging term is applied to any person who shows quick enthusiasm in anything but in a few days loses interest and soon gives it up.

Matsuri yori mae no hi: "Happier on the eve rather than on the day of the festival." (Lit., "More than the festival, the day before.") In other words, expectation gives more pleasure than the reality.

Mizukara anadotte nochi hito kore wo anadoru: "If you despise yourself people will afterwards despise you." You must first respect yourself in order to win respect from other people. English parallel: Trust thyself only and another shall not betray thee.

Neko no me no yō ni kawaru: "To change like the eyes of a cat." This expression is often used to describe a changeable and fickle person.

Saru mono wa hibi ni utoshi: "He who departs is forgotten daily." This proverb, which originated in China, states the well-known fact that people with whom you were intimate are often forgotten when not seen for a long time. English parallels: Out of sight, out of mind. Seldom seen, soon forgotten.

Tanki wa sonki: "A quick temper results in loss." The Japanese do not admire a person who is short tempered and irascible.

Tanryo kō wo nasazu: "A quick temper does not bring success." Like nearly all other people, the Japanese highly regard a person who can govern his temper and keep calm under most trying circumstances. English parallel: Haste makes waste.

Tate ita ni mizu: "Great fluency." (Lit., "Water on a standing board.") This expression is often used to describe a person who is quick to speak and to act.

Tatsu yori henji: "Be prompt in your reply before you stand up." (Lit., "Before you stand, reply.") The figure is that of a group of *samurai* who are seated on the floor in front of their lord who has called them for a conference. When their leader calls on any one or more of them by name, the courteous and loyal thing to do is to reply *"hai"* ("yes") promptly, and then rise and go to him. This proverb also suggests that one should be quick to say and do good.

Te no ura wo kaesu yō: "Like turning the hand over." This expression is descriptive of a person breaking his promise or changing his attitude.

Ten ni noboru kokochi: "To be transported with joy." (Lit., "The feeling of ascending to heaven.")

Toki ni aeba nezumi mo tora to naru: "When the time comes even a rat becomes a tiger." The fortunes of a person are often advanced by seizing the opportunity at the right time. English parallel: Put a coward on his mettle and he will fight the devil.

Tonde hi ni iru natsu no mushi: "He flies into the flame, the summer insect." This expression is used when a rash man of little strength or military skill attacks his more powerful enemy and is killed. Thus, by his recklessness he brings misfortune upon himself. English parallel: The fluttering moth about the candle flame at last gets burned.

Uyo-kyokusetsu no jinsei: "Human life is full of vicissitudes." (Lit., "The rope-remainder twisting of human life.") That is, life is not a straight and easy path, for it is full of strange twists and turns, ups and downs.

Utsurugi no aru otoko wa seikō shinai: "A capricious man does not succeed." (Lit., "A man with a changeable spirit is not successful.") English parallal: A rolling stone gathers no moss.

Yakan konjō: "A changeable nature." (Lit., "A tea-kettle disposition.") That is, soon hot or soon cold.

Yasu-ukeai no haya wasure: "Easily promised, quickly forgotten." English parallel: A man apt to promise is apt to forget.

FAMILY

JAPANESE SOCIETY is family centered. The family is a rigid hierarchy in which each individual has his niche and must find his precise status in every situation. The father is the head of the family, and prior to the adoption of the new constitution, exercised great power over the other members. Even with the newly-gained freedoms the wife and children more often than not follow the old customs and practices, for it is hard, especially in Japan, to go against social usage and the dictates of filial piety. The Japanese have a deep love of children, who in their early years are very much pampered and petted. As the child grows older, more restrictions and disciplinary measures are added until he is able and ready to live up to all the obligations of an adult. In urban areas among the rising generation the present tendency is to play down filial piety and to play up parental duties and responsibilities. Still, in rural areas and among middle-aged to older people the time-honored customs and practices of the hierarchical family prevail. The following proverbs dealing with various aspects of family life were in use long before the present days of modern Japan.

MARRIAGE:

Nakōdo wa waraji senzoku: "A go-between needs a thousand pairs of sandals." Because he must go many times back and forth to the homes of the prospective bride and groom until both families are satisfied.

Aien kien: "A marital union goes by strange chances." (Lit., "United affinity, strange affinity.")

En wa ina mono, aji na mono: "Affinity is a mysterious thing but it's spicy!" There is no accounting for taste, but it is delightful to have it satisfied. English parallel: Marriages go by destiny.

Azuma otoko ni Kyō onna: "A Kyoto woman for an Azuma man." The word Azuma means "east." In old Japan the Azuma man was distinguished for martial traits and physical stamina, while the Kyoto woman was considered very beautiful. So an Azuma man and a Kyoto woman were believed to make a good match in marriage.

En to tsuki-hi wa sue wo mate: "For marriage and time wait for the final moment." It is better to wait for the propitious time than to hasten a marriage. English parallel: Marry in haste, repent at leisure.

Chōchin ni tsurigane: "An ill-assorted match." (Lit., "A paper lantern against a hanging temple bell.") Buddhist temple bells frequently are quite large and hang in strongly-built belfries, while a paper lantern is generally small and often seen hanging in some dark place to give needed light. Though similar in shape there is a great difference in their uses. In Japan an unequal match is believed to bring misfortune.

Nejiri-gama ni nejiri-buta: "A crooked top on a crooked kettle." This saying, applied to a man and wife, teaches that like should go together.

Oshitsuketa en wa tsuzukanu: "A compulsory marriage does not endure." In spite of this proverb many a father has forced his daughter to marry the man of his choice.

Tsuri-awanu wa fuen no moto: "An ill-assorted match is the source of discord." An ill-matched couple makes for divorce.

Muko wa zashiki kara, yome wa niwa kara: "Choose the bridegroom from the parlor and the bride from the yard." In matchmaking it was considered preferable for a woman to take a man of high birth ("from the parlor") for her husband, but for a man to take a woman of humble origin ("from the yard") whose father's occupation was farming, because she will then prove to be an industrious and thrifty wife.

Nyōbō wa hakidame kara: "Choose a woman from the rubbish heap." The reason for this is that if you marry a woman from a lower class she will tolerate whatever difficulties life may bring.

Tsuma wa shita yori erabu beshi; tomo wa ue yori erabu beshi: "Choose a wife from a position lower than your own, and choose friends from a higher status." English parallel: Go down the ladder when you marry a wife; go up when you choose a friend.

Yome to tanmono wa hiruma erabe: "Choose a bride and piece goods in the daytime." English parallel: Choose neither a woman nor linen by candlelight.

Nyōbō wa ie no takara da: "A wife is a household treasure." See Proverbs 31:10: "A good wife who can find? She is far more precious than jewels."

Awase mono, hanare mono: "What is joined may be separated." Here we see the Buddhist idea of fate, the above expression being generally used in reference to a divorce after it has taken place. It is also said of a husband and wife who disagree.

Fūfu-genka to nishi-kaze wa yūkata ni naru to yamu: "The quarrels of married couples and the west wind stop at evening." This proverb humorously observes that when night comes the quarrels of the couple naturally cease.

Fūfu-genka wa inu mo kuwanu: "Even a dog will not eat a quarrel between husband and wife." Though dogs and pigs eat anything, so unpleasant is a domestic quarrel that even a dog does not care to touch it.

Kaminari ga fūfu-genka wo wajukusase: "Thunder will bring to a peaceful end a quarrel between husband and wife." Perhaps because they are so badly frightened they will stop quarreling. Most Japanese, especially in rural areas, are afraid of thunder.

Kanai no kenka wa bimbō no tanemaki: "Family quarrels sow the seeds of poverty." English opposite: Poverty breeds strife.

Nita mono fūfu: "Resembling each other are husband and wife." A man and his wife after they have been married a long time, will often look alike and have similar character and tastes.

Omae hyaku made, washa kujūku made: "You may live up to one hundred years and I up to ninety-nine." An expressed wish of a husband that he and his wife may have a long life together. Note that it is considered desirable for the husband to die first, thus enabling the wife to mourn for her spouse and pray for and to his departed spirit.

Otoko wa chie onna wa nasake: "Man for his head, woman for her heart." (Lit., "As for man wisdom, as for woman affection.") It is man's part to use his noble faculty of judgment, while woman's part is to express her love and sympathy. English parallel: In the husband wisdom, in the wife gentleness.

Otoko wa dokyō, anna wa aikyō: "Man for his courage, woman for her attractiveness." A man is esteemed for his bravery while a woman is admired for her charm.

Otoko wa matsu, onna wa fuji: "Man is a pine tree, woman a wisteria vine." The former provides the strong base around which the latter may twine.

Musume miru yori haha wo miyo: "Look at the mother rather than her daughter." In selecting a woman for your wife you should watch her mother first in order to get some idea of the character of her daughter. English parallel: Like father, like son.

Nabe kama uttemo ii kaka tore: "Take a good wife even if you have to sell your pots and kettle." Although a good pot and kettle are most important kitchen utensils, a good wife is even more important to the home.

Nyōbō jūhachi ware hatachi: "My wife is eighteen and I am twenty." These ages are considered by young farmer boys as being an ideal matrimonial arrangement.

Nyōbō to kutsu wa furui ga ii: "Wives and shoes are better when old." They are comfortable and easy to get along with after you have had them for some time.

Nyōbō to nabe-kama wa furui hodo ii: "Wives and pots and kettles are better when old."

Nyōbō to tatami wa atarashii hodo ii: "A wife and floor matting are better when new."

BRIDES:

Aki-nasu wa yome ni kuwasu na: "Don't feed the bride autumn eggplant." Since a bride is proverbially hateful to the parents of her husband she should not be permitted to eat such a delicacy as eggplant in autumn.

Aki-saba wa yome ni kuwasu na: "Don't let the bride eat autumn mackerel." This is advice to the mother-in-law to be as unkind as possible to the bride.

Akusai wa rokujū nen no fusaku: "A bad wife is a poor harvest for sixty years." This same proverb with exactly the same meaning sometimes appears as: *Nyōbō no warui no wa rokujū nen no fusaku.* English parallel: A bad wife is the shipwreck of a house.

Iniato e yuku tomo, shiniato e yuku na: "Though you may become the wife of a divorced man, don't become the wife of a widower." The reason behind this common saying is that a widower will always hold dearly the memory of his dead wife, but the man who has sent away his first wife will love his new wife better.

Isshō no kuraku tanin ni yoru: "The joys and sorrows of a whole life depends on a stranger." According to the old Japanese custom of marriages arranged by parents, the bride and groom are often strangers, having seen each other only once or twice before the wedding ceremony. The above proverb applies to a woman's life, for she will be happy or miserable according to her husband's character and fortunes.

Iya na nyōbō wo sareba sambyaku mon son shita kokochi: "If you send away your wife, whom you dislike, you will feel that you have lost three hundred 'mon.'" A *"mon"* is an old coin worth one hundredth of a *"sen,"* but neither the *"mon"* nor the *"sen"* are now in use in Japan. The *"sen"* before World War II was worth one hundredth of a *"yen."*

Kinō no yome kyō no shūto: "Yesterday's bride is today's mother-in-law." According to Japanese customs, a bride who is severely treated by her mother-in-law will soon become a mother-in-law herself and accord similar harsh treatment to the bride of her son.

Kojūto wa oni sembiki: "A sister-in-law is as fearful as a thousand devils." The Japanese word for sister-in-law, *"kojūto,"* literally means "a small mother-in-law." In old Japan the husband's unmarried sister, staying under the same roof, was popularly reputed to be as formidable to the young bride as a thousand devils, because her ill will often proved strong enough to cause her brother to send away his wife. However, under the new constitution this seldom happens, for human rights are much more respected than they were prior to World War II.

Moto-ki ni masaru ura-ki nashi: "No branch surpasses the trunk." No fountain can rise higher than its source. A second husband or wife is not better than the first one. Generally, the first wife or husband is considered superior to the second one.

Oni no nyōbō no kijin ga naru: "The wife of a devil becomes a devil." In most cases where the husband is a bad man the wife also is bad.

Rakka eda ni kaerazu, hakyō futatabi terasazu: "Fallen flowers do not return to branches, a shattered mirror does not again reflect." Things done cannot be undone. After the wife has sought and obtained a divorce the second half of the above proverb is frequently quoted.

Sōkō no tsuma wo sarazu: "Don't divorce your refuse-and-bran wife." That is, don't cast off the woman married in poverty and with whom you have eaten a miserable diet of refuse and bran, even though you may now have come into prosperity.

Teifu wa ryōfu ni mamiezu: "A faithful wife does not marry again." She remains faithful to her deceased husband.

Yome to shūto wa inu to saru: "Brides and mothers-in-law are like dogs and monkeys." That is, they are always on bad terms with each other.

Yome wa kita toki ni shikome: "Train the bride when she first comes." The mother-in-law is here advised to give full instructions to the new bride in the beginning of her married life so that she will fit into the ways of the family.

HUSBAND:

Geta wa hanao kara, teishu wa nyōbō kara: "The clogs are set off by their thongs, a husband by his wife." Just as clogs made a good appearance when furnished with beautiful thongs, so a husband appears to good advantage when his wife is a beautiful and intelligent woman.

Nyōbō wa hito no ga ii, setchin wa uchi no ga ii: "As to a wife another man's is better, but as for a privy my own is good." This expresses the thinking of a husband who deems the wives of other people better than his own.

Tonari no hana wa akai: "My neighbor's flowers are red." In the above proverb the phrase "are red" means "look more beautiful than mine." The man is clearly envious of his neighbor's wife and family.

Tonari no nyōbō wa utsukushii: "The neighbor's wife is beautiful." English parallel: Better is the neighbor's hen than mine.

Uchi no kome-no-meshi yori tonari no mugi-meshi: "More preferable than the rice meal at home is the barley meal at the neighbor's." Boiled rice is admittedly more expensive and tasty than barley food, yet when eaten at a neighbor's home the latter is preferred. The viewpoint of a man who does not appreciate the good things he has at home. English parallel: My neighbor's goat gives more milk than mine.

Hinkei no ashita suru wa kore ie no motorurunari: "It is contrary to the house (family) where the hen announces the dawn," i.e., the man should always be the head of the house. English parallel: A cackling rooster and a crowing hen always come to some bad end.

Nyōbō no shiri ni shikareru: "To be henpecked"; "to be tied to a wife's apron strings." (Lit., "To be spread over the buttocks of one's wife.")

Teishu wo shiri ni shiku: "To have a husband tied to her apron strings." To be henpecked. (Lit., "To have the husband spread on her buttocks.") The Japanese feel that this is the situation in most American homes, for they note that women have a more dominant part than in theirs. With the adoption of the new constitution the legal rights of women in Japan and the part they play both in the home and in the outside world has been tremendously enlarged. English parallel: Petticoat government.

Kage-Benkei: "A shadow Benkei." Benkei was a warrior-priest of extraordinary strength who lived at the end of the twelfth century and performed many feats of valor in which he righted numerous wrongs. In general, he took the part of the poor and oppressed and cut down their enemies, thus becoming their ideal and hero. The above phrase describes a man who is a despot at home, or one who brags of his courage when the enemy is away, but actually is just an ordinary fellow. English parallel: A cock on his own dunghill.

Uchi-Benkei: "A Benkei at home." In their own home men of small valor can be as formidable as Benkei, the famous priest-warrior. English parallel: At home an elephant, abroad a cat.

Uchi ni icha hamaguri-gai, soto e decha shijimi-gai: "At home a clam, abroad a corbicula." While both shellfish are eaten by the Japanese as food, the clam is by far the larger. Hence, while one may appear very big and important at home, when he goes out he is quite small and insignificant. English parallel: A lion at home, a mouse abroad.

Uchi ni kaereba Tenka Sama: "On returning home he becomes the Lord of the World! Unfortunately there are many Japanese husbands who are quite despotic and rule their households with an iron hand.

Uchi no mae no yase-inu: "A scrawny dog before his master's house." Even a lean dog is valiant at the door of his master. Likewise an ordinary person appears brave and important at home. English parallel: Every dog is a lion at home.

Teishu no sukina aka eboshi: "There is no accounting for tastes." (Lit., "The favorite red *eboshi* of the master.") This proverb arose in ancient times when the *"eboshi,"* a hat with a long top worn by nobles on formal occasions, was in vogue. The wife is urged to let her husband follow his desires even to wearing a red *"eboshi,"* when custom and practice dictated only black as formal attire. In old Japan the whole family was expected to approve and admire everything the husband and father did. Latin parallel: De gustibus non est disputandum.

Wara de tabane temo, otoko wa ippiki: "Even though he were a bundle of straw, a man counts for one." That is, a man is of some value even though he may appear quite useless. This saying reflects the thinking of old Japan, in which the male was always the dominant sex. English parallel: A man of straw is worth a woman of gold.

PARENTS:

Fubo imaseba tōku asobazu: "If your parents are living, don't go on a long trip." This Confucian maxim teaches the duty of children towards their parents not to make them anxious, the idea being that children should always be near aged parents to take care of them and especially to be at their deathbed.

Go-uchi wa oya no shinime ni awanu: "The go-player cannot arrive on time at the deathbed of his parent." The word *"shini-me,"* translated "deathbed" is literally "death-eyes." It is the duty and privilege of the eldest son, or if he is not present, some other child, to close the eyes of the parent after he dies. The above proverb is quoted to describe a person so intent on his game that he omits the doing of highly important things.

Hato ni sanshi no rei ari: "The dove shows its filial piety by sitting three branches below its parents." This is a Chinese-derived proverb inculcating respect for parents.

Hidari uchiwa de kurasu: "To live with a fan in the left hand." This proverb describes the easy circumstances of a sottish father, who has sold his daughter to be a concubine or courtesan, thus permitting him to live in such ease that (in summer) he holds a fan in his left hand and a cup of liquor in his right. The saying also delineates a man who has a successful son who will look after him when he retires.

Ishi ni futon mo kiserarezu: "Don't try to cover the stone with a quilt." The stone referred to is a gravestone. The moral is that we should show kindness to our parents while they are living, because it will be useless after they are dead to show filial piety by covering their gravestones with warm quilts.

Jishin, kaminari, kaji, oyaji: "Earthquake, thunder, fire, father." These four things named in ascending order of severity were proverbially feared by the Japanese. Prior to World War II and especially during the feudal period, the father as head of the house had almost complete control of the family and all in it.

Ko wo miru koto oya ni shikazu: "The parents can see best the character of the child." This saying from an ancient Chinese classic teaches that parents, from long personal observation, are best able to judge the character of their children.

Ko yue no yami: "Darkness because of the child." A parent, because of his love for the child, is often in the dark concerning his real characteristics and what should be done for him. Note that the teaching of this proverb is the reverse of the preceding saying.

Ko wo suteru yabu aredo, oya wo suteru yabu nashi: "Although there may be a bamboo jungle where you may cast off your children, there is no jungle where you can cast off your parents." In ancient times in order to prevent overpopulation, a form of infanticide known as *"mabiki"* (lit., "thinning out") was practiced, in which young babies, generally girls, were thrown away in some lonesome spot. The proverb refers to this cruel practice and states that filial love to parents is more important than love to children.

Kodomo ni kikin nashi: "There is no famine to children." Despite the cruel practice described in the preceding proverb, most parents did not follow it even during times of famine for they would starve themselves rather than let their children starve. In ancient Japan, where communications and transportation were poor, a rice-crop failure meant famine for the area, and this frequently was the case.

Kō wa hyaku kō no moto, shūzen no hajime nari: "Filial piety is the source of many (lit., 'one hundred') good deeds and the beginning of all virtue." This is one of the most frequently-quoted proverbs that teach reverence for parents.

Kōkō no shitai jibun no oya wa nashi: "When one would be filial one's parents are gone." A warning against waiting too long to show filial love.

Kōkyō de oya no kao wo utsu: "Adding insult to injury." (Lit., "Striking the parent's face with *The Book of Filial Duty.*") Confucius, whose teachings are the basis of Japanese morals and social usage, repeatedly inculcated the importance of respect to parents by their children, and especially emphasized it in his volume, *The Book of Filial Duty.*

Oya no yokume: "The partial eyes of parents (for their children)." Sometimes the eyes of love are blind to the faults of the children.

Oni no yō na oya: "A fiendlike parent." In every culture there will be occasionally such a parent.

Oya no ḳao ni doro wo nuru: "To smear with mud the faces of one's parents." That is, to bring shame and disgrace upon them.

Oya no inga wa ḳo ni muḳuu: "The fate of one's parents is returned to their children." That is, the *ḳarma* effects of parents visit their children with retribution. English parallel: The sins of the fathers are visited upon the children.

Oya no hiḳari wa nana hiḳari: "Parental influence is lasting." (Lit., "The light of parents is worth seven lights.") That is, the glory parents may have adds a sevenfold luster to the glory of their offspring. The word "seven" *("nana")* is not just a number, but as in many Oriental countries, has the meaning of "completeness." The Japanese have always held that the success and the distinguished attainments of a parent greatly help in the advancement of the children.

Oya no ḳoḳoro ḳo shirazu: "Children do not understand the hearts (minds) of parents." It is difficult for children to appreciate and understand the love that parents have for them. It is also difficult in these modern days for children to comprehend fully the thinking of parents. The reverse, too, is true for with all the new teaching that children are receiving, parents have difficulty understanding them, and children often consider their parents "old fogies."

Oya no omō hodo ḳo wa omowanu: "Children do not have as much affection for parents as parents have for them."

Oya no senaḳa demo tada wa ḳaḳanu: "He won't even scratch his parent's back without a fee." This figure of speech describes an avaricious man.

Oya wa senri yuḳu tomo ḳo wo wasurezu: "Although parents go a thousand 'ri' away they do not forget their children." As explained elsewhere, the Japanese *"ri"* is a unit of distance of about two and one-half miles. The above proverb well describes the solicitude of parents for their children.

Oyo wa ḳurō shi, ḳo wa raḳu wo shi, sono mago wa ḳojiḳi suru: "Parents labor hard, children live at ease, and grandchildren go begging."

Oya wo omō kokoro ni masaru oya-gokoro: "Surpassing the affection of children for their parents is parental love."

Oya wo narō ko: "Children learn from their parents." They do this by imitating them. English parallel: As the old cock crows, so crow the young.

Oya-ko no naka demo kinsen wa tanin: "Even between parents and children money matters make strangers." That is, money is money and business is business even between parents and children.

Umi no on yori sodate no on: "Obligation to one's foster parents is greater than to the parents who gave birth to him." Hence, the child should be more grateful to the former than to the latter.

Umi no oya yori sodate no oya: "More valuable than the child's own parents are the foster parents." That is, the foster parents are more appreciated and loved by the child they have loved and reared.

Waga ko no akuji wa mienu mono: "One cannot see the evil deeds of one's own children." English parallel: The neighbor's children are always the worst.

CHILDREN:

Amayoshi ko wo sutsuru: "To pamper children is to desert them." English parallel: Spare the rod and spoil the child.

Bimbōnin no kodakusan: "Poor men have many children." (Lit., "The many children of a poor man.")

Bimbōnin no kodakara: "Poor men's treasures are their children." English parallel: Children are poor men's riches.

Hakoire musume ni mushi ga tsuku: "Vermin will attack one's beloved daughter." The idiom in Japanese for beloved or pet daughter is *"Hako-ire-musume"* (lit., "daughter-in-a-box"). Even daughters who are jealously guarded may sometimes be enticed away and taken by someone else.

Hara wa kari mono: "The womb is a hired (borrowed) thing." Japanese feudal law decreed that the head of each family should have a male child, whether by his legitimate wife or by his concubine, to perpetuate his line of descent. Thus, the idea arose that a woman is a mere utensil for producing male offspring. Hence, the womb was thought to be something that could be hired or borrowed.

Hatsumago wa ko yori kawai: "The first grandchild is more beloved than one's own child." This is especially so if the child is a boy, for then the family name can be carried on.

Hito maseba mizu masu: "The larger the family the greater the expense." (Lit., "As the people increase water increases.") Extra water is needed not only for drinking, cooking, and washing purposes, but also in rural sections, for watering an increased area of paddy fields so that rice may be grown to feed the extra mouths in the family.

Ichi hime, ni Taro: "First a girl, then a boy." (Lit., "First a princess, second the first son.") This is believed by the Japanese to be the lucky order of births in a family, probably because the older sister can help care for baby brother and assist mother in household duties.

Ima naita karasu ga mō warau: "The crow that has just been crying is now laughing." This common expression is used to banter a child who has been crying but begins to smile as soon as he finds some cause to delight him.

Katawa no ko hodo kawaii: "A deformed child is the dearer to his parents."

Karasu ni hampo no kō ari: "The filial duty of feeding one's parents is known even to the crow." This proverb of Chinese origin exhorts children to carry out their filial duty to their parents.

Kawaii ko ni wa tabi saseyo: "Send the beloved children on a journey." This should be done to give him strength, wisdom, and experience which will enable him to deal with all sorts of problems.

Kawaii ko wa bō de sodateyo: "Bring up your beloved child with a stick." English parallel: Spare the rod and spoil the child.

Ko ni masaru takara nashi: "There are no better treasures than children."

Ko wa sangai no kubi-kase: "Love of children is an eternal encumbrance." (Lit., "A child is a neck-shackle to the three worlds.") In Buddhist lore the three worlds are: "the world of desire, the world of form, and the world of formlessness," roughly corresponding to the worlds of the past, present, and future. The above proverb explains that children may be the source of much trouble and anxiety to the parents.

Kodomo no nedoi: "The root questions of children." Children are very inquisitive and often ask questions that go to the root of matters.

Kodomo wo chō yo hana yo to itsukushimu: "To love a child as if it were a butterfly or a flower." English parallel: To love one's child like the apple of one's eye.

Ko-dakara sune ga hosoru: "Riches in the shape of children make one's shank thin." English parallel: Having many children makes one lean.

Kono oya ni shite kono ko are: "With such a parent there is such a child." English parallel: Like father, like son.

Komochi no hara ni wa uma no waraji mo hairu: "A pregnant women's stomach will hold the straw sandals of a horse." Because giving nourishment to her baby she is constantly hungry and could eat anything as large and unappetizing as a horse's sandals. In ancient Japan horses were not shod with iron shoes but wore specially-woven sandals on their hooves.

Ko-musume to kobukuro wa yudan wa naranu: "It will never do to be careless of a little girl and a small bag." English parallel: A girl, a vineyard, an orchard, and a bean field are hard to watch.

Me no naka e iretemo itaku nai: "Even though I let him into my eye there is no pain." This common expression is used to express great love for a darling child.

Musume wa koware mono: "Daughters are fragile ware."

Musume sannin areba shindai ga tsubureru: "If you have three daughters your estate will go to ruin." Probably because in Japan a father often spends much money, even beyond his means, in providing a rich trousseau and household equipment for his daughters when they marry.

Naku ko to jitō ni wa katarenu: "You can't win over a crying child or a provincial magistrate." In early feudal times the *"Jitō"* (provincial magistrate) had predominant power and was often despotic. A crying child also insists on having his way and will not listen to reason.

Neko yori mashi da: "It is better than a cat." That is, a child can be taught to do what he is told, but not a cat.

Nikumarekko yo ni habakaru: "A hated child is shunned by the world." A bad boy, though disliked, will often develop into a man of strong personality.

Nikumarekko yo ni habikoru: "A hated child runs wild in the world." Therefore he prospers in the world and lives to a great age, often becoming arrogant.

Oeba dakareru to iu: "If you give the child your back it will ask to be carried in your arms." There is no pleasing some people.

Ōta ko yori daita ko: "Rather than the child on your back, the child in your arms (is most dear)." The wet nurse carried her employer's child on her back, but even more dear is her own child whom she carries in her arms.

Oya baka, ko rikō: "The parent is a fool and the child wise." English parallel: An ill cow can have a good calf.

Oya ga nakutomo ko wa sodatsu: "Even without parents a child will grow up." English parallel: Nature is a good mother.

Otoko no ko wa chichi ni shitagai, onna no ko wa haha ni shitagō: "Let sons follow their fathers and daughters their mothers." When parents agree to separate, sons are generally taken under the father's care and daughters under the mother's.

Oyaji ga mōkerya musuko ga tsukau: "Father earns and son spends."

Richigi (Ritsugi) mono no kodakusan: "An upright man's many children." That is, a sincere and honest man is rewarded with a large family.

Sannen ni shite ko naku wa saru: "A bride who bears no child after three years of marriage should be divorced." (Lit., "Having no child after three years, separate.") The Civil Code during the Tokugawa period provided for such a procedure, for the law aimed at securing an heir or heiress for every family, and thus to maintain the traditional family system.

Sobo sodachi wa sambyaku yasu: "Those who have been reared by grandmothers are cheaper by three hundred (coins)." That is, they are so thoroughly spoiled that they are not of much value.

Sōryō no jinroku: "The eldest son is a blockhead." In Japan it is commonly believed that the eldest son is not as gifted intellectually as his younger brothers.

Tameru nara wakagi no uchi: "If you would bend the tree do it while it is young." A correction in the character of a person should be done in youth. English parallel: As the twig is bent the tree is inclined.

Toshi wo toru to kodomo ni kaeru: "When advanced in age we become children again." English parallel: Old age is a second childhood.

Wakai toki ni do nai: "One is not young twice." That is, since you are young only once, make the best of your youth. English parallel: Gather roses while ye may.

HOME AND FAMILY:

Chi wa chi dake: "Blood is only blood." Though they may quarrel a great deal, brothers settle their differences and help each other when either is in deep trouble. However, don't depend on it for everything. English parallel: Blood is thicker than water. A direct Japanese translation of this English proverb and accepted by the Japanese as one of their own is: *Chi wa mizu yori koshi.*

Enja no shōko: "The evidence of relatives." Relatives and friends cannot be trusted as witnesses in a lawsuit. Thus the above is applicable to all situations in which interested witnesses appear.

Keitei kaki ni semege domo, hoka sono anadori wo fusegu: "Older and younger brothers may quarrel within their enclosure, but they oppose the affronts of outsiders." This is a maxim from Chinese sources exhorting members of a family to present a united front against outsiders, no matter how much they may quarrel among themselves.

Konuka sangō mottara yōshi ni yuku na: "If you have as much as three 'gō' of rice bran, don't go into a family as an adopted son." Three "gō" is about one pint. Thus the proverb means: If you have even the smallest amount of property, don't become an adopted son, since the lot of such is not an enviable one.

Kyōdai wa ryōte no gotoshi: "Brothers are like both hands." They should help each other in good times as well as in bad.

Kyōdai wa tanin no hajimari: "Brothers (and sisters) are the forerunners of strangers." Too often brothers and sisters are apt to disagree and become worse than outsiders. As one gets a family, the blood relationship between brothers and sisters grows lighter.

Sekiaku no ie ni yoō ari: "The family that has done many wicked deeds has great misfortune." This proverb, taken from the writings of Confucius, teaches that misfortune is sure to come to the family that has been guilty of evil deeds.

Sekizen no ie ni wa yokei ari: "The family that has done many virtuous deeds has abundance." That is, a virtuous family has long prosperity. This Confucian saying states that good deeds are rewarded by happiness.

Tanin yori miuchi: "Better than strangers are relatives." English parallel: Blood is thicker than water.

Tōzai katei ni masaru tokoro nashi: "East, West, there is no place that surpasses home." English parallel: East, West, home is best.

Uchi hodo ii tokoro nai: "No place is as desirable as home."

Uji yori sodachi: "Better than birth is upbringing." In character development, upbringing and training is more important than birth.

Waga ya ni hisubeki tokoro nashi: "There is no place to be compared to my house." English parallel: There is no place like home. Whether the house be a crowded tenement in a big city, a beautiful villa surrounded by lovely landscaped gardens in the suburbs, or a humble straw-thatched cottage in the midst of rice fields, the love of the Japanese for his home is just as warm and deep as that of an Englishman or American for his.

FATALISM

THE NUMEROUS NATURAL DISASTERS—typhoons, floods, earthquakes, and fires—with which the Japanese are frequently afflicted have made the people fatalistic. Their most common expression, *"shikata ga nai"* ("there is nothing that can be done,") denotes resignation to fate. The phrase generally used on taking leave, *"sayōnara,"* translated "good-bye," literally means "well, if it must be so." This also has a clearly defined fatalistic suggestion. In the philosophy of Buddhism there are strong fatalistic and pessimistic elements. It is, therefore, not surprising that fatalistic beliefs are also found in the proverbs and sayings of the Japanese.

Aoide tsuba wo haku: "To spit against the sky." (Lit., "Looking up, he spat.") The general meaning of this proverb is that one who attempts mischief against others will bring it upon himself.

Asu ari to iu koto nakare: "Don't say there's a tomorrow." Don't put off to tomorrow what can be done today, for there may never be a tomorrow for you.

Dekita koto wa shikata ga nai: "What is done is done." (Lit., "Regarding what has taken place, nothing can be done about it.") This proverb is often given as an excuse for not doing something about a given situation or problem. English parallel: What is done cannot be undone.

En naki shujō wa doshigatashi: "People with no *karma* relation are irredeemable." That is, there is no salvation for those who lack the inborn Buddhist nature to be good. This abusive statement is frequently made when the person we admonish makes no effort to reform.

Ichiju no kage, ichiga no nagare: "The shade of the same tree, the flowing of the same stream." To sit under the same shade tree or to drink from the same stream is, according to the Buddhist idea, predestined by fate.

Inga ōhō: "Poetic justice." (Lit., "*Karma* retribution.") This is the Buddhist and Hindu doctrine that a cause is requited with an effect. *"Inga"* is the Japanese word for *"karma."* English parallel: "As a man sows, so will he reap."

Inga tekimen: "Immediate *karma.*" Cause and effect are swiftly shown. English parallel: Swift is heaven's retribution.

Inga to kageboshi wa tsuite mawaru: "Karma and shadows follow one everywhere." The Japanese word *"inga"* is their translation for *"karma,"* a Sanscrit word for cause and effect.

Inga wa meguru kuruma no wa: "Karma is the turning of a wheel." English parallel: The wheel of fortune is ever in motion.

Kafuku wa azanaeru nawa no gotoshi: "Fortune and misfortune are like the twisted strands of a rope." That is, good luck and bad luck are closely entwined.

Kane no kireme ga en no kireme: "The end of money is the end of love (affinity)." English parallel: When poverty comes in at the doors, love leaps out at the windows.

Kaze ni mukatte tsuba suru: "To spit against the wind." If you do wrong to others you will surely suffer retribution. English parallel: Who spits against the wind, spits in his own face.

Mizu no nagare to hito no yukusue: "The flow of water and the future of human beings are uncertain." Life is truly indefinite. Though governed by *karma,* man does not know what is in store for him.

Nanji ni izuru mono wa nanji ni kaeru: "What comes out of you will return to you." A wrong done to a person will come back to the doer.

Shōhai wa toki no un: "Victory or defeat is the destiny of the moment."

Sode no furiawase mo tashō no en: "Even the swinging together of sleeves is preordained by destiny." The Buddhist concept is that all things are determined in a former world.

Sode surio mo tashō no en: "Even the brushing of your sleeves against another is due to the *karma* relations from a previous life." The Buddhist doctrine of *karma,* sometimes loosely called destiny or predestination, states that even a chance acquaintance is a divine ordinance.

Sōden henjite umi to naru: "Mundane things are subject to sudden change." (Lit., "The mulberry fields change into the sea.") Because of the volcanic nature of the land and the frequency of earthquakes in Japan, fields have often been known to slide into the sea.

Temmō kai-kai so ni shite morasazu: "Heaven's net is very great and coarse, but it does not let anything through." English parallels: Heaven's vengeance is slow but sure. Justice has long arms.

Ten naru kana, toki naru kana: "It is the will of heaven and also of the times." In this and succeeding proverbs where the word *"Ten"* ("heaven") is used we see the influence of Confucian classics in which the same word is used to indicate the supreme moral rule or order in the universe.

Ten ni kuchi nashi, hito wo shite iwashimu: "Heaven has no mouth but causes man to speak." English parallel: The voice of the people is the voice of God.

Ten ni mukatte tsuba wo haku: "To spit against heaven." That is, retribution is sure to follow if you do wrong to others. English parallel: Who spits against heaven spits in his own face.

Ten nibustu wo ataezu: "Heaven bestows no two things (at the same time)." It rarely happens that heaven endows a person with two advantages. For example, a beautiful woman often is not wise.

Tenka wa tenka no tenka: "The world is the world for the world." The world does not belong to any individual. No ruler is justified in ruling the world for his own interests alone, but for the promotion of the welfare of all the people.

Tenka wa mawarimochi: "The world is a wheel." (Lit., "Beneath the heavens things go by turns.") English parallel: Fortune knocks at our doors by turns.

Tsumazuku ishi mo en no hashi: "Even the stone upon which you stumble is a part of fate." The Buddhist idea of "fate" *("en")* is based on the *karma* relation in which "the whole ethical consequence of one's acts is considered as fixing one's lot in the future existence."

Umpu-tempu: "Lucky or unlucky." (Lit., "Fate no, or heaven's distribution." This phrase is used to indicate what we would term "trusting to chance," or "to run the risk." English parallel: Sink or swim.

Un satte, eiyū jiyū narazu: "With his luck gone, a hero is not free." (Lit., "Parted from his destiny, a great man is not at liberty.") English parallel: The mill cannot grind with the water that is past.

Un wa ten ni ari: "Fate is with heaven." Man cannot control his future, since that is in the hands of heaven. Here again, as in some of the preceding proverbs, is the Confucian idea of heaven as the supreme moral order in the world.

FRIENDSHIP

THOUGH OUTWARDLY POLITE and friendly, smiling and co-operative, the Japanese are inwardly on guard against slights, criticisms, ridicule, or discourtesies. Mutual distrust, suspicion, and readiness to criticize do not make for many deep and lasting friendships. This being the case, very few Japanese have friends with whom they can be absolutely open and frank. School friendships, especially in junior or senior high schools, probably come closer than anything else to what Americans mean by the term "intimate friend" or "chum."

Aite no nai kenka wa dekinu: "Where there is no antagonist you cannot quarrel." Even if insulted few Japanese will quarrel openly, for a loss of emotional control would subject them to the ridicule and censure of others. English parallels: It takes two to make a quarrel. When one will not, two cannot quarrel.

Akuyū wa nashi ni shikazu: "No company is better than bad company." (Lit., "A bad friend is no better than no friend.")

Chikashii naka ni mo reigi: "Proper courtesy (decorum) should be observed even between close friends." One should not behave too familiarly even towards one's closest friends. In Japan the rules of social conduct and ceremonial politeness constantly form barriers to close friendships. English parallel: Familiarity breeds contempt.

Fūki ni wa tanin mo atsumari, hinsen ni wa shinseki mo hanaru: "When prosperous, even strangers visit you; when poor and obscure, even relatives desert." (Lit., "When you have wealth and fame even strangers gather around; in time of poverty and lowliness even relatives depart from you.") English parallel: In time of prosperity, friends will be plenty, in time of adversity not one in twenty.

Hito ni sennichi no yoshimi naku, hana ni hyaku nichi no kurenai nashi: "With humans there is no intimacy lasting a thousand days, nor does the scarlet of a flower continue a hundred days." This proverb clearly indicates that no intimacy is expected more than three years.

Hito wa furuki ni shikazu; koromo wa atarashiki ni shikazu: "Old friends are better than new ones; new clothes are better than old ones." (Lit., "As to people the old are best; as to clothing new are best.")

Hōyū ni shibashiba sureba utonzeraru: "Go often to your friend and you'll be treated coolly." That is, you will be neglected if you go too often to the home of your friend.

Inaka mono ni tanin nashi: "To a rustic there are no strangers." People in rural areas are more friendly than those who live in urban centers. This is probably true all over the world.

Kannan ni itte tomo wo shiru: "In hardship you know your friends." English parallel: Adversity is the true scale on which you weigh your friends.

Ki ga karui to ashi mo karui: "When the spirit is light the foot also is light." This light-hearted friendliness is more often found in the country than in cities. English parallel: A willing mind makes a light foot.

Ki-ō wa togamezu: "To reproach not what is past and gone." (Lit., "The past is not to be blamed.") Let us forgive and forget faults committed against us by someone in the past. English parallel: Let bygones be bygones.

Kyō no imōto ni tonari kaezu: "I won't exchange my neighbor for my younger sister in the capital." English parallel: A near neighbor is better than a distant cousin.

Kyūyū ni masaru kagami nashi: "There is no better mirror than an old friend." An old friend will not hesitate to tell you when you are in the wrong and help you to live up to your true and better self.

Mizu no morasanu naka da: "They are so close that even water would not leak between them." This expression is generally used in describing friendship between the sexes and is a favorite figure for the intimacy of lovers.

Mukai sannin ryō-donari: "Three houses opposite and one on each side. The closest neighbors a person has, according to Japanese beliefs and practices, are the three houses directly across the street or road, and the house to the left and right of your house. A new arrival always calls first at these places and leaves a small gift at each. Gifts are also exchanged with these close neighbors on New Year's Day and on the occasion of weddings, funerals, and other special events.

O wo furu inu wa tatakarezu: "The dog that wags its tail cannot be beaten." When a person is affable and conciliatory we cannot treat him unkindly.

Shitashii naka ni mo kaki wo tsukure: "Put up a fence (wall) between even intimate friends." A certain amount of reserve is necessary among close friends even though you may have known them for many years. English parallel: A hedge keeps friendship green.

Suigyo no majiwari: "The intimacy of water and fish." This figurative expression describes a very close friendship such as Damon and Pythias.

Tōi shinrui yori chikaku no tanin: "Better than a distant relative is a nearby stranger." Because when help is needed relatives living at a distance can do little, but a kind friend or neighbor can do much.

Tomo to saké wa furui hodo yoshi: "Friends and wine, the older the better." Age matures and improves both friends and wine. English parallel: "Old friends and one wine are best.

Yūjō wa seishin no kekkon nari: "Friendship is the marriage of the soul."

Yūjō wa ittai dōshin: "Friendship is the same heart in one body."

Yoi naka ni kaki wo seyo: "Build a fence between intimate friends."

Zennin no teki to naru tomo, akunin no tomo to naru na: "Even though you become the enemy of a good man, don't become the friend of a bad man." It is always well to avoid bad society.

GENEROSITY AND HOSPITALITY

As a NATION and as individuals the Japanese are generous and hospitable. They are most punctilious in the giving and returning of presents. Nearly every visit or call is accompanied with a gift, be it large or small. When invited to a meal the guest brings a gift. Also at weddings, funerals, receptions, anniversaries, and on New Year's Day—the birthday celebration for all Japanese—gifts are presented. This custom leads to considerable expense and involves much time in selecting suitable gifts, but the Japanese bear it with good grace, accepting it as a necessary part of their social life. When guests or even strangers call at the home, tea and little cakes are always served by the host or hostess irrespective of the time of day or night.

Not long after my wife and I had moved to the city of Waka-yama, a Japanese lady, Mrs. Takeshita, called with a gift of cake and asked to see the newly-built missionary home. She was taken over the whole house and showed great interest and curiosity. Two weeks later she called again with a small gift, and this was repeated several times. Finally, she asked Mrs. Buchanan whether on a certain day she could bring a friend and also her architect, since she was erecting a new house and wished to make use of some American ideas and architectural principles. Consent being given, Mrs. Takeshita arrived the afternoon of the appointed day with the architect and nine other people, much to the consternation of the hostess, who had prepared sandwiches, cakes, cookies, and tea for only three guests! Mrs. Take-shita reasoned that she was fully justified in doing this, since she had given many presents and had built up *"on"* or "obligation" on the part of the American lady which the latter was repaying by enter-training so many guests. Sometimes generosity is shown for the pur-pose of getting more in return.

Atōru wa toran ga tame: "Giving is for the purpose of taking." First give and then you will be given in return. Be kind to others and they will be kind to you. English parallel: The hand that gives gathers.

Toran to seba mazu ataeyo: "If you would take, first give." English parallel: He who would take must give.

Chinkyaku mo mikkame ni wa isōrō: "Even a welcome guest becomes a parasite on the third day." Even in Japan there is the pos-sibility of overstaying your welcome. English parallel: The first day a guest, the third day a pest.

Chōja no mandō, hinja no ittō: "Rather than ten thousand lan-terns from a wealthy man is one lantern from a poor man." The lanterns mentioned refer to those generally made of stone or bronze which decorate the premises of shrines and temples and serve as votive offerings. The poor man's gift is appreciated more than the million-aire's because of the donor's sincerity and sacrifice. See in the New Testament the story of the widow's mite: Mark 12:41-44.

Ichi ryū nambai: "One grain, ten thousand fold." A figurative expression used to denote a munificent recompense for a small act of kindness.

Itadaku mono wa natsu demo kosode: "As a gift a wadded silk garment is acceptable even in summer." A wadded silk robe *("kosode")* is used only in the cold season, nevertheless, if presented during the hot season it will be gladly accepted. Another wording of the above proverb is:

Kudasaru mono nara natsu demo kosode: "If it is something to be received, a wadded silk garment even in summer (is acceptable)." English parallel: Don't look a gift horse in the mouth.

Nikui taka ni eba wo kae: "Give food to the hawk you do not love." Be generous even to the person you dislike. English parallel: Return good for evil.

Tera kara sato e: "From the temple to the village." This expression is used when after calling on a person your host calls back on you and brings a gift much larger than the one you had taken. In former times in Japan it was the custom for villagers to make gifts twice a year to the Buddhist temple in which they were registered. But if presents were given "from the temple to the village" as sometimes was the case, the usual process of social practice would be reversed. Hence, the above proverb is quoted when there is a reversal of the ordinary arrangement between the giver and the recipient.

GREGARIOUSNESS

THE JAPANESE are fond of crowds. They like to travel in the company of others and are unhappy and suspicious when left alone. School excursions to places of historical or aesthetic interest are indulged in twice a year and considered an important part of education. Family and village outings for flower viewing are common. Business and professional groups often travel together to hot springs or places of scenic interest. Although flower arrangement, tea ceremony, and *"haiku"* composing still have many devotees, gregarious amusements and sports such as baseball, *"sumō"* (Japanese wrestling), and skiing draw far larger crowds. There is a strong urge to conform, and those who don't are viewed with suspicion. The average person is unwilling to make individual decisions and frequently will consult some friend or superior before determining his course of action. At small conferences and committee meetings voting is seldom the procedure. Rather there is full and lengthy discussion of the subject until there is general agreement, after which the chairman will announce the decision of the group. This method is sometimes employed in much larger gatherings. One may say, without fear of contradiction, that the herd instinct is much stronger in Japan than in Western countries; and even in the neighboring lands of Korea and China there is much more individualism and independence of thought and action.

Bannin no koe wa kami no koe nari: "The majority's voice is the voice of the gods." (Lit., "The voice of ten thousand people is the voice of the gods.") The Japanese word *"ban"* or *"man,"* though literally translated "ten thousand," has the meaning of "a great number" or "all."

Dōbyō ai awaremu: "Sorrow loves the society of sorrow." (Lit., "Patients of the same disease sympathize with each other.") English parallel: Misery loves company.

Dōki ai motomu: "Like draws like." (Lit., "People of the same temperament desire each other.") English parallel: Birds of a feather flock together.

Gaki wo ninzu: "Even little imps when numerous are strong." Trifles sometimes prove of some use when there are a number of them. English parallel: Even tender creepers when united are strong.

Hito no zen-aku wa sono majiwaru tomo ni yotte shirareru: "Whether a person is good or bad can be known by the friends with whom he associates." English parallel: Tell me the company you keep and I'll tell you what you are.

Hitotsu nabe no mono wo kū: "They are accomplices." (Lit., "They eat from the same pot.")

Ichijō no ya wa orubeku, jūjō wa orubekarazu: "A single arrow is easily broken, but not ten in a bundle." English parallel: In union there is strength.

Ichi mō shū mō wo hiku: "One blind man leads many blind men." Sometimes blind men go in groups for mutual assistance and protection. Likewise people who are not too able or strong can help each other.

Inu mo hōbai, taka mo hōbai: "Dogs are companions, hawks also are companions." Dogs and hawks are companions when they are taken hunting together by their master. So people of various rank and occupations should assist each other and work together.

Ippiki no uma kurueba, sembiki no uma mo mata kurū: "If one horse becomes wild, then a thousand horses become wild." That is, one evil man can influence a crowd to do evil. English parallel: When one sheep is over the dam, the rest follow.

Itsubō no arasoi wa gyofu no ri: "A fight between a kingfisher and a clam is profitable to the fisherman." That is while they are fighting the fisherman comes and takes both. The moral of the proverb from Chinese sources is obvious. English parallel: When two dogs fight for a bone, a third runs off with it.

Ka wa shū ni teki sezu: "A few are no match for the many." There is no use in going against the wishes of the majority. (Lit., "The minority cannot oppose the majority.")

Ittō kusarite hyaku tō sonzu: "One rotten peach spoils a hundred peaches." (Lit., "One peach rotting one hundred are damaged.") English parallel: One rotten apple will spoil a barrel.

Kazu ōkereba anzen nari: "If there are great numbers, there is safety." This is the Japanese translation of the English proverb: There is safety in numbers.

Kyōjin hito wo hashirasu: "A madman makes people run." Somewhat similar to this is the next proverb.

Kyōjin hashireba fukyōjin mo hashiru: "When a madman runs, sane people run." The above two proverbs illustrate the tendency of people to follow the example of others whether it be good or bad. English parallel: One coward makes ten.

Kyōson kyōei: "Existing together, thriving together." This phrase, which may also be translated "co-existence and co-prosperity" was a slogan much used in Japan before and during World War II. It was used as an excuse for Japan's seizure of Manchuria and other parts of China, and her excursions into the South Seas, in order to prevent the ABCD (American, British, Chinese, and Dutch) Powers from encircling her economically and politically. English parallel: Live and let live.

Mizu wa hōen no utsuwa ni shitagai, hito wa zen-aku no tomo ni yoru: "As water lends itself to the shape of the vessel which contains it, so a man is influenced by his good or bad friends."

Mujina no ana de kitsune wo toru: "To catch a fox in the hole of a badger." Men of similar bad character associate together. English parallel: Birds of a feather flock together.

Mukade wa shindemo taorenu: "A centipede though dead will not fall." Because some of its numerous legs will cling to the former position and keep the centipede from falling. This figure is applied to a person who is not likely to experience utter failure in his trade or other undertakings because he has numerous relatives and friends backing and supporting him.

Odawara hyōjō (hyōgi): "A long and fruitless discussion." (Lit., "An Odawara conference.") Some two hundred and fifty years ago the great general, Toyotomi Hideyoshi sent to the Lord of Odawara Castle a summons to surrender. The latter called together his lieutenants to confer with them concerning whether they should surrender or fight to the last. For many days they discussed the matter but arrived at no decision. Finally Hideyoshi tired of waiting, attacked the castle, and utterly destroyed it and its occupants. Thus the term "An Odawara conference" came to mean "an endless discussion resulting in nothing." The uselessness and danger of indecision is clearly illustrated in this story.

Rui wa tomo wo yobu: "Like attracts like." (Lit., "Like kinds call companions.")

Rui wo motte atsumaru: "Like kinds gather together." English parallel: Birds of a feather flock together.

Sannin yoreba kugai: "Three persons together, bitter world." Because the three are likely to disagree and quarrel.

Sannin-zure kenka no moto: "Three persons together is the foundation of a quarrel."

Sannin yoreba Monju no chie: "Three persons together produce the wisdom of Monju." "Monju" is the Japanese name for Maitreya, the Buddhist deity of wisdom and intellect. English parallels: Two heads are better than one. As many heads, as many wits.

Taiko mo bachi no atari guai: "The drums sound according to the way they are struck." Much depends on the way you approach and solve a problem. English parallel: Laugh and the world laughs with you.

Tsurai sadame: "A trying decision." To come to a decision alone is very painful for most Japanese, who would much rather consult a friend, teacher, or some older relative.

Zako no toto majiri: "Small fish mingle with big fish." That is, nobodies among somebodies. Men of no importance will have no influence mingling with men of much greater importance, for the former will be ignored by the latter. English parallel: It does not become the sparrow to mix in the dance of the cranes.

HONESTY

THE JAPANESE have not always been distinguished for their honesty. During the feudal period and in the early years of the Meiji era there was much dishonesty among the merchants, samples often being of far better quality than the goods when delivered. In the fivefold classification of people instituted by the Tokugawa rulers—nobles, warriors, farmers, artisans and merchants—those who sold articles or engaged in trade were lowest in the social scale. Nobles and warriors felt that it was beneath their dignity to handle filthy lucre, while farmers and artisans seldom had any. Since they were so despised and treated as inferiors it is not surprising that merchants should act accordingly and engage in shady business deals. However, with the opening of Japan to the Western world, much of the dishonesty rampant in business and commercial deals began to disappear, so that now there is a high standard of honesty among most of the merchants of Japan. The Japanese have learned through experience that honesty is the best policy and that in the long run dishonesty does not pay. In my thirty-five years in Japan I have met with fewer cases of dishonesty than here in the United States.

Akusen mi ni tsukazu: "Ill-gotten money does not remain with one." English parallel: Ill-gotten goods seldom prosper.

Fugi no fūki wa fuun no gotoshi: "Ill-gotten wealth will be gone all too quickly." (Lit., "Riches and honors unjustly gained are like floating clouds.")

Kasshi temo tōsen no mizu wo nomazu: "Although dying of thirst, I drink not the water of a stolen fountain." This dictum from the Chinese classics is quoted as a warning against living dishonestly no matter what good remuneration may be offered. Honest poverty is far better than dishonest riches.

Kōbaisha wa nusubito to dōzai: "The purchaser of stolen goods is equally criminal with the thief." This is the Japanese translation of the English proverb: The receiver is as bad as the thief.

Kokoro tadashi kereba koto tadashi: "If the heart is right the deeds will be right." English opposite: A crooked stick will have a crooked shadow.

Nuka wo neburite kome ni oyobu: "Licking up the bran they come up to rice." A sin or bad habit begins in a small way, like taking a little bran from a rice container, but if unchecked it develops into something really serious, like stealing rice or something even more valuable.

Shinri wa kami no musume nari: "Truth is the daughter of the gods."

Shinri wa tsune ni chūyō ni sonsu: "Truth is always in the middle way." This proverb is taken from the Confucian Doctrine of the Mean—a teaching that is highly prized and widely followed in Japan.

Shin-yō wa mukei no zaisan: "Credit is invisible fortune." Confidence is wealth without form. English parallel: Credit is better than gold.

Shōjiki wa saijō no seisaku: "Honesty is the very best policy." This proverb is a translation of the English one and came into use during the Meiji era when merchants began to be more honest.

Sode no shita: "A bribe." (Lit., "Under the sleeve.") The giving and receiving of bribes or "presents" is still quite common in Japan. For example, hearing that a certain wealthy man is planning to erect a new business office or build a mansion, a contractor will call on him with a present of a box of cake. On opening the box, an envelope is revealed containing four or five thousand yen or more. Sometimes a gift certificate of a prominent department store is enclosed in the box of cakes.

Tadashiki mono wa kannan ōshi: "The honest man has numerous difficulties." (Lit., "The righteous man has many hardships.")

Taka wa shi shitemo ho wo tsumazu: "The hawk will die before it pecks the ears of grain." That is, a noble person will die rather than be dishonest.

Taka wa uete mo ho wo tsuibamazu: "The hawk though hungry will not peck at the ears of grain." That is, a true gentleman would prefer to die rather than live by dishonest means. The Japanese word *"taka"* in the above two proverbs is the trained hawk or falcon who accompanies and assists his master, the warrior or nobleman, on his hunting trips.

HONOR

ONE OF THE MANY FINE CHARACTERISTICS the Japanese have is a high sense of honor. The Japanese word *"makoto,"* which may be translated "sincerity" or "genuineness," is rated as one of the highest of virtues and signifies utter devotion to the codes of conduct. The anthropologist Ruth Benedict has defined *"makoto"* as "zeal to follow the 'road' mapped out by the Japanese code and the Japanese spirit." The strongest condemnation that a Japanese can make is to say that such and such a person or country lacks *"makoto"* (honor). During the feudal period the *samurai* or warrior was considered the living embodiment of honor. When taken prisoner in battle or captured under other embarrassing circumstances, he would be given the privilege of committing suicide by disembowelment (*"seppuku"* or *"hara-kiri"*) and thus maintaining his honor. His liege lord and his family could rejoice that he died like a gentleman with his name untarnished. Even in these modern days the Japanese maintain a strong feeling for *"makoto"* and the need for maintaining it under all circumstances.

Aoide ten ni hajizu, fushite chi ni hajizu: "Looking up we are not ashamed in the presence of heaven, nor bowing down are we ashamed in the presence of earth." In other words, neither in the presence of the gods nor before man have we any cause for shame. This is the expression of a man who has a clear conscience.

Boro wo kitemo kokoro wa nishiki: "Though wearing rags his heart is brocade." Inwardly a prince though outwardly a pauper. English parallel: Under rags there often beats a heart of gold.

Bushi ni nigon wa nai: "A *samurai* or warrior *(bushi)* does not have a double tongue." Good faith was considered a prime virtue of a *samurai* in old Japan, and even today when a Japanese wants to attest to his veracity he will quote the above proverb. English parallel: An honest man's word is as good as his bond.

Bushi no ichigon kintetsu no gotoshi: "A warrior's single word is as unchanging and reliable as gold and steel." His promise is as dependable as the gold in his purse and the steel of his priceless, untarnished sword.

Bushi no inochi wa gi ni yorite karushi: "A warrior deems life a light thing when compared to honor."

Inochi wa gi ni yorite karushi: "Life is light when compared to honor." This proverb is the abbreviated form of the preceding one. *"Gi,"* the Japanese word for "honor" may also be translated "duty."

Bushi no ko wa kutsuwa no oto ni me wo samasu: "A warrior's child awakens at the noise of a bit." The sound of a horse champing his bit puts the child of a warrior on the alert.

Bushi no sambō: "Three things a warrior must forget (home, family, and self)." For to the warrior loyalty to his lord *(chūgi)* is of supreme importance. Thus will he show that he has *"makoto,"* that is, sincerity or utter devotion to his code of conduct.

Bushi to kogane wa kyūkei shite mo kuchinu: "Warriors and gold may take a rest but never decay."

Chitoku wa kuruma no ryōrin no gotoshi: "Wisdom and virtue are like the two wheels of a cart." That is, they are always inseparable.

Dōri ni mukō yaiba nashi: "Against reason no sword will prevail." Everything is conquered by reason.

Doko no karasu mo kuroi: "Everywhere the crows are black." This means that since men everywhere have the same principles in the conduct of life, we must always act honorably.

Hana wa sakura, hito wa bushi: "The cherry blossom among flowers, the warrior among men." The cherry is first among flowers, as the warrior is first among men. Both are supreme in their line. This proverb which originated during the feudal period gives pre-eminence to the status of the warrior class in Japan, for their moral character was regarded as the model of perfection and the highest ideal for all men. To this day, many Japanese families are proud to trace their lineage to some warrior ancestor, although the five-class system enforced by the Tokugawa overlords has been abolished for one hundred years.

Hito wa ichidai, na wa matsudai: "Man is for one generation; his name (fame) is for all ages to come." Man is mortal, but his good name is immortal.

Mi wa ichidai na wa matsudai: "Life is for one generation; a good name (fame) is forever." This proverb is another form of the one before.

Hōritsu wa hito wo erabazu: "Law does not make choice of persons." This is taken from the English proverb: Law is no respecter of persons.

Iki-haji wo sarasu: "To live in dishonor." (Lit., "To expose oneself to living dishonor.") To the warrior, death is preferable.

Intoku aru mono wa yōhō ari: "Good deeds done by stealth will be openly rewarded." Good offices done in secret will receive open compensation. English parallels: He who lends to the poor gets his interest from God. What is done by night appears by day.

Jingi ni hamukau yaiba nashi: "Virtue commands respect." (Lit., "There is no blade that can contend against humanity and justice.")

Katana wa bushi no tamashii, kagami wa onna no tamashii: "The sword is the soul of the warrior, the mirror is the soul of a woman." From ancient times both objects were deemed valuable and sacred things. Two of the Imperial regalia are a sword and a mirror: the first, the symbol of male virtues—courage and honor; the second, the symbol of female virtues—chastity and affection.

Kimono Masamune, hada Muramasa: "My garment is a Masamune, my skin is a Muramasa." A warrior, though poor, has nothing left but valuable blades. Masamune and Muramasa were famous swordsmiths who lived in the thirteenth and fourteenth centuries and gave their names to the blades they forged. These blades are still considered the finest in the world. Unfortunately the secret of making such wonderful cutting steel has been lost.

Kōgen reishoku sukunashi jin: "Flattery and servile looks show a lack of benevolence." English parallel: Grand eloquence, little conscience.

Kokyō ni nishiki wo kazaru: "To return to one's native place attired in brocade." This proverb describes a man who revisits his native place laden with worldly success and honor. During the feudal period only those in high official position and who also had great wealth could wear gold and silver threaded brocade.

Mime yori kokoro: "Better a good heart than a fair face." A person whose character is fine is preferred to one who has only good looks. English parallel: Handsome is that handsome does.

Mime-yoki mono wa kokoro mo uruwashi: "A good-looking person has also a beautiful heart." The fine character of a person is shown in his face.

Minamoto kiyokereba nagare kiyoshi: "If the fountain-head is clear, the stream will be clear." That is, the heart must be clean to produce good deeds. English opposite: Muddy springs will have muddy streams.

Mune ni kugi: "A twinge of conscience." (Lit., "A nail into the breast.")

Nimai no shita wa tsukawarenu: "One cannot be deceitful." (Lit., "One cannot use a double tongue.") Because the moral code of the warrior does not permit double talk, and his high sense of honor prevents him from stooping to anything so low.

Ryōshin wa seigi no ima nari: "Conscience is the living room of righteousness."

Ryōshin wa tokugi no bampei nari: "Conscience is the sentry of virtue and righteousness."

Saya wa naku tomo mi wa hikaru: "Though the scabbard is lacking, the blade gleams." True worth needs no adornment and can easily be seen. The scabbards of the swords of the warriors were generally richly decorated with beautiful gold and silver ornaments, but the blades were prized above all else.

Seigi ware ni ari to omoeba soko ni yūki ga shōzuru: "Consciousness of right gives us courage." (Lit., "If it is thought that justice is with us it will give birth to courage.")

Shi wa yasuku, sei wa katashi: "To die is easy, to live is hard." It is much easier to die in a worthless cause than to live nobly.

Tadashii mono wa kannan ōshi: "The righteous person has many hardships."

Tama ni kizu: "A flaw in a gem." That is, an imperfection in an almost perfect character. English parallel: A fly in the ointment.

Tama to kudaketemo kawara no mattaki ni narawaji: "Better be a broken jewel than a whole tile on the housetop."

Tama to natte kudaken yori kawara to natte mattakaran: "Better to remain an unbroken tile on the housetop than a broken jewel." Note that this proverb is exactly opposite in meaning to the one preceding it.

Tatsu tori ato wo nigosazu: "A bird taking wing does not leave muddy water behind." So a person departing from office or some job should behave honorably at his resignation and leave a happy memory behind him.

Toku ko narazu, kanarazu tonari ari: "Virtue is not an orphan, it will always have neighbors." This Confucian saying states that a benevolent deed will never remain unencouraged or unrewarded.

Toku wa shiru ni yorazu okonō ni ari: "Virtue is not knowing but doing." Knowledge of what is right is important, but more important is to do it.

Toku wa sore jishin ni oite mukui ari: "Virtue is a reward in itself." English parallel: Virtue is its own reward.

Tōdo no tora wa ke wo oshimi, Nippon no bushi wa na wo oshimu: "Tigers of Cathay value their fur, warriors of Japan value their names (honor)." In this proverb the Japanese word *"na"* literally "name" has also the meaning of "reputation" or "honor." This is also true of the next proverb.

Tora wa shi shite kawa wo todome, hito wa shi shite na wo nokosu: "A tiger dies and leaves his skin; a man dies and leaves his name." It is better to leave after death an honorable name than an ignoble wealth.

Yaiba ni tsuyoki mono wa rei ni suguru: "A skillful swordsman surpasses in decorum." In the feudal period the members of the warrior classes were not only the most skillful fighters, but they were generally also the best educated and most advanced in politeness. Many of the scholars of that day were of *samurai* lineage.

Yama takaki ga yue ni tattokarazu, ki aru wo motte tattoshi to nasu: "Mountains are not esteemed because they are high but because they have trees." So men are honored and esteemed not because they are big and strong but because they are wise and noble.

Zen naru mono kanarazu bi narazu: "What is good is not necessarily beautiful." Goodness and beauty do not always go together.

IMITATION

THE JAPANESE are both borrowers and preservers. They are imitative rather than original, but selective, not slavish, in their imitation. In their early history the Japanese borrowed extensively from China and to a more limited extent from India. In later times large borrowings were made from Europe and America, but frequently improvements and adaptations were made to the object or culture borrowed. In all of her borrowings and imitation, basic Japanese traits and cultural characteristics were not lost. It is the boast and belief of many Japanese that their culture has absorbed and used all that is best in both the East and the West.

Asa ni tsureru yomogi: "The hemp on which hangs the sagebrush." The hemp *(asa)* is straight, while the sagebrush *(yomogi)* is bent and crooked. When the hemp and sagebrush grow together, the latter follows the straight growth of the former. So men of weak character are helped by association with those whose character is upright. English parallel: With the good we become good.

Gō ni itte wa gō ni shitagae: "In a village do as the village does." This proverb of Chinese origin, encourages us to follow the customs of the place where one resides. English parallel: When in Rome do as the Romans do.

Hotoke no mane wa suredomo, chōja no mane wa naranu: "Though you may imitate Buddha, don't imitate a wealthy man." Good may come from trying to be like Buddha, but only sorrow and great financial loss will ensue if you try to ape the rich.

Kage no katachi ni shitagō ga gotoshi: "As the shadow follows the form." This is said of persons or things that are inseparably connected.

Karasu ga u no mane shite mizu ni oboreru: "The crow imitating the cormorant drowns in the water." This teaches the danger of too close imitation, and also the peril of sailing under false colors.

Monzen no kozō narawanu kyō wo yomu: "The shopboy (acolyte) before a temple gate reads a sutra untaught." Having heard them so often he knows them by heart, although they are in Sanscrit, a language he has never learned. The Japanese word *"kozō"* may mean either "acolyte" or "shop-boy." English parallel: The scholar's maid quotes Latin.

Ni-no-mai: "To make the same mistakes." (Lit., "To do the second dance.") That is, "a repetition" in a humorous and blundering way. This expression is taken from an ancient dance in which the first movement, called *"Ama,"* is followed by a second movement known as *"Ni-no-mai."* In this second dance the movements of the first dancer are repeated in a ludicrous, maudlin manner. Hence, if a person makes the same mistakes of another, he is described as "performing the second dance" *("Ni-no-mai wo enzuru").* He is doing a repetition.

Yūshō no moto ni jakusotsu nashi: "Under a brave general there are no cowardly soldiers." This saying describes the power of a good example. English parallel: A good officer will make good men.

IMMATURITY

WHILE BY NO MEANS TRUE OF ALL, many Japanese have an unrestrained childishness of outlook, call it immaturity or naïveté, which is quite refreshing. This is especially true of people living in rural areas or those whose educational opportunities have been limited.

Akaru kerya tsukiyo to omō: "Thinking it is moonlight because it is light." This is an idiomatic saying for a one-track mind.

Amma no megane: "Spectacles for a blind massagist." This is an expression to denote what is unnecessary, since nearly all massagists are blind.

Aonisai: "A raw youth." (Lit., "Green two years old.") This idiomatic expression is used to describe a young person who has little knowledge and less experience.

Aru wa iya nari, omō wa narazu: "What we have we dislike, what we long for we cannot get." That is, things often do not go as we wish in this world. English parallel: If wishes were horses, beggars would ride.

Ato no matsuri: "Faulty timing." (Lit., "After the festival.") A *"matsuri"* (festival) in a village, town, or city is a time of great importance, but the day after is too late to enjoy or benefit from it. English parallel: After death the doctor.

Baji tōfū: "Utter indifference." (Lit., "The horse's ear, east wind.") Unwanted advice is as useless and unwanted as the east wind to the horse's ear. To the farmer, the east wind may be most welcome as the precursor of rain, but to the horse it is a matter of complete indifference. English parallel: Water on a duck's back.

Chōsan-boshi: "That's humbug." (Lit., "Morning three, evening four.") This expression comes from the writings of the Chinese philosopher Chuang Tzu. A certain monkey showman told his animals that they would get three fruits in the morning and four in the evening. Since they were dissatisfied with the offer, he reversed the order and said that he would give them four in the morning and three in the evening. This ruse proved quite satisfactory. Hence the expression *"Chōsan-boshi"* came to mean, "That's humbug" or "That's applesauce," since it was a case of "six of one and half a dozen of the other."

Dasoku wo soeru: "To do something superfluous." (Lit., "To add legs to a snake.") According to a Chinese story, a certain man drew a snake and then added legs to the picture. English parallel: "To put a fifth wheel to a coach.

Dorobō ni kagi wa azukeru: "To court disaster or a great loss." (Lit., "To entrust your key to a thief.")

Dorobō wo mite nawa wo nau: "Precautions that are too late." (Lit., "To start making a rope after seeing the robber.") English parallel: To lock the stable door after the horse is stolen.

E ni kaita botamochi no yō: "A useless article." ("Like a sweet rice cake in a picture.") A rice cake in a painting is of little use for it cannot be eaten; so often what we wish for we cannot get. English parallel: The wine in a bottle does not quench thirst.

E ni kaita mochi wa kuwaren: "You can't eat the rice cake in a picture."

Enkō suigetsu wo torō: "A monkey attempting to catch the moon in the water." An expression to denote a foolish and dangerous undertaking.

Ensui kinka wo sukuwazu: "Distant water will not extinguish the neighborhood fire." English parallel: Water afar does not quench a fire at hand.

Ese-bushi no katana ijiri: "An empty threat." (Lit., "A sham warrior toying with his sword.")

Eyō ni mochi no kawa wo muku: "To be too much of a spendthrift." (Lit., "Pampered people peel the crust of the rice cake.") English parallel: Vetches seem bitter to the full-cropped pigeon.

Futoku mijikaku: "A short and reckless life." (Lit., "Bold and short.") A person who unlawfully gains wealth and is executed for his crime is spoken of as having led "a bold and short life." See *Hosoku nagaku:* "Slender and long," p. 141.

Geta ni yaki-miso: "A foolish and useless deed." (Lit., "To smear wooden clogs with roast bean paste.") Roast bean paste if eaten is delicious, but to smear it on wooden clogs is both foolish and wasteful.

Gummō zō wo saguru: "A group of blind men groping for an elephant." This proverb is based on a story in Aesop's Fables of five blind men who each felt a different part of the animal's body and came to very different conclusions concerning what an elephant was like. The saying is quoted when different people look upon a problem from different points of view and fail to obtain the correct full picture.

Hairu koto hayaku, deru koto hayashi: "What enters quickly, departs quickly." In many people this is especially true of learning. What is learned with ease often is not long retained.

Hayaku juku sureba hayaku kusaru: "Fast ripe, fast rotten." An accomplishment or knowledge that is quickly acquired will also be lost quickly. English parallel: Quick come, quick go.

Hayari mono wa sutari mono: "What's in fashion will be out of fashion." Anything that you may make or buy according to changes in fashion will soon be out of fashion.

Heta no yokozuki: "Fond of it but unskillful." (Lit. "The partiality of the unskillful person.") That is, an unskillful person's attempt is sure to be a failure.

Inu no kawabata aruki: "An aimless stroll." (Lit., "A dog's riverside stroll.") This expression is used to describe a person who wanders about the streets without purchasing anything. English parallel: Window shopping.

Inu no kenka ni kodomo ga de, kodomo no kenka ni oya ga deru: "One thing comes from another." (Lit., "Dogfights draw children, children's fights draw parents.") From small incidents frequently come larger consequences.

Ippan wo mite zempyō wo shiru: "You may judge the whole from a part." (Lit., "By seeing one spot you know the entire leopard.") English parallel: You may know the lion by its claws.

Kaeru no tsura ni mizu: "Something that is ineffectual." (Lit., "Water on a frog's face.") English parallel: Water on a duck's back.

Kaji ato no pompu: "A belated and unnecessary thing." (Lit., "After the fire, the engine pump.")

Kaji ato no yōjin: "To be too late in doing something." (Lit., "Precautions after the fire.")

Kappa ni suiei wo oshieru: "Unnecessary and foolish effort." (Lit., "Teaching a river goblin to swim.") The *"kappa"* is a river goblin that swims far better than any man.

Kappa ni suiren: "Swimming instructions to a river goblin." The meaning and use of this proverb is the same as the one above.

Katsu ni nozonde ido wo horu: "To do something too late." (Lit., "In the presence of thirst you dig a well.")

Ke wo mite uma wo sōsu: "To judge a thing by its looks only." (Lit., "To look at the hair and judge the horse.")

Kenka sugite no bō chigiri: "To pick up sticks after the fight is over." It is too late to pick up clubs when there is no longer a fight.

Kizu motsu ashi no kimi warushi: "A guilty conscience gives one an ominous feeling." (Lit., "An injured foot's bad feeling.")

Kojiki wo mikka sureba yamerarenu: "One who has been a beggar for three days cannot stop." Probably because it is an easier way to make a living than by working hard. English parallel: Once a beggar always a beggar.

Kinjiki kanarazu shimo ōgon narazu: "Golden color is not infallibly gold." This is the Japanese translation and adaptation of the English proverb: "All is not gold that glitters."

Kōto shishite sōku niraru: "A case of base ingratitude." (Lit., "The sly rabbit is dead and the hound is cooked.") When there is no longer any need of the hound, the hare having been caught or killed, the very means of success is disposed of. English parallel: When the danger is past the guardian saint is derided.

Kūchū rōkaku: "Castles in Spain." (Lit., "Castles in the air.") The expression *"kūron"* (lit., "air argument") means "an empty (academic) theory or discussion."

Kyūchō eda wo erabazu: "A sorely pressed bird is not choosy about branches." English parallel: Any port in a storm.

Mae e futa ashi, ushiro e mi ashi: "Not an advance but a retreat; not success but a failure." (Lit., "Two steps forward, three steps backward.")

Mekura-hebi mono ni ojizu: "A blind snake fears nothing." That is, one who knows nothing fears nothing.

Mekura, hebi ni ojizu: "Blind men are not afraid of snakes." English parallel: Fools rush in where angels fear to tread.

Mino-uri kasa ni te hiru: "Not to make use of the conveniences one has." (Lit., "The straw-raincoat dealer winnows with a bamboo basket hat.") Instead of using a straw basket of which he has many, he uses a bamboo umbrella hat which is less convenient and more expensive.

Mizukake-ron: "An endless and fruitless discussion." (Lit., "A water-splashing argument.") The idea comes from the playful contest of groups splashing each other in a river or sea.

Moeru aburagami no yō ni shaberu: "To be a chatterer." (Lit., "To talk like burning oilpaper.") English parallel: To talk like a house on fire.

Moyuru hi ni abura wo sosogu: "To increase a given situation or condition." (Lit., "To pour oil on a burning fire.")

Muika no ayame, tōka no kiku: "Something that is too late." (Lit., "Irises on the sixth day, chrysanthemums on the tenth day.") At the Boys' Festival on May 5 irises are used as decorations, and at the Chrysanthemum Festival on September 9 that flower is used in the home. In each case on the day after the festival the flowers serve no purpose. English parallel: A day after the fair.

Nesshi-yasuku mono wa hie- (same-) yasushi: "An easily heated thing is easily cooled." This applies to persons as well as to things. English parallel: Soon hot, soon cold.

Nete ma wa gokuraku: "When asleep it is heaven." The implication being that when one is awake and working it is hell.

Nigeru mono wa michi wo erabazu: "A fleeing person is not choosy about his road." Because his only aim is to escape as quickly as possible.

Nochi no senkin: "Belated relief." (Lit., "A thousand gold pieces later.")

Nusubito ni kagi watasu: "To do a foolish and dangerous thing." (Lit., "To hand over the keys to a robber.") That is, to do something exceedingly dangerous and foolish as placing a dishonest person in charge of valuables.

Nusubito (Dorobō) ni oisen: "Throwing away good money after bad." (Lit., "To give pursuing money to a robber.") To give more money to a departing thief. That is, to spend unnecessary money after sustaining a loss in some undertaking. English parallel: Throwing the handle after the blade.

Nusubito toraete nawa wo nau: "To twist straw into a rope after the thief is caught." After the robber is captured it is too late to make a rope for tying him. English parallel: To lock the stable door after the horse is stolen. See "After the robber has gone you string a bow," p. 131.

Nusubito wo toraete mireba waga ko nari: "A sudden and most unpleasant discovery." (Lit., "Having caught the thief and looked at him I found that he was my child!")

Nusumi-gui wa umai: "Stolen things eaten are delicious." English parallel: Stolen fruit tastes sweet.

Oboreru mono wa wara wo mo tsukamu: "A drowning person

will clutch at even a straw." That is, a man in a dangerous situation will resort to any means. The above proverb is probably a direct translation of the English one, "A drowning man will catch at a rush (straw)."

Ō-kaze ni hai wo maku: "The utterances of an irresponsible talker." (Lit., "To scatter ashes in a big wind.") Just as ashes thrown away in a strong wind are widely scattered and cannot be recovered, so the utterances of an irresponsible person are widely spread and cannot be regained.

Shōchū no tama wo torareta yō: "As though a jewel in one's hand has been taken away." This expression is used to describe a great disappointment, such as the loss of some valued person or thing.

Shōmon no dashi okure: "To bring out a bond too late." This proverb is used to describe a case in which action is too late to be of use. English parallel: To plead after sentence is given.

Sōrei sugite isha banashi: "To talk about doctors after the funeral is over." English parallel: After death, the doctor.

Tou ni ochizu, kataru ni otsu: "When asked he does not tell, but when he speaks he tells tales." This often happens in the cross examination of a suspect.

Tsukiyo ni chōchin: "An unnecessary thing to do." (Lit., "To carry a paper lantern on a moonlight night.")

Udo no taiboku: "A big, gawky fellow." (Lit., "A big asparagus tree.") This expression is a metaphor for a big, good-for-nothing person.

Uma no mimi ni nembutsu: "Something utterly unavailing." (Lit., "A chanted Buddhist invocation into the ear of a horse.") English parallels: Preaching to the wind. Preaching to deaf ears.

Ushi no mae no koto shirabe: "To do something that is neither understood nor appreciated." (Lit., "Playing a harp before an ox.") The "*koto*" is a long, recumbent harp with thirteen strings. It is the aim of all cultured Japanese young ladies to learn to play it well. A beautiful Japanese girl attired in a formal flowing kimono and playing the koto with true musical appreciation is a feast for both the eyes and ears.

Wana ni kakeru: "To catch in a trap." This expression is used both literally and figuratively.

Yake-ato no yōjin: "Caution after a fire." English parallel: When the house is burnt down, you bring water.

Zoku satte hari-yumi: "After the robber has gone, you string the bow." This proverb describes a preparation that is too late. See "To twist straw into a rope after the thief is caught," p. 129.

INDIRECTNESS OF SPEECH

FROM SOME OF THE PROVERBS that have been given and those which follow in this section it will be seen that indirectness in speech and action is an outstanding trait of the Japanese. It is much more admired and practiced than directness. This is probably due to the desire not to bring shame on oneself or others. In many Japanese expressions the principle of understatement is used, and the hearer or reader is left to draw his own conclusions. Figurative language is also widely used in both prose and poetry.

Abura wo kakeru: "To egg on a person; to instigate." (Lit., "To pour on oil.") This is a popular and idiomatic phrase for setting a person to do something.

Abura ga noru: "To put on fat." This expression is literally applied in the case in which the fish fattens in its "season." Metaphorically it means "to warm up to a subject"; "to be interested"; or "to be in the height of one's skill and power."

Abura wo shiboru: "To rebuke; or to take to task." (Lit., "To squeeze out oil.") This phrase is frequently used in daily conversation.

Baka wo shōchi no yakuza demo: "Even a worthless fellow can obtain the consent of a fool." To get the consent of a fool is so easily done that even worthless fellows take advantage of it.

Gomame no hagishiri: "Impotent rage." (Lit., "The teeth gnashing of a small dried sardine.") English parallel: The frog flew into a passion, and the pond knew nothing about it.

Hachi monji wo fumu: "To walk parrot-toed." (Lit., "To walk the figure eight.") This means to walk modestly for a Japanese woman and drunkenly for a man.

Hana iki wo kagu: "To curry favor, or to consult another's pleasure." (Lit., "To smell another's nasal-breathing.")

Haru-aki ni tomu (Shunjū ni tomu): "To be still young." (Lit., "To be rich in spring and autumn.") *"Shunjū"* is the Japanese-Chinese pronunciation of *"Haru-aki."*

Inochi no sentaku: "Recreation; refreshment." (Lit., "Laundering of life.") This expression is used to indicate the recreation a person takes after a long period of work.

Ishi de tamango wo tsubusu yō: "An easy thing to do." (Lit., "Like smashing an egg with a rock.")

Jigoku de hotoke ni au yō: "Like a Buddha met with in hell." This phrase is frequently used to express great relief when a quick way of escape is found from some looming disaster. English parallel: An oasis in the desert.

Jūnin-nami: "Average, ordinary, or mediocre." (Lit., "Ten persons in a row.")

Jūmoku no miru tokoro, jisshi no yubisasu tokoro: "It is positive proof." (Lit., "It is just what ten (all) eyes see and ten (all) fingers point to.")

Kabuto wo nugu: "To acknowledge defeat." (Lit., "To take off one's helmet.") This idiomatic expression is taken from the battlefield in the feudal period.

Kago no tori kumo wo shitō: "A person deprived of his liberty desires freedom." (Lit., "A caged bird longs for the clouds.") The above proverb is more often applied to women than to men. In the late 1930's a very popular sentimental song was entitled *"Kago no Tori"* ("A Bird in a Cage.")

Kan-oke ni kata ashi wo tsukkomu: "To be at the point of death." (Lit., "To have one leg in the coffin tub.") This expression is frequently said of a person who is quite old, or has a serious illness. In Japan the casket in which the deceased is put for burial or cremation is tub shaped, especially if the funeral is to be a Buddhist one. English parallel: To have one foot in the grave.

Kawa ni mizu wo hakobe: "To do something unnecessary." (Lit., "To carry water to the river.") English parallel: To carry coals to Newcastle.

Kayui tokoro ni te ga todokanu: "Not to know where the trouble is." (Lit., "The hand cannot reach the place that itches.")

Ki kara ochita saru no yō: "A helpless condition." (Lit., "Like a monkey fallen from a tree.") This saying is often used to describe a person who is no longer in his familiar environment, and hence open to the attacks of his enemies.

Kikai wa eyasuku, ushinai yasushi: "Easily had opportunities are easily lost." English parallels: Easy come, easy go. Make hay while the sun shines.

Kojiki ga uma wo moratta yō: "An unwelcome gift." (Lit., "Like a beggar who has received a horse.") The gift is unwelcome because if he tried to sell the horse, he would probably be accused of having stolen it. Not having any money, the beggar would be unable to purchase food for the animal. English parallel: A white elephant.

Kusai mono ni hai ga takaru: "Foul-smelling objects swarm with flies." Just as flies gather on stinking things, so men of small ability and character are attracted by lucrative though disreputable projects. English parallel: Where the carcass is the ravens will gather.

Kutsu wo hedatete kayuki wo kaku: "To get at the seat of trouble with difficulty." (Lit., "To scratch the itching place through the shoe.") The inefficiency of certain measures for dealing with a difficult situation is thus described.

Kyō no yume, Ōsaka no yume: "Once upon a time." (Lit., "This is a dream of Kyōto and a dream of Ōsaka.") In old times Japanese folk stories were often begun with the above expression, just as fairy tales and stories written a generation ago for American and English children would frequently start with "Many, many years ago . . ." or "Once upon a time . . ."

Kyūshi issei wo eru: "To have a narrow escape from death." (Lit., "To gain one life from nine deaths.") The expression *"Kyūshi"* (nine deaths) is the idiom for "certain death." Hence, the above saying may be translated: "to have a narrow escape from the very jaws of death itself."

Makura wo takaku shite neru: "To sleep tranquilly." (Lit., "To sleep on a high pillow.") Centuries ago pillows with a wooden base three to six inches high came into use. The base of the head or neck being placed on the pillow, the sleeper can relax, confident in the knowledge that the elaborate hair-do would not be disturbed during the night. Since the hair arrangements of women were much more intricate than those of men, the high pillow finally came to be used only by the former.

Mambyō ichiyaku: "A universal remedy; a panacea." (Lit., "Ten thousand illnesses, one medicine.") Here the word *"man"* or *mam,"* translated into English "ten thousand," has also the meaning of "many" or "all."

Maruku osameru: "To smooth over a quarrel or dispute." (Lit., "To suppress roundly.") This phrase means to come to an amicable settlement by removing the sharp corners of differences, each side making concessions. English parallel: To square it. Here the curves of well-rounded arguments are removed, i.e., making concessions, so that the square sides of each can come together, and an agreement is reached.

Miso no miso-kusai wa jō-miso ni arazu: "The highest art is concealed art." (Lit., "The bean paste that smells like bean paste is not the best bean paste.") English parallel: The perfection of art is to conceal art.

Mizu no awa to natta: "It has come to naught." (Lit., "It has become water froth.") That is, the scheme or plan has failed or fallen to the ground.

Mizunomi-byakushō: "A poor peasant or petty farmer." (Lit., "A water-drinking farmer.") The term probably arose from the fact that in ancient times peasants were not permitted to drink rice wine (*saké*) and were too poor to purchase it even if allowed to do so.

Mizu wo hanareta uo no yō: "A helpless person." (Lit., "Like a fish separated from water.") This expression is used to describe a person who has lost all his resources and does not know where to turn for help. English parallel: A fish out of water.

Moto no Mokuami: "To be no better than before." (Lit., "Mokuami remained as he was.") The following story is told as the origin of this proverbial expression. To keep secret the death of a certain general until his son was old enough to take over the headship of the family, a blind man, Mokuami, who greatly resembled the general, was chosen to pose as the bed-ridden sick warrior. The ruse succeeded. In due time the son came to power, and Mokuami became again a blind beggar in the street. Hence, the phrase *"moto no mokuami"* has come to mean, "to return to one's former position," "to remain as one was," or "to be no better than before."

Moto no saya e osameru: "To reinstate a person." (Lit., "To put back into the former scabbard.") This proverb, drawn from ancient military life, means "to reinstate a person in his former position." In domestic life it has the meaning of "recalling a separated wife to her husband's home."

Motte tazan no ishi to subeshi: "Anything that can be put to use." (Lit., "Having brought it, let it be a stone from another mountain.") Though the stone may not be a valuable gem, it may prove useful in polishing more precious stones. Hence, something that can be used, or anything that can be put to profit.

Muchi nagashi to iedomo bafuku ni oyobazu: "The power or authority of government has its limitations." (Lit., "Though the whip is long it does not reach the belly of the horse.") English parallel: The king has long arms, but they do not reach all places.

Mushi no iki: "To be breathing faintly." (Lit., "The breath of an insect.") This expression is used to describe the faint breathing of a dying person.

Musume hitori no muko hachi nin: "Much to be desired." (Lit. "Eight sons-in-law for one young woman.") This expression is often used to describe a good berth or position which is being sought after by a number of persons. It also depicts a popular beauty or heiress who has many candidates for her hand.

Neko mo shakushi mo: "Everyone." (Lit., "Both cats and dippers.") English parallels: All the world and his wife. Every man Jack.

Ningyō wo tsukau: "To pull wires (behind the scene)." (Lit., "To use a puppet.") English parallel: To make a catspaw of a person.

O-cha wo nigosu: "To speak ambiguously; to prevaricate." (Lit., "To make the tea cloudy.") This expression is probably taken from the tea ceremony in which powdered green tea is put into a big bowl over which warm water is poured. The mixture is then stirred or whipped into a green froth by an implement of finely-split bamboo and shaped like a shaving brush, before being offered to the guest. The purpose of the stirring may be to gain time, or to obscure the quality of the tea. When a person takes temporizing measures in spite of a pressing need he is said "to stir the tea."

Ō-kaze no ato no yō: "A sudden stillness after a great commotion." (Lit., "As after a great windstorm.") Another reading of the characters for *"ō-kaze"* (great wind) is *"taifū"* from which we get the now frequently used word "typhoon" or hurricane. When such a great windstorm has blown over there is frequently a period of absolute stillness, which scientists now explain as passing through the eye of the hurricane, or rather the center of the hurricane passing over a given place. This extreme quietness is often compared to the calm that follows a terrible family quarrel or some other great commotion.

Ō-mizu no hiita ato no yō: "A great stillness following much commotion." (Lit., "Just as after a great flood has subsided.") This proverbial phrase and the one preceding it have much meaning to the people of Japan, for each year that country is subjected to terrible hurricanes and disastrous tidal waves and floods which take a great toll of life and property.

Oni ni kanabō: "As strong as can be." The word *"oni"* may be translated either "devil" or "ogre." When, as in Japanese painting or sculpture, the devil is represented as carrying an iron rod, he is considered invincible. So a very strong man when heavily armed, has a double advantage, and the saying "an ogre with an iron rod" is applied.

Oni no kakuran: "The illness of a very healthy person." (Lit., "The devil's cholera morbus.") Even devils fall ill. So the above phrase is used when an unusually strong and healthy person succumbs to some sickness.

Oni no ude: "Great fondness." (Lit., "The devil's arm.") For example, a man's only son of whom he is extremely fond, is often referred to as "the devil's arm." Just as the devil without his strong arms would have all the fight taken out of him, so a person deprived of some greatly beloved object would be rendered powerless.

Ryōjin wo ugokasu: "To move the dust on the beams." This phrase of Chinese origin, is used to describe the voice of a fine singer or chanter as: "His voice is so powerful and beautiful that it moves the dust on the beams of the building."

Ryōmata wa kakerarenu: "One cannot run on two crotches." This is similar in meaning to the English proverbial phrase: "You cannot have your cake and eat it too."

Ruiran no gotoko ayaushi: "In great peril." (Lit., "As perilous as piled-up eggs.") In Japanese markets one often sees dozens of eggs piled in a great pyramid. Since the eggs may tumble down and be broken to pieces at any moment, the above proverb means "in imminent danger."

Samben mawatte tabako ni sho: "Let me go round three times and take a puff at the pipe." This expression is used to give a slight hint to a person who bores you with his tedious talk to wind up his discourse.

Sekihin arau ga gotoshi: "To be reduced to abject poverty." (Lit., "As though washed red poor.") English parallel: As poor as a church mouse.

Sembei ni kanazuchi: "An iron hammer struck against toasted rice cake." This phrase indicates something quite easy to do. *"Sembei"* is a very thin, crisp, roasted rice cake which can easily be broken in the fingers and reduced to crumbs by a single blow of an iron hammer.

Sembei no yō ni pechanko ni naru: "To be crushed or flattened." (Lit., "To be laid flat by a blow like a thin rice cake.")

Senaka ni mizu wo abiseraru yō: "An unpleasant or disagreeable experience." (Lit., "To feel as if cold water were poured down one's back.")

Sojō no koi: "A carp on the chopping board." This describes a fish about to be killed and cut up by the cook. The expression is used to describe a man who has been overpowered by and is at the mercy of his enemy, or a person who is made to face disciplinary action.

Suna wo kamu: "To have an unpleasant experience or feeling." (Lit., "To chew sand.")

Suzumushi wa uta no tame ni kago ni kawaru: "A bell cricket is kept in its cage on account of its song." In Japan various species of insects are kept in cages as pets and for the chirping sounds they make. One of the best-liked is the *"suzu-mashi"* (bell cricket), so called because its chirpings resemble the tinkle of a silver bell. The above saying means that one's own talents are sometimes the cause of one's misery.

Tomoshibi wa ķien to shite sono hiķari wo masu: "A light when about to go out increases its brilliance." A sick person may suddenly get better before he dies. An author or scientist often does his best work just before death.

Tosho no hitsuji: "A sheep on the way to the slaughterhouse." This phrase describes the sad, crestfallen looks of a doomed prisoner on his way to the place of execution.

Tsuķiyo ni ķama wo nuķu: "To hoodwink a person." (Lit. "To remove a cauldron on a moonlight night.") The *"ķama"* is the large iron pot or kettle in which rice is daily boiled, hence one of the most important vessels in the kitchen. To let it be stolen on a bright moonlight night amounts to almost criminal negligence. Thus the above proverb describes the careless loss of important possessions and the deception of the owner.

Udonge no saita yō: "A rare happening." (Lit., "As if the plantain had flowered."). The *"udonge"* or "plantain" is the Japanese word for the Sanscrit *"Udambara,"* an imaginary plant said to bear flowers once in 3,000 years. This rare happening is also believed to be a very good omen.

Ugo no taķe-no-ķo: "Bamboo sprouts after a rain." After a heavy rain the bamboo grove will be seen to have numerous sprouts which seem to have suddenly appeared above the ground; so a multitude of things of the same kind sometimes appear all at once in the world. English parallel: Like mushrooms in the rain.

Washi no ķo: "The eagle's young." This expression like, "The devil's arm," q.v., is used to indicate great fondness.

Watari ni fune: "A timely occurrence or rescue." (Lit., "At the ferry, a boat.") When in a great hurry to cross a bridgeless river we arrive at the ferry just in time to take the boat which is about to go to the opposite shore; so when in great need a friend may give us just the assistance and encouragement we need.

Yabure-gutsu wo suteru yō: "Like throwing away torn shoes."

This is a figurative expression for getting rid of things that have out-worn their use.

Yake-ishi ni mizu: "Water on a heated stone." That is, a small amount of anything is not sufficient to fill a great need. For example, a short shower after a long spell of dry weather does little good and is as useless as pouring a small amount of water on a scorched rock. English parallel: All is lost that is put in a riven dish.

Yama ni tsumuzukazu shite ari-zuka ni tsumazuku: "Though we do not fail in big undertakings we are not successful in small things." (Lit., "Though not stumbling over a mountain, we stumble over an anthill.") English parallel: To stumble at a straw and leap over a block.

Yamiyo ni teppō: "An aimless effort; a fruitless undertaking." (Lit., "Shooting with a gun on a dark night.") This expression is used to describe a hazardous act with no definite end in view.

Yase-uma muchi wo osorezu: "A lean horse fears not the whip." That is, starving people do not fear punishment and will often rise up against their oppressors. English parallel: A hungry dog and a thirsty horse take no heed of blows.

Yase-uma ni omoni: "A heavy burden on a lean horse." That is, entrusting to a mediocre man a task greater than his ability.

Yō ni yotte koro wo egaku: "In the usual way he draws a bottle-gourd." This saying is applied to the person who speaks, writes, or acts in a conventional manner.

Yūdachi wa uma no se wo wakeru: "A hard and sudden summer shower." (Lit., "A summer shower parts the mane of a horse.") This describes a summer shower which in Japan frequently comes suddenly and with great force.

Yuki to sumi hodo chigau: "As different as snow from charcoal." English parallel: As different as white from black.

Zatō no tsue wo ushinatta yō: "To be absolutely helpless." (Lit., "Like a blind man who has lost his staff.")

INDUSTRY

CONSTANT TOIL during working hours is the lot of most Japanese. They are among the most industrious folk in the world, and one sees few loafers or indolent people. The farmer and artisan work from sunrise to far into the night. The merchant and business man keep long office hours and often bring home work to be done. The professional man's hours for work are generally longer than those of his confreres in the United States. The student spends the day in the lecture room or laboratory and then studies until a late hour. During examinations, of which there are many in Japan, students will frequently go for a week without sleep while "cramming" their lecture notes and textbooks. The housewife's work may often keep her busy from four in the morning to long after midnight, and this is most likely to be the case if she is a bride living with her husband in the home of his parents. With the increasing use of modern conveniences, working hours have been somewhat shortened, but one may say without fear of contradiction that Japan is by far the most industrious nation in Asia and one of the most industrious in the world. Though hard working, the Japanese are fond of play. They make good use of their holidays, festivals, and recreation periods.

Asa oki wa nanatsu no toku ari: "Early rising has seven advantages." Here the word *"nanatsu"* (seven), as in numerous other countries of both the Far East and the Near East, has the meaning of "many." English parallel: The early bird catches the worm.

Asa oki wa san mon no toku: "Early rising makes the profit of three *mon*." A *"mon"* had the value of one tenth of a *"rin"*; the *"rin"* was worth one tenth of a *"sen"*; and the *"sen,"* one hundredth of a *"yen."* For more than fifty years the *mon* and *rin* have not been in use in Japan, and because of depreciated currency, the *sen* is also out of circulation. English parallel: Early to bed and early to rise makes a man healthy, wealthy, and wise.

Asobi-nin hima nashi: "Pleasure seekers have no leisure." Though they do not work, they are too busy having a good time. English parallel: Idle people have the least leisure.

Bon to shōgatsu to ga issho ni kita yō: "To be extremely busy." (Lit., "As if the Festival of the Dead and the New Year arrived at the same time.") *"Bon"* is the Buddhist Festival of the Dead—All Soul's Day—when the spirits of the dead revisit their homes and are feasted. It is celebrated about the middle of July. The exact date differs slightly in different parts of Japan. Just before this festival nearly all stores have special sales, and there is a general settling by merchants and shopkeepers of all semiannual bills. This is also done before the coming of *"Shōgatsu"* (the New Year). Thus at these two times of the year everyone is extremely busy and happy. English parallel: As busy as if all quarter days had come together.

Ete no ho wo age: "To give scope to one's skill." (Lit., "To hoist the sail before one's strong points.") This proverb encourages people to follow up their natural advantages and make full use of their abilities. English parallel: To give sail to dexterity.

Hajime kara chōja ni wa narenu: "One cannot be a wealthy man from the first." Great wealth is generally not amassed suddenly. It is necessary for a person to go through all the stages of advancing prosperity by accumulating a fortune little by little. Being thrifty and hard working each day of the year will bring financial reward and success. English parallel: Step after step, the ladder is ascended.

Heta no dōgu shirabe: "An unskillful person inspects his tools." Since he lacks natural ability, a poor workman is doubly dependent on his equipment. English parallel: A bad workman quarrels with his tools.

Hosoku nagaku: "Slender and long." This saying describes a long and frugal life. An honest person does not wish to get rich quickly by dishonest means but is satisfied to lead a long and easy life by being frugal. His motto, "Slender and long," is just the opposite of those who desire to amass a fortune quickly even by dishonest means and whose motto is "Bold and short" (*"Futoku mijikaku,"* q.v., p. 126.)

Ikiuma no me wo nuku: "To pluck out the eyes of a live horse." This metaphor is used to describe a very wide-awake and shrewd person; or the bustling condition of a busy street.

Ima no hito-hari, nochi no tō-hari: "Better a stitch now than ten stitches later." Early care saves wear. English parallel: A stitch in time saves nine.

Kōbō wa fude wo erabazu: "Kōbō is not choosy about his writing brush." Because he is such an able calligraphist he can write well with any brush-pen. That learned Buddhist priest was famed for his great skill in calligraphy, painting, sculpture, and scholastic studies. English parallel: The cunning workman does not quarrel with his tools.

Kōkoku wa shōgyō no haha nari: "Advertising is the mother of commerce." Because honest and attractive advertisements give birth to more and more business, and increase sales.

Meijin fude wo erabazu: "An expert does not choose his brushpen." Because he can do good work even with poor implements. The word *"meijin,"* translated "expert," is written with the Chinese ideographs for "name" and "person"; i.e., one who has made a name for himself.

Nai ga iken no sō-jimai: "There is no further need for advice." (Lit., "To have nothing is the advice for going out of business.") When everything is gone reproofs are at an end. English parallel: An empty purse makes a man wise, but too late.

Namake mono no sekku-bataraki: "Useless show in lieu of quiet perseverance." (Lit., "The lazy person works at festival time.") Although he does not work on regular days, he makes a show of work at festivals when no one else is working. English parallel: The lazy becomes industrious towards evening.

Neko no te mo karitai: "To be extremely busy." (Lit., "We wish to borrow even the paws of a cat.") When our hands are full of work anybody's help would be most welcome, even the assistance of a cat's paws.

Nōsho fude wo erabazu: "The good calligrapher is not choosy about his writing brush." Even with poor tools a good workman can do excellent work. That is, talent and ability count for more than implements.

Rō sezu shite nani mono ka wo en: "Without working what can a person get?" That is, honest labor is what everyone should do.

Ryōkō wa zai wo erabazu: "A skilled artisan is not fussy about the material." For even with second-rate material he can have good results.

Saifu karukereba genki nashi: "When the purse is light there is no vitality." Without a certain amount of money for his needs, a person is apt to be depressed.

Shakkin nakereba kiken nashi: "With no debt there is no danger."
Shindai wa kamaboko ni naru: "A wasted fortune." (Lit., "A fortune gone to fish gelatin.") *"Kamaboko"* is a gelatin made of ground-up boiled fish and is a cheap but nourishing food.

Shōjin kankyo shite fuzen wo nasu: "Small men leading an idle life will do wrong." This proverb is taken from the teachings of Confucius. Since most people are "little men," that is, unimportant persons, it is well to keep busy. English parallel: The devil finds mischief for idle hands to do.

Tonari no takara wo kazoeru: "To count the treasures of your neighbor." It is useless to estimate the wealth of your neighbor while you do nothing to increase your own through hard work.

Yoine asaoki chōja no moto: "Early sleeping and early rising are essentials for becoming a millionaire." English parallel: Early to bed and early to rise makes a man healthy, wealthy, and wise.

Zashite kuraeba yama mo munashi: "Even a mountain of riches is not enough for an idle person." (Lit., "When a man just sits and eats, even a mountain becomes nothing.") To always eat the bread of idleness will reduce great wealth. English parallel: Idleness makes the fullest purse empty.

Zeni kane wa waki mono: "Money quickly flows away." (Lit., "Money is a thing that gushes forth.") Hence, the need for industry and hard work.

KINDNESS

THOUGH THEY DO NOT OUTWARDLY DISPLAY THEIR FEELINGS, since from early childhood they are taught to conceal them, the Japanese are basically kind. The two words most frequently used for kindness are *"shinsetsu,"* written with two Chinese ideographs meaning "friendship constantly," and *"nasake,"* written with one Chinese ideograph having the two components of "heart" and "green." *"Nasake"* may also be translated "pity" or "compassion" and is an important element in Buddhist teaching. This gave rise in the Tokugawa period to a group known as *"Kyōkaku"* or *"Otokodate,"* whose aim was the protection of the weak and oppressed against the strong, in particular the swashbuckling *samurai,* who were quick to cut down any who displeased them. The basic chivalrous attitude of the *"Kyōkaku,"* who rebelled against the injustice of the times and defended the downtrodden masses, was known as *"kikotsu"* (Lit., "spirit bone"). Thus, to this day kindness as displayed by the Japanese is not a mere feeling but has very strong and positive features.

Jizen wa katei ni yori hajimaru: "Doing good to humanity should first be practiced at home." This proverb is a translation of the English one: Charity begins at home.

Kai-inu ni te wo kamareru: "To have your hand bitten by your pet dog." The experience of a kindly man who suffers wrong from an ungrateful person to whom he has been especially helpful is thus described.

Kyūchō futokoro ni ireba ryōfu mo kore wo korosazu: "When a bird in distress flies into his bosom even the hunter will not kill it." This proverb of Chinese origin was much valued by the warriors of feudal Japan, for it commanded them to spare, when requested to do so, the life of a weaker enemy who was at their mercy.

Mushi ippiki koroshita koto ga nai: "A guileless and kindly person." (Lit., "Not even one insect has he ever killed.") English parallel: He has never harmed an insect.

Mi wo koroshite jin wo nasu: "To sacrifice one's life for a benevolent deed." This Confucian maxim encourages a person to do good deeds to others without regard to his own interests. English parallel: A candle lights others and consumes itself.

Nasake ni hamukau yaiba nashi: "There is no blade that can offer resistance to kindness."

Nasake ni mukau yaiba nashi: "There is no sword that can oppose kindness." Both proverbs are two versions of the same popular saying. English parallel: Kindness is the noblest weapon with which to conquer.

Nasake wo hito no tame narazu: "Kindness is not just for the sake of others." A kind deed has also a favorable reaction on the doer. It is never lost. English parallels: He who gives to the poor lends to the Lord. The hand that gives gathers.

Ninjō ni kokkyō nashi: "There are no boundaries to humanity (kindness)." *"Ninjō,"* which is here translated "humanity" or "kindness," has also the meaning of "sympathy" or "fellow-feeling."

Nasake wo shiru ga makoto no bushi: "He who knows kindness (compassion) is a true (sincere) warrior."

Rōsoku wa mi wo herashite hito wo terasu: "Candles exhaust themselves to give light to men." That is, great men unselfishly devote themselves to promoting the welfare of others. English parallel: A candle lights others and consumes itself.

Senri no uma wa aredo Hakuraku nashi: "Though you may have a horse that can travel a thousand *ri* (2,440 miles), you cannot find Hakuraku." Kindness to friends, for which Hakuraku was famous is not to be found nowadays. Hakuraku (the ideographs mean "chief happiness") is the name of a famous horse expert who lived in days of yore and was noted for kindness to his friends.

Sokuin no kokoro wa jin no hajime nari: "A heart of sympathy is the beginning of benevolence." This proverb, taken from Confucian writings, informs us that a feeling of compassion is the root of philanthropy. English parallel: Pity's akin to love.

Sono tsumi wo nikunde sono hito wo nikumazu: "Hate the sin but do not hate the person." This Confucian teaching states that a man should condemn the offence but be generous to the offender.

Tabi wa michizure, yo wa nasake: "On a journey a companion, in the world kindness." Good company in travel and compassion in life are greatly to be desired. This proverb originated in ancient times when travel was both hazardous and unpleasant. Men should not live separately in this world. They must help each other. English parallels: No road is long with good company. Company in distress makes trouble less.

Tabi wa ui mono, tsurai mono: "Travel is a gloomy and trying experience." Travelers learn much of what is sad and inconvenient. After all, home is more pleasant and restful.

Tōka kore wo atatamuru mo ichi nichi ni shite yoku kore wo samasan: "Though you may warm an object for ten days, it will be perfectly cooled in a day." That is, a long kindness is soon forgotten. English parallel: One hour's cold will suck out seven years' heat.

Uramazu kisezu: "Don't bear a grudge and don't record it."
English parallel: Forgive and forget.

Urami ni mukuyuru ni toku wo motte seyo: "To repay a grudge do it with virtue." That is, pay good for evil.

Waga mi wo tsunette hito no itasa wo shire: "Pinch yourself and you will know the pains of others." We must try to sympathize with other people by undergoing or imagining the pain they experience. English parallel: Do as you would be done by.

Yo wa aimochi: "Life in this world consists in mutual helpfulness." Give and take is the rule of the world. English parallel: Live and let live.

Zen wa isoge: "Hasten to do good." Don't wait to do good, but do it quickly. English parallel: Make hay while the sun shines.

LEARNING

MORE THAN PERHAPS ANY OTHER PEOPLE the Japanese are studious and zealous in their search for knowledge. The teacher, the professor, and the scholar are highly respected and honored. The student spends long hours in study both in and outside the classroom. Top ranking students on graduating get the best positions in government and business. Because of their studious habits and their love of learning, Japanese who go abroad for graduate study and research generally do outstanding work.

Bun wa hito nari: This is the Japanese translation of the English proverb: "The style is the man."

Furuki wo tazunete atarashiki wo shiru: "Through inquiring into old things we learn the new." This is a Confucian saying which teaches that by a thorough study of old things new ones will be discovered. English parallel: There is nothing new under the sun.

Gakumon ni kokkyō nashi: "There are no national frontiers to learning." Scholarship knows no boundaries between countries.

Gakumon ni chika-michi nashi: "There is no short cut to learning." English parallel: There is no royal road to learning.

Gakushi ni totta tenka nashi: "There is no scholar who has taken control of the whole country." A man of learning is not suited to wield political power, for experience has shown that scholars make poor rulers.

Hachijū no te-narai: "To study penmanship at eighty." English parallel: It is never too late to learn.

Hon no mushi: "A bookworm." The Japanese phrase is a direct translation of the English one and has the same connotation.

Iki-jibiki: "A living dictionary." English parallel: A walking dictionary.

Jūnen ichi-jitsu no gotoshi: "Ten years as one day." This means, "without intermission for ten years"—a phrase signifying continued application for many years.

Keisetsu no kō wo tsumu: "To pursue one's studies by the light of fireflies and snow." (Lit., "To pile up merit by fireflies and snow.") This expression describes the successful completion of studies by needy students. In ancient China two such young men diligently pursued learning by reading books in the summer by the light of fireflies gathered for the purpose, and in winter by the reflection of starlight from a quantity of snow. English parallel: To burn the midnight oil.

Manabazareba shirazu: "Without learning there is no knowing." English parallel: Learn not and know not.

Oshieru wa manabu no nakaba: "To teach is the center of to learn." English parallel: Teaching others teacheth yourself.

Rokujū no te-narai: "To study calligraphy at sixty." English parallel: It is never too late to learn.

Ruri mo hari mo teraseba hikaru: "Emeralds as well as glass will shine when light is shed on them." This proverb teaches that when education is given to them, both a clever man and a foolish one will become wise.

Saishi tabyō: "Talented men have poor health." (Lit., "A talented person, many illnesses." This is probably due to the fact that they were careless about proper diet and exercise. A large percentage of students, teachers, and scholars in Japan have or have had tuberculosis.

Saishi tammei: "Talented persons are short lived." English parallel: Whom the gods love die young.

Shisō wa chimmoku nari: "Thought is silence." That is, ideas come through quiet meditation. Hence, in Japan as well as in other countries learned men have withdrawn from the noisy and demanding world.

Shomotsu wa hozon-sareta kokoro nari: "Books are preserved minds."

Shōnen oi yasuku, gaku nari gatashi: "Youth easily grows old, yet becomes learned with difficulty." In other words, while young we should make every effort to acquire learning and experience. English parallel: Art is long, life is short.

Yoku manabi, yoku asobi: "Study well, play well." A good rule for students: After studying diligently, relax by playing hard.

LOYALTY

IN THE FEUDAL PERIOD the highest virtue was that of loyalty. One was expected to be loyal to his friend, to his family, to his teacher, to his employer or master, and to his feudal lord. This last-named loyalty was by far the most important and one that might demand the sacrifice of all lesser loyalties and even of one's life. With the abolition of feudalism in the Meiji period, loyalty to a liege lord was transferred to loyalty to the Emperor, a loyalty expected of and held by all Japanese. This gave tremendous power and authority to the group that surrounded and influenced the Emperor. In modern times loyalty, though still practiced by many, is not held to be so important. However, its concomitant, obedience to authority, still remains a leading characteristic of the Japanese.

Chūkō wa karada no yōsei: "Loyalty and filial piety are the training of the body." That is, the duty of all Japanese is to build up strong bodies so that they can better serve the Emperor in peace and war and carry out their obligation to their parents by supporting them when they get too old to work.

Chūkō no michi wa ichi ni shite, ni narazu: "The ways of loyalty and filial duty are one and the same thing." That is, there should be no conflict between duty to one's lord (country) and duty to parents.

Chūshin wa ni kun ni tsukaezu: "A loyal subject does not serve two lords." This proverb, much quoted during the feudal period, is taken from the writings of Ssu-ma Ch'ien, a famous historian of ancient China. English parallel: No man can serve two masters. See Matthew 6:24.

Danji wa onore wo shiru mono no tame ni shishi; joshi wa onore wo aisuru mono no tame ni katachi-zukeru: "A man dies for the one who appreciates him; a woman does her make-up for the one who loves her." That is, men and women have their respective concerns.

Iza, Kamakura to iu toki ni wa: "When an emergency arises." (Lit., "When it is said: 'Come now to Kamakura!'") This well-known proverb is taken from the *"Nō"* drama, "Hachi-no-ki" ("The Potted Trees"), in which a poor but hospitable warrior, Genzaimon Sana, burns his valuable potted trees to provide warmth for his disguised guest, the retired Regent Hojo Tokiyori, and tells him that if the summons should suddenly be received: "Come to Kamakura (the seat of military government)," he, as a warrior, would do his duty and promptly answer the call. Thus, this expression, *"Iza, Kamakura to iu toki ni wa,"* now bears the meaning of "When an emergency arises," or, "At the critical moment."

Jō-i wa kuni wo iyasu: "A good physician heals the illness of his country." English parallel: A wise statesman saves the country.

Kimi hazukashime-rarureba shin shisu: "When the liege lord is put to shame, his vassals will die avenging it." In the feudal period in Japan, loyal retainers would avenge with their lives any insult to their lord. This is best illustrated by the true story of "The Forty-Seven *Rōnin.*" A *"rōnin"* was a masterless *"samurai"* (warrior) or lordless retainer. See elsewhere in this volume for a further explanation of "The Forty-Seven Rōnin." See pp. 59 and 187.

Kuni midarete chūshin arawaru: "When a country is in disorder loyal men appear." At a time of emergency men who love their country will come forth to save it. English parallel: The night brings out the stars.

Oya-ko wa isse, fūfu wa nise, shū-jū wa sanse: "Parents and children are for one generation, husband and wife for two generations, lord and liege are for three generations." This proverb points out that in feudal times the relation between lord and retainer was more important than all others.

Ryō-kin wa ki wo erande sumu: "Good birds make their nests upon choice trees." (Lit., "Wise birds live in carefully chosen trees.") This dictum from Chinese sources teaches that a wise man carefully chooses his master and does his best to serve him.

Taikan wa chū ni nitari: "A traitor is generally in the disguise of a patriot." (Lit., "A great villany resembles a loyalty.") That is, an extremely wicked person may pass off as a very good person.

MEMORY

JAPANESE EDUCATION up to 1946 laid great emphasis on memory, the best student being one who could memorize the textbook or the lectures of the professor. In cramming before examinations, the students accomplished marvelous feats of memory, but the knowledge thus acquired was often soon forgotten or not put to practical use. More recently, modern education in Japan encourages individual initiative and originality.

Ashi no ura ni meshitsubu: "Cooked rice grains sticking to the soles of the feet." This homely expression is used to describe any person or thing we have difficulty in shaking off. Just as we have difficulty in removing grains of cooked rice on which we have accidentally stepped, so at times we find it hard to rid ourselves of some situations or people.

Dokushō hyappen onozukara tsūzuru: "Read it aloud one hundred times and it becomes spontaneously understandable." Some writings cannot be fully comprehended at first glance or the hidden meaning appreciated. Repeated perusal of difficult passages will reveal much that is worthwhile.

Mitsu-go no tamashii hyaku made: "A three-year-old's soul remains unchanged for a hundred years." Habits formed in early childhood continue through life. Hence, the importance of early direction and training. English parallels: Habits in youth continue through life. The child is father of the man.

Mukashi totta kinezuka: "To take up again one's old and accustomed business." (Lit., "The pestle which one had handled years ago.") The *"kinezuka"* or "pestle referred to here is the one used for pounding boiled rice in the preparation of *"mochi"* ("rice cakes"), a favorite dish on New Year's Day or other festive occasions. Thus the expression "to take up the old pestle" means that a man is again going about his old business with his accustomed skill.

Narai sei to naru: "Habit becomes one's nature." That is, constant repetition and practice of something makes it second nature. English parallels: Habit is second nature. Practice makes perfect.

Suzume hyaku made odori wo wasurezu: "Sparrows, though they live to be a hundred, do not forget their dance." So people long retain the important lessons learned in childhood. Hence, the need for early training and indoctrination.

Ten shiru, chi shiru, hito shiru: "Heaven knows, the earth knows, man knows." This is a warning that nothing that has been done can be concealed.

Ten shiru, chi shiru, ware shiru: "Heaven knows, the earth knows, and I know." This proverb is another version of the preceding one. The old Chinese philosopher who originated the saying here teaches us that we should not participate in anything that we would be ashamed to have known.

OBLIGATIONS

EVEN A SHORT RESIDENCE in Japan will reveal that the people are exceedingly obligation conscious. The Japanese word *"on"* may be variously translated "obligation," "favor," or "debt of gratitude." Every Japanese is involved in an endless and complicated mass of obligations to those above him, to those on his own level, and to those below him. There are also obligations to one's self, to conduct oneself in the proper way expected by society. Repayment for each obligation is expected, else one loses face or standing and is thus put to shame. To repay these countless obligations, be they little or big, requires unlimited effort on the part of every Japanese as long as he or she lives. No conscientious Japanese ever feels free from all his obligations.

Ada wa on de hō-zeyo: "Repay your enemy with a favor." Requite an injury with kindness, and thus your opponent will be put under obligation to you. English parallel: Return good for evil.

Chōchin wo karita on wa wasurenaku tomo, tentō no on wo

wasureru: "Though one does not forget the kindness of a friend who lends a paper lantern, he forgets the kindness of Providence (lit., the Way of Heaven)." The word *"on,"* here translated "kindness," has the fuller meaning of "an obligation which one must pay."

Inu neko mo sannen kaeba on wo wasurezu: "Even a dog or cat if kept for three years does not forget its obligation." This saying is an admonition to ungrateful persons and is often used to insinuate that they as human beings should remember their obligations *("on").*

Inu wa mikka kaeba on wo wasurezu, neko wa sannen no on wo mikka ni wasureru: "Keep a dog for three days and he will not forget your kindness, but three years kindness shown to a cat is forgotten in three days." Here the word *"on"* translated "kindness" is "an obligation owed because of kindness received."

Ko wo motte shiru oya no on: "When you have your own children you will understand your obligation to your parents." The best way to know your debt of gratitude to your parents is to have a child of your own. English parallel: He that has no children knows not what is love.

On wo ukeru wa jiyū wo uru nari: "To receive a favor *("on")* is to sell one's liberty." This proverb is a good illustration of the strong sense of obligation which a Japanese has. When he has repaid the obligation, the Japanese feels that he has regained his freedom so far as that person is concerned.

Oya no on wa yama yori takaku, umi yori fukashi: "Duty to parents is higher than the mountains, deeper than the sea." Here the word *"on"* or "obligation" is best translated "duty." This proverb is learned and quoted by Japanese children from the time they are able to speak.

On wo shiranu mono: "An ungrateful wretch." (Lit., "One who knows no obligation.") To hurl such an accusation against a person is considered a terrible insult. *"Kono on shirazu me!"* ("You ungrateful rascal!")

OPTIMISM

IN SPITE OF THE PESSIMISM of Buddhist philosophy, the hierarchical state of society, and the tremendous weight of duties and obligations, most Japanese are quite cheerful and optimistic. This is especially true in the case of peasants and day laborers, who though they work long, hard hours get a lot of fun out of life. See the section WIT.

Aku ni tsuyokereba zen ni mo tsuyoshi: "Those strong in doing evil are also strong in doing good." When an evil person turns over a new leaf he will do many good deeds to expiate his past life. Every deep dyed scoundrel has the possibility of becoming a saint. A strong enemy will make a strong friend.

Ame futte ji katamaru: "After rain the ground gets firm." This may be interpreted both literally and figuratively. English parallels: After rain comes fair weather. Good comes out of evil.

Anjiru yori umu wa yasui: "To give birth to a child is easier than even an anticipated safe delivery." Things are not as difficult as they seem. English parallel: All things are difficult before they seem easy.

Aru ichi mon nai sen ryō: "Having one *mon* is better than not having a thousand *ryō*." One *"mon"* is one-tenth of a *"rin,"* one-hundredth of a *"sen,"* or one-thousandth of a *"yen."* In Japan the *"mon," "rin,"* and *"sen"* are no longer in use. In old Japan the *"ryō,"* also no longer in use, had the purchasing value of about twenty *"yen."* Hence, one *"ryō"* was twenty thousand times the value of a *"mon,"* and one thousand *"ryō"* was twenty million times the worth of one *"mon."* English parallel: A bird in hand is worth two in the bush.

Bombu sakari ni kami tatari nashi: "The ordinary man in his prime gets no curse from the gods." That is, a good healthy man generally gets along pretty well in life. English parallel: The gods have no power over a man in his prime.

Botamochi de hoppeta wo tatakareru yō: "Something exceedingly good." (Lit., "As good as having one's cheek patted with sweet rice-dumpling.") English parallel: As good as having one's bread buttered on both sides.

Botamochi wa tana ni ari: "Good things are sure to come." (Lit., "Sweet rice-dumplings are on the shelf.") That is, good fortune is in heaven and will fall to some one.

Byōshin nagaike: "An invalid lives long." Probably because he is cared for carefully. English parallel: A cracked vessel often lasts longest.

Ejiki ni doku nashi: "There is no poison in food one eats with relish." Nothing comes amiss to the man who eats with a good appetite. English parallel: Content works all ambrosia.

Fukōchū ni saiwai ari: "There is blessedness in adversity." English parallel: Every cloud has its silver lining.

Fuku wa uchi, oni wa soto: "Good luck inside, devils outside." This formula is used when beans are thrown around the house on *"setsubun"* (the days of the vernal equinox), to drive out evil influences and bring in good ones. The master of the house, early in the morning, goes from room to room, scattering beans to the four corners while shouting the phrase: "In fortune, out devils." Special services on this day are also held in many Buddhist temples, and crowds gather to catch the beans scattered to them by the priests.

Fumareta kusa ni mo hana go saku: "Even downtrodden weeds will bear flowers." This proverb indicates the possibility of a downtrodden person rising to prosperity and honor, so there is no need to be pessimistic about the future.

Furarete kaeru kahō mono: "Fortune favors the person (man or woman) who has been jilted." "The person who has been rejected and returns home is lucky." This saying generally applies to marriage proposals but it is sometimes used when work or business applications have been refused. English parallel: When Venus does not smile on you Fortune does.

Go ni makete shōgi ni katsu: "To lose at *go* and win at *shōgi.*" Both are Japanese games allied to chess and checkers. The above proverb means to lose in one thing but gain in another.

Hikaru hodo naranu: "The rumbling is not so bad as the flash." That is, what follows is not so much to be feared as what went before. Nevertheless, many Japanese are terrified by thunderstorms.

Ie hin ni shite kōshi izu, kuni midarete chūshin izu: "A family in poverty produces a dutiful son; a country in disorder brings forth a loyal subject." Just as a family in adverse circumstances will often produce a son who will reverse conditions and bring it to prosperity, so a land in confusion frequently brings out a subject who will put down disorder and advance the glory of the country. English parallel: Adversity brings out a man's virtue.

Ikimi ni ejiki: "Food never fails to the living." As long as a man lives he can get food somehow or other. English parallel: God never sends mouths but he sends meat.

Inu ni mo hōnen ari: "Even a dog will have a bountiful year." So a person no matter how distressing his circumstances will have better times. English parallel: Every dog has his day.

Itsu-mo yanagi no shita ni dojō wa nai: "Loaches are not always under a willow." This small fish is frequently found in flooded rice fields or muddy streams and is a staple article of food for poor peasants. The above proverb means that one may hope for the best but one must not expect good luck all the time. English parallel: The fox is not caught twice in the same snare.

Kaikatsu wa kenkō ni saku hana da: "Cheerfulness is the very flower of health." From long observation and experience, the Japanese have concluded that cheerfulness and good health are closely related—a fact that medical science has proved.

Kawara mo migakeba tama: "If you polish even a tile it becomes a gem." There is hope, therefore, for even the ignorant and uncultured person who can become wiser and refined through education and training.

Kega no kōmyō: "A lucky mistake." (Lit., "An accidental great exploit.") Sometimes we do things not expecting success but it comes anyway.

Ki ni mochi ga naru: "Rice cakes grow on trees." This is a figure of speech for an unexpected happy occurrence.

Kirin mo oite wa doba ni shikazu: "Even a giraffe when old is little better than a jade." English parallel: A live dog is better than a dead lion.

Ku onozukara tanoshimi to naru: "Pain spontaneously becomes pleasure." Suffering, courageously borne, will sometimes lead to joy. English parallel: Sweet are the uses of adversity which like a toad ugly and venemous wears yet a precious jewel in its head.

Ku wa tanoshimi (raku) no tane: "Pain is the seed of pleasure (ease)." Affliction is the source of joy. English parallel: No cross, no crown.

Kyū sureba tsūzu: "When in an extremity there is a way out."

That is, a person may find himself in an impasse, but there is a solution. English parallel: When things are at their worst they will mend.

Me to hana ga areba miyako e noboru: "If you have eyes and a nose you can go to the capital." That is, a man with ordinary faculties can do ordinary things.

Mi no naru ki wa hana kara shireru: "A fruit-bearing tree is known by its flowers." This saying teaches that a man who is destined to be a great person shows promise even in his youth.

Ningen banji Saiō no uma: "An evil sometimes turns out to be a blessing in disguise." (Lit., "People and all things are like Saiō's horse.") According to an ancient Chinese story, an old man, Saiō by name, had a horse that ran away but returned some days later bringing another horse with him. The old man's son, while riding this second steed, fell off breaking his leg. But this mishap really proved advantageous, for because of his lameness the young man was not called to military duty and thus could stay happily at home with his parent. The future often provides happy solutions of difficult problems.

Ō-bune ni notta yō: "A feeling of great security." (Lit., "As if aboard a large ship.")

Oni mo tsuno wo oru: "Even the devil sometimes breaks his horns." The implication is that even a bad man will sometimes change and become a good person.

Oni no kubi demo totte ki da: "To feel as happy as can be." (Lit., "He feels as if he has beheaded a devil.")

Tayori ga nai no wa buji na no da: "No communication indicates safety." This is the Japanese version of the English saying: No news is good news.

Tayori no nai no wa yoi tayori da: "No news is good news." This is a direct Japanese translation of the English proverb.

Ten kara yoko ni furu ame nashi: "There is no rain that falls horizontally from heaven." That is, man's character is originally good. No one is born originally evil.

Ten wa mizukara tasukuru mono wo tasuku: "Heaven helps those who help themselves." This is a direct Japanese translation of the English proverb: "God helps those who help themselves."

Tendō hito wo korosazu: "The way of heaven does not kill man." God is merciful to the just who are suffering under an injustice. English parallel: God tempers the wind to the shorn lamb.

Tendō zen ni fuku su: "The way of heaven brings good fortune to the good." That is, heaven blesses the right. English parallel: God defends the right.

Tentō Sama to kome no meshi wa tsuite mawaru: "The sun and rice food follow one everywhere." That is, wherever one goes one can get a livelihood. No matter where one goes if one works hard he will get enough to eat.

Ukiyo wa kokoro shidai: "The transient world is what we wish it to be." In other words man's willpower can control his environment considerably.

Waratte kurasu mo isshō, naite kurasu mo isshō: "It is one life whether we spend it in laughing or in weeping." Hence, the implication is that it is better to go joyfully through life without being too vexed by cares.

Waratte son shita mono nashi: "No one has ever suffered loss because of laughter." Good humor has never caused a person to lose out, for a smiling face always gives pleasure to other people.

Warō kado ni fuku kitaru: "Good luck comes in at a smiling gate." Fortune comes in by a merry gate. A happy countenance is more likely to be the precursor of a successful life than a scowling mien.

Wataru sekai (seken) ni oni wa nai: "In the world we pass through there is no devil." In other words, there is kindness and good will everywhere if we only keep looking for it.

Yamai wo shireba naoru ni chikashi: "If you know the disease recovery is near." Correct diagnosis is of first importance in medicine. This proverb is both literally and figuratively true. When a man is aware of his faults, he can take measures to overcome them. English parallel: A disease known is half cured.

PATIENCE

MORE THAN MOST OTHER RACES the Japanese are patient and persevering They have little respect for impatient and short-tempered people. In the peasant type especially, there is a mulish stubbornness that makes them impervious to new ways. This dislike for change causes them to hold to old customs and ways of procedure. However, while retaining the old, the average Japanese does not hesitate to try new ways, if such seem more practical and beneficial. This has enabled the nation to rise in a little more than a hundred years from a relatively unknown country to one of the world's great powers.

Arasō suzume hito wo osorezu: "Quarrelling sparrows do not fear man." Because they are so busy fighting they do not have time to consider other things.

Awanu futa mo areba au futa mo ari: "If there is a lid that does not fit there is a lid that does." The point is to keep on patiently looking until you find what you want. English parallel: Every shoe fits not every foot.

Bonnō no inu oedomo sarazu: "Though the dogs of worldly passions have accomplished their purpose, they do not depart." To get rid of earthly desires requires patient and unceasing effort. English parallel: It is hard to get rid of worldly passions.

Chiri mo tsumoreba yama to naru: "Even dust when accumulated makes a mountain." English parallel: Little and often makes a heap in time.

Dorobō mo jūnen: "Even a thief takes ten years (to become proficient)." To become skilled in any occupation takes many years of patient training.

En no shita no take-no-ko: "A bamboo sprout under the veranda." This is descriptive of a person who is mediocre and cannot rise to fame despite persistent efforts.

Go ni tsuyoi mono wa shōgi ni mo tsuyoi: "A good *go* player is also a good player of *shōgi*." One who is an expert at any kind of work is nearly always good at any other similar type of work. Both *go* and *shōgi* are Japanese games somewhat like but more intricate than chess and checkers and require a tremendous amount of patience and concentration.

Heta teppō mo kazu uchi ya ataru: Even a poor gunner if he shoots many times will hit it. English parallel: If at first you don't succeed, try, try again.

Ichi ka bachi ka: "Ace or loss." This is a gambling expression. *"Ichi"* here means "chance." It is the ace at dice. *"Bachi"* (lit., "punishment") signifies "loss." The whole of the above proverb is used adverbially with the meaning "at any price" or "at any cost." No matter whether he will get good luck or not the gambler will patiently keep on trying. English parallel: Sink or swim.

Ichi-nichi sen-shū: "One day a thousand autumns." To a person who looks forward with impatience to a thing or event (such as his own wedding), one day will seem as long as a thousand autumns. English parallel: One day is as long as a thousand winters.

Ikkyo ryōtoku: "A single stroke with double gain." (Lit., "One effort two gains.") English parallel: To kill two birds with one stone.

Inu mo arukeba bō ni ataru: "Even a dog if he walks about will hit on a club." That is, a person who exerts himself will obtain success somehow or other. The negative interpretation of the above proverb is misfortune will sooner or later hit a person. English parallel: Every dog has his day.

Ise e nanatabi, Kumano e mitabi: "Seven times to Ise, three times to Kumano." This proverb characterizes a great zeal for making pilgrimages, Ise being the Great Shrine dedicated to the sun goddess, Amaterasu Ō-mikami, the ancestress of the Imperial family; and Kumano, the sacred place where the deity Kumano Gongen (a manifestation of Buddha) is worshiped. The first is the most sacred place of *Shintō,* the indigenous religion of the Japanese; the second, one of the sacred places of Buddhism which was imported to Japan from India via China and Korea at about the sixth century A.D.

Ishi no ue ni mo sannen: "Sit patiently for three years even on a rock." Perseverance will win through any difficulty, for even a cold stone will get warm if you sit on it a long time. You must not expect your undertakings to succeed immediately. English parallel: Perseverance brings success.

Ittembari: Lit., "One point stretching." This frequently used phrase has the meaning of: "sticking to," "concentrating one's energies upon," or "relying entirely on" some plan or thing.

Jinji wo tsukushite temmei wo mate: "Do the best you can and await the decree of heaven." After we have done the best that is humanly possible, we must patiently leave the result to God. English parallel: Man proposes, God disposes.

Kahō wa nete mate: "For good luck sleep and wait." That is, everything comes to him in time who can sleep and patiently wait.

Kannin wa isshō no takara: "Patience is a life-long treasure." English parallel: Patience is a virtue.

Kannin-bukuro no o ga kireru: "The drawstring of the bag of patience is broken." On the whole the Japanese people are very patient, but both as individuals and as a nation this virtue at times is exhausted.

Kenteki atsumatte taikai to naru: "Drops from rivulets put together form the ocean." English parallel: Little drops of water . . . make the mighty ocean.

Kotte wa shian ni atawazu: "Too much concentration of thought does not produce a plan." When a person deliberates excessively he will not hit upon a good plan. Hence, he should patiently await the right time to do or say anything.

Kusare nawa mo yaku ni tatsu: "Even a rotten rope can be put to use." That is, an apparently useless thing if patiently kept for a while will be found useful.

Kyūjin-no-kō wo ikki ni kaku: "To stop short of the one thing needful." (Lit., "A meritorious deed nine fathoms high lacks one basketful.") In constructing a hill of a certain height many baskets full of earth must be carried until the desired altitude is reached. If one basketful is lacking the desired height is not attained. So the above proverb means the failure of any plan at the last moment.

Mateba kairo no hiyori: "If you wait patiently excellent weather will come for your sea journey." English parallel: All things come to him who waits.

Mateba kanro no hiyori ari: "If you wait there will come nectar-like fair weather."

Nana-korobi-ya-oki: "The vicissitudes of fortune." (Lit., "Seven falls and eight rises.") There are many ups and downs in life, but patient perseverance will win in the end. English parallel: He that falls today may be up again tomorrow.

Naranu kannin suru ga kannin: "True patience consists in bearing what is unbearable." When the Emperor of Japan broadcasted the order to surrender to the Allied Powers, he quoted this proverb.

Nintai wa nigashi saredo sono mi wa amashi: "Patience is bitter but its fruit is sweet."

Nani goto wo suru ni mo nintai ga nakute seikō senu: "In whatever you do unless you have patience you will not succeed."

Nintai wa iwa wo mo tōsu: "Patience will pierce even a rock."

Nori-kakatta fune da: "It's a ship you have embarked on, you know." That is, you are now undertaking something where there is no turning back. No matter what the risks may be, the project must be continued. A slightly different form of the above proverb with about the same meaning is:

Nori-dashita fune: "A ship that has already set sail." English parallel: We are in for it.

Oni ga deru ka, hotoke ga deru ka? "Will a devil come out or a Buddha?" Will the results be good or bad? Only patient waiting will give the answer.

Rekishi wa kurikaesu: "History repeats itself." This is a direct Japanese translation of the English proverb.

Ro sannen ni sao shichinen: "Three years for managing an oar, seven years for the pole." In propelling a junk the use of the oar or a pole are not as easy as they seem. Hence patience and perseverance are needed.

Rokai ga nōte fune de watarenu: "Without oars you cannot cross in a boat." To succeed in life you need money or other materials. The Japanese word *"rokai"* is a combination word of two kinds of oars— *"ro,"* a long single oar that is pivoted on a knob at the stern of the boat, and *"kai,"* a short single oar that works in a loop or on a cord. Hence the expression *"rokai ga nai"* ("without any oars of either kind") means "to be thrown on one's own resources."

Rokai no tatanu umi mo nashi: "There is no sea where oars are not used." Here again the word *"rokai"* refers to both types of oars. Hence, to cross the sea of life every resource must be used.

Rōma wa ichijitsu ni shite narazu: "Rome was not done in a day." This is the Japanese translation of the much-quoted English proverb.

Sandome ni wa me ga deru: "The third time it prospered." (Lit.,

"On the third time buds came forth.") English proverb: Third time does the trick.

Sei daseba, kōru ma mo nashi mizuguruma: "If a water wheel exerts itself it has no time to get frozen." That is, a busy person has not time for useless activities or play.

Senri no michi mo ippo yori su: "Even a journey of a thousand *ri* must start with one step." A *"ri,"* the unit of distance in Japan, is 2.44 miles. The above proverb means everything must be done patiently in regular sequence.

Shika wo ou ryōshi wa yama wo mizu: "The hunter pursuing the deer sees not the mountain." Since the hunter is intent on gains and nothing else, the beautiful scenery is lost on him. English parallel: He who is in hot pursuit is blind to reason.

Shimbō suru ki ni kane ga naru: "Money grows on the tree of patience."

Shippai wa seikō no motoi nari: "Failure is the source of success." One failure will not discourage an earnest man but rather put him on his metal to try again patiently and persistently until he attains success.

Shōbai wa ushi no shidare: "Business is like the froth from an ox's mouth." That is, it is slow and the result of patient, hard labor.

Shūkan wa dai ni no tensei: "Habit is the second nature." The English have a proverb exactly like this, but it appears that both proverbs originated separately.

Sode wo toraeru: "To buttonhole a person." (Lit., "To seize the sleeve.")

Sōgyō wa yasuku shusei wa katashi: "The commencement is easy but the maintenance is difficult." It is easy to start an undertaking or business but to maintain it successfully requires much perseverance and patience.

Somemonoya to kajiya wo sannen sureba shusse ga dekiru: "If you become a dyer or a blacksmith for three years you will advance in life." These occupations are so hard that if a person patiently and persistently works at them for three years he will succeed.

Sono hi gurashi: "A hand to mouth existence." (Lit., "To live from day to day.")

Son shite toku tore: "Make the best of a bad bargain." (Lit.,

"Take a profit from your loss.") English parallels: A hook is well lost to catch a salmon. You must lose a fly to catch a trout.

Sorosoro ittemo ta wa nigoru: "It is best to work patiently and slowly." (Lit., "Even though you tread slowly over your rice field it will become muddy.") That is, the rich soil will be mixed with the water from the irrigation ditch and the paddy field will be ready for the planting of the rice seedlings.

Taikai no mizu mo itteki kara: "The water of even the great ocean comes from one drop at a time." So a person must not be impatient to see results quickly. English parallel: The whole ocean is made up of single drops.

Takaki ni noboru wa hikuki yori su: "Be willing to start with a low position if you wish to attain a high one." (Lit., "To climb to a high spot begin from a low place.") English parallels: Learn to creep before you run. Step after step the ladder is ascended.

Tenteki ishi wo ugatsu: "Falling drops pierce the stone." English parallel: Constant dropping wears the stone.

Uma ni noru made ushi ni nore: "Ride an ox before you ride a horse." We must be willing to use an inferior substitute at hand rather than wait interminably for something better. Be patient and content to use first a slow means of travel, and then you will be ready for a faster one. English parallel: He who cannot get bacon must be content with cabbage.

Wazawai mo sannen tateba yaku(yō) ni tatsu: "Even a misfortune will prove useful if you bear it for three years." Bearing a misfortune for a long time will develop patience which will be an asset in the development of a strong character and future success. English parallel: Keep a thing seven years and you will find a use for it.

Wazawai tenjite fuku to nasu: "To turn one's misfortune to account." (Lit., "A misfortune being changed becomes good fortune.") English parallel: Bad luck often brings good luck.

Yo ni hi wo tsuide: "Unremitting labor." (Lit., "Night followed by day.") To engage in such labor demands unending patience.

Yomichi ni hi wa kurenu: "The day is not ended for him who makes a night journey." The meaning of this proverb is that if you go about your business in a patient, slow, and steady manner, you will not need to expose yourself to the dangers and discomforts of a journey by night.

PESSIMISM

IN A PREVIOUS SECTION of this book it was pointed out that there is much optimism in Japanese character. Their cheerful outlook on life, however, does not prevent them from frequently showing considerable pessimism. Such a negative outlook on life is partly the result of the Buddhist teaching, that, since all existence is ephemeral and fleeting, the greatest good is cessation of being. The prevalence of natural calamities—earthquakes, typhoons, fire, and floods—have also added to the uncertainty of life, and thus contributed to basic Japanese pessimism.

Akete kuyashuki tamate-bako: "A treasure box is opened with resulting regret." When opened it is like Pandora's box. The above proverb probably comes from the fairy tale of the Japanese Rip Van Winkle, Urashima, the fisherman who leaves his home and lives happily with Otohime, a charming sea princess. After a long absence he returns to his village bearing a treasure box presented to him by Otohime as a farewell gift. In spite of her parting injunction not to open the box, Urashima does so. A puff of white smoke comes from it, and the young fisherman instantly turns into a decrepit old man who is not recognized by any in his native village. Thus, this proverb is used when a person is disappointed with the actual result on which hopes have been built.

Aona ni shio: "Greens sprinkled with salt." Just as greens sprinkled with salt wilt, so a man when depressed or cowed looks wilted.

Ashita no kōgan, yūbe no hakkotsu: "A rosy face in the morning, white bones in the evening." This proverb, of Chinese origin, points to the frailty of life. A rosy youth will all too soon grow old and die, for life is fleeting. English parallels: Today red, tomorrow dead. Change and decay in all around we see.

Au wa wakari no hajimari: "To meet is the beginning of parting." This saying can be traced to the pessimistic philosophy of Buddhism which teaches that in this world we meet only to separate.

Fuchi kawa ni futa wa naranu: "You cannot put a lid on a deep pool or a river." Those who wish to drown themselves cannot be prevented. If a person is bent on destroying himself nothing can stop him.

Fukuro no naka no nezumi: "A cornered person." (Lit., "A rat in a bag.") That is, there is no way of escape. English parallel: The mouse that hath but one hole is quickly taken.

Fukusui bon ni kaerazu: "Spilt water never returns to its tray." This saying is popularly ascribed to a well-known Chinese historical character, Tai Kung-wang, who told his divorced wife that he would reinstate her provided she put spilled water back into the tray. The proverb teaches that a wife who got her divorce at her own request cannot be received back by her husband. English parallels: Done cannot be undone. Things past may be repented but not recalled.

Futatsu ii koto wa nai: "Good fortunes seldom come together." (Lit., "There are no two good things.") English parallel: You cannot have your cake and eat it too.

Fūzen no tomoshibi: "Very hazardous and uncertain." (Lit., "A candlelight before the wind.") This saying is used to describe the precarious state of someone or something on the verge of ruin. The full proverb is *"Jinsei wa fūzen no tomoshibi,"* q.v.

Hi kurete michi tōshi: "The day comes to an end, but the destination is distant." (Lit., "The sun has set, but the road is far to go.") This is a quotation from a Chinese poem that suggests the thought that a man has grown old, yet he has not attained half the success that he had hoped to get in life. English parallel: The days are short and the way is long.

Hi wo sakete mizu ni ochiru: "Avoiding the fire, he falls into the water." We escape one trouble only to fall into another. English parallel: Out of the frying pan into the fire.

Hito no inochi wa tsuyu yori moroi: "The frailty of life." (Lit., "Life is more fragile than the morning dew.") English parallel: Life is but a bubble.

Hito no uwasa mo shichijūgo nichi: "Even gossip about a person lasts but seventy-five days." Rumor of a man's words and deeds do not last long. It is soon forgotten. English parallel: A wonder lasts but nine days.

Hyaku nen kasei wo matsu: "To wait a hundred years for the river to clear." The river referred to here is the Hwang-ho or Yellow River of China, whose waters are always muddy. This proverb suggests the least possibility of anything being completely changed for the better.

Honeori-zon no kutabire mōke: "Your pains for your trouble." (Lit., "Hard work lost, exhaustion earned.") This very common Japanese expression is used when a person's efforts have resulted in a waste of labor.

Ichi nan satte mata ichi nan: "One trouble is followed by another." (Lit., "One calamity taken away, again another calamity.") English parallel: To get out of one mire to run into another.

Ikimi wa shinimi: "To live is to die." (Lit., "A living body is a dying body.") This saying teaches that man must die sooner or later. English parallel: Our birth is nothing but our death begun.

Ima-mairi hatsuka: "Hard work at a new job." (Lit., "Just arrived, twenty days.") A new servant works very hard when he first comes, but after twenty or thirty days his diligence falters and he begins to be idle. English parallel: A new broom sweeps clean.

Inu honeotte taka no ejiki: "One person gets rewarded for another's hard work." (Lit., "The dog works hard and the hawk gets the food.") To the jaundiced eye of a pessimist, the above seems to to be true too often. English parallel: Asses carry the oats and horses eat them.

Isha mo saji wo nageru: "A hopeless case." (Lit., "Even the physician throws away his spoon.") The "spoon" is the one used in giving medicine to the patient. This common expression is used to indicate that the doctors in despair have given up the patient. The saying is also used figuratively to point out that those who are trying to solve a difficult problem have given up.

Ishi wo idaite fuchi ni iru: "To bring certain death." (Lit., "To leap into a deep pool embracing a stone.")

Isogiwa de fune wo yaburu: "To break down or fail at the psychological moment." (Lit., "The ship breaks up on the edge of the beach.") English parallel: There's many a slip 'twixt cup and lip.

Jinsei wa asa tsuyu no gotoshi: "Man's life is like the morning dew." It soon evaporates. English parallel: Our life is but a span.

Jinsei wa fuyū no gotoshi: "Man's life is like the May fly." Like the ephemera which lasts but a day, man's life is short and uncertain. English parallel: Life is but a bubble.

Jinsei wa fūzen no tomoshibi: "Man's life is like a light before the wind." In ancient Japan, most night lights were candles; hence the above proverb could be translated: "Human existence is like a candle flickering in the wind." It may be extinguished any time.

Jinsei wa shichijū koro mare nari: "Man's life rarely attains seventy years." In days of yore the average life span was much shorter than it is now, and seventy was a great age.

Jinsei wa sōma-tō no gotoshi: "Man's life is like a kaleidoscope." That is, it has many aspects both bright and dark. English parallel: Life has its ups and downs.

Jinsei wa wazuka gojū nen: "Man's life is barely fifty years." Life expectancy in Japan, prior to World War II, was much shorter than in the United States.

Kado-matsu wa meido no tabi no ichiri-zuka: (Lit., "Corner pine trees are but milestones on our journey to Hades.") At New Year's time every Japanese home places pine branches or trees on each side of the front door or gate. The pine signifies constancy and long life, and expresses the hope that the occupants of the house will have long and useful lives. New Year's Day is also celebrated as the birthday of each individual Japanese and is a time of great rejoicing and feasting. Therefore, to state that the pine-tree decorations, at this time of great happiness, are "but milestones to Hades" is a startling example of the pessimistic teaching of Buddhism. The above proverb is said to have originated some five hundred years ago from the sayings of Ikkyū-oshō, a celebrated priest of the Rinzai sect.

Kani ga tsume wo mogareta yō: "Like a crab that has had its claws torn off." This is a metaphorical allusion to a person who has lost his hope, or his only resource.

Kinka ichi-jitsu no ei: "The splendor of the rose of Sharon is but a day." This saying expresses the brevity of life. English parallel: Today a king, tomorrow nothing.

Kinō no hana wa kyō no yume: "Yesterday's lovely flower is but a dream today." A beautiful maiden or a promising youth of yesterday is but a mound of ashes today! This is another example of extreme pessimism inculcated by Buddhism. English parallel: Who today was a haughty knight, is tomorrow a penniless wight.

Kinō no fuchi wa kyō no se: "The world is full of changes." (Lit., "What was a deep pool yesterday is but a shallows today.") One can never tell what each day may bring forth. English parallel: Yesterday's red, today's dead.

Kinō no tsuzure, kyō no nishiki: "Yesterday in rags, today in gold brocade." English parallel: A nobody today, a prince tomorrow.

Kyōji mon wo idezu, akuji sen-ri wo hashiru: "News of evil travels far faster than news of good." (Lit. "Good deeds won't even go out the gate, but evil deeds will speed a thousand *ri.*") Since the *ri,* the Japanese unit of distance, is 2.44 miles, one thousand *ri* is not merely 2,440 miles, but signifies a tremendous or immeasurable distance.

Kōkai saki ni tatazu: "Repentance always comes too late." (Lit., "Repentance never comes beforehand.") English parallels: It is no use crying over spilt milk. No weeping for shed milk.

Koketsu wo nogarete ryūkutsu ni iru: "Fleeing out of a tiger's den he enters a dragon's hole." That is, from bad to worse. English parallel: From the frying pan into the fire.

Ku wa raku no tane: "Cares are the seeds of ease." People who work and live under hardships may in later years attain a life of ease. English parallel: No pains no gains.

Ku wa iro kawaru, matsu no kaze: "Trouble has changed into winds blowing through the pine trees." One may not evade anxiety (trouble) by withdrawing into a forest, for even there he will be disturbed by the winds blowing through the pine trees.

Kuni ni nusubito, ie ni nezumi: "No country or house is perfect." (Lit., "Robbers in every country, rats in every house.")

Kurō wa hito ni tsuku mono: "Anxieties are things that cling to people." Once attached they are hard to shake off.

Kurō wa mi no doku: "Anxieties are poison to a person." This proverb originated hundreds of years ago, long before scientists discovered that excessive worry produced large amounts of hydrochloric acid in the stomach which ate into its lining, thus resulting in gastric ulcers. English parallel: Care will kill a cat.

Miira-tori ga miira ni naru: "The biter is bit." (Lit., "The hunter of mummies becomes himself a mummy.") The taker is taken. Hence, the word *"miira-tori"* ("mummy-taker") has the meaning of "a messenger who never comes back." English parallel: Many go for wool and come back shorn.

Mikka minu ma no sakura: "Cherry blossoms though in full bloom will soon fade." (Lit., "Not being viewed for three days the cherry blossoms are gone.") Life is indeed as fleeting and fragile as the cherry bloossoms. Here again, we see the strong influence of Buddhist pessimism.

Mitsureba kakeru, yo no narai: "All persons have their ups and downs." (Lit., "When the moon is full it begins to wane, such is the way of the world.") English parallel: Every tide has its ebb.

Mono shite mono saru: "The uncertainty of everything." (Lit., "Losing what you have just acquired.")

Nagai tsuki-hi ni mijikai inochi: "For long months and days there is a short life." Sometimes the months and days seem to drag on, but life itself is actually short.

Nagai ukiyo ni mijikai inochi: "Time is long but life is short." (Lit., "In this long transitory world life is short.")

Omō koto naranu ga ukiyo: "What you deeply desire cannot be attained; such is this fleeting world." Here again in this proverb we see the Buddhist pessimistic view of life. Art is long and life is short.

Raku areba ku ari: "After pleasure comes pain." (Lit., "Where there is pleasure there is pain.") English parallel: No pains, no gains.

Raku wa ku no tane, ku wa raku no tane: "Pleasure is the seed of pain, pain is the seed of pleasure." English parallel: Rest comes from unrest, and unrest from rest.

Rōshō fujō wa yo no narai: "For old and young, uncertainty, such is the way of the world." That is, death comes to the aged and young alike.

Sangai wa kataku no gotoshi: "The three worlds are like a house on fire." In Buddhist teaching the three world are "the world of desire," "the world of form," and "the world of formlessness," which roughly correspond to the worlds of the past, present, and the future. Hence, the above proverb may be interpreted to mean "the world is a living Hell."

Sayōnara: "Good-bye"; "farewell." (Lit., "If it must be so.") This is one of the most pessimistic of leave-taking expressions in the world. Compare this with the English "Good-by" (a contraction of "God be with ye") and "Farewell" (a contraction of "Fare ye well"); the French "Adieu" ("I commend you to God"); the Spanish "Adios" ("I commend you to God"); and the German "Auf wiedersehen" ("Until I see you again") and "Lebewohl" ("Live you well").

Seija hitsumetsu esha-jōri: "Living persons are doomed to decay, those who meet are bound to part." Life is short and partings come all too soon.

Shikata ga nai: "There is no help for it." It is inevitable. As already pointed out in the section FATALISM, this most frequently heard expression, *"shikata ga nai,"* well illustrates the pessimistic philosophy of despair or fatalism held by most Japanese.

Shinda ato no matsuru: "Something that is done too late." (Lit., "After death, the festival.") The festival—a time of joy and feasting —which you expected to attend, comes after your death, so that you did not get to enjoy it.

Shinda ko no toshi wo kazoeru: "To count the age of a dead child." This expression is used to describe some foolish or useless undertaking. English parallel: To cry over spilt milk.

Shinin ni kuchi nashi: "A dead person has no mouth." English parallel: Dead men tell no tales.

Shinu ko wa mime yoshi: "The dead child had good features." One should not waste time in vain regrets or crying over opportunities that are gone.

Shinu mono bimbō: "The lot of the dead person is wretched." (Lit., "The dead person is poor.") Since the dead have no wealth, fame, or friends, they are much to be pitied. The above expression is often used in reference to the death of a person whose living spouse is enjoying a rising fortune.

Shōja hitsumetsu esha-jōri: This is the same saying but different pronunciation of *"Seija hitsumetsu esha jōri"*: "Living beings are doomed to decay, and those who meet are destined to part." This statement from a Buddhist sutra well illustrates the pessimistic nature of that religion.

Sōjuku sōrō: "Early maturity, early senility." Precocity is followed by rapid aging. English parallel: Soon wise, soon foolish.

Sue no tsuyu moto no shizuku: "The final dewdrop (on the branch) and the drip on the trunk (will both evaporate in the end.") The world is but a fleeting show. Here again, we have the Buddhist idea that the world or life is ephemeral and will soon dissolve.

Takai tokoro e tsuchi-mochi: "Bring earth to a high place (to make it higher)." That is, poor people are laboring to increase the wealth of rich people, thus making the rich richer and the poor poorer.

Tō de shindō, hatachi de saishi, sanjū sugireba tada no hito: "A prodigy at ten, a genius at twenty, but after thirty years an ordinary person." Sometimes early promising characteristics are not fulfilled in later life. English parallel: A man at five may be a fool at fifteen.

Tsuki ni murakumo, hana ni arashi: "A cluster of clouds to the moon, a storm to flowers." Both destroy beauty and satisfaction. Hence, there is no perfect condition or enjoyment in this world. English parallel: No rose without a thorn.

Tsuki ni murakumo, hana ni kaze: "To the moon, gathering clouds; to flowers, the wind." A slightly different version of the preceding proverb. Beauty and prosperity do not last long. English parallel: Change of fortune is the lot of life.

Ukiyo no tabi: "The journey of this transitory life." This is generally regarded by the Japanese as unpleasant because of its uncertainties.

Yuku mizu ni kazu kaku yori mo hakanashi: "More transient than to write on running water." Such is life, according to Buddhist beliefs.

Yume no ukihashi: "The floating bridge of dreams." This phrase also illustrates the Buddhist view of the uncertainty of life.

PRACTICALITY

A VERY PRACTICAL PEOPLE, the Japanese do not hesitate to use and adapt to their own needs the inventions and ways of other races and civilizations. Since almost the dawn of their history the Japanese have borrowed and in their own way put to good use anything that could be of value to them. As a race they are somewhat lacking in inventiveness and originality, but whatever they adopt they frequently modify extensively to serve their own needs. Though faithful copiers, they do not hesitate to make changes where an improvement is called for, thus often resulting in a superior product.

Abura tsukite hi kiyu: "When the oil is exhausted the flame goes out." Therefore, it is well to be prepared. English parallel: They hurt themselves who wrong others.

Akuji senri wo hashiru: "An evil deed runs a thousand *ri.*" The *ri,* the unit of distance in Japan, is 2.44 miles. The rumor of a bad action spreads rapidly and far. The above frequently-quoted proverb is of Chinese origin. English parallel: Bad news has wings.

Ami nakushite fuchi ni nozomu na: "Without a net don't face the pool." English parallel: It is hard to catch birds with an empty hand.

Ari no haideru suki mo nai: "There is not even a hole that an ant could go through." This saying describes a place that is closely guarded, or packed with people.

Ami no uo: "A fish in a net." This expression is used to describe a person who has been hunted and will soon be captured.

Aru wa naki ni masaru: "To have is better than nothing." English parallel: Anything is better than nothing.

Arisō de nai no wa kane, nasasō de aru mo kane: "The thing one seems to have but really has not, is money; and the thing that one seems to lack but really has is money, too." Appearances are deceptive, so one should be careful in making judgments.

Ashimoto ni tsukekomu: "To take a person at a disadvantage." (Lit., "To take advantage of a person's feet.") This is a term of swordsmanship. It means to lunge at your opponent when his feet are unsteady, in order to defeat him.

Ashimoto no akarui uchi ni: "A thing should be done before it is too late." (Lit., "While there is yet light at the feet.") Since the night is full of danger it is much safer to undertake a thing in the daytime; that is to say, while there is sufficient time in which to do it. Hence, this proverb is frequently used to warn or exhort people.

Asu wa asu no kaze ga fuku: "Tomorrow blows tomorrow's wind." English parallel: Sufficient unto the day is the evil thereof.

Asu no hyaku yori kyō no gojū: "Better than a hundred tomorrow, (give me) fifty today." English parallel: Better an egg today than a hen tomorrow.

Asu wa asu, kyō wa kyō: "Tomorrow is tomorrow, today is today."

Atama wo soran yori wa kokoro wo sore: "Rather than shave your head, better shave your mind (heart)." To "shave your mind" means to "polish your mind." That is, it is more important to cultivate the doctrines of Buddhism than to be careful in shaving your head. English parallel: It is not the cowl that makes the friar.

Ate koto to Etchū-fundoshi wa mukō kara hazureru: "Our expectations and the stringed loincloth come off from the other side." The meaning is that the results are sometimes surprising. English parallel: He that lives on hope has but a slender diet.

Bimbō hima nashi: "The poor have no leisure." This is because poor men must always be working to make ends meet.

Bimbō kowai mono nashi: "The poor have nothing to fear." Robbers will not attack them since the former have nothing to gain. English parallel: A penniless traveler will sing in the presence of a robber.

Bimbō taka-makura: "The poor sleep soundly." (Lit., "The poor high pillow.") Having no possessions, the poor are not worried lest they be stolen. *"Taka-makura"* (lit., "high pillow") is the idiom for "to sleep peacefully." In old Japan, sleepers usually placed under their necks hard pillows, often with a wooden base three to five inches high, to keep intact their elaborate coiffure.

Bonnin (bonjin) nakuba ijin nakaran: "Without ordinary men, there would be no great men."

Chabara mo ittoki: "Even a cup of tea will stay hunger for a time." English parallel: When hungry any food is fit for a while.

Chōshū yoku mai, tasen yoku kau: "Long sleeves dance well, much money buys well." *Chōshū* ("long sleeves") refers to the formal kimono of young women whose sleeves almost touch the floor. Though very beautiful, the dress is impractical except for Japanese dancing. The above proverb means "to have what is necessary for success," that is, luxurious clothing and plenty of money.

Daidō-shōi: "Almost identical." (Lit., "Great similarities and small differences.") English parallel: Six of one and half a dozen of the other.

Daiji no mae no shōji: "Before a great matter a small thing (can be omitted)." You must overlook comparatively small matters when endeavoring to do great things. For example, even wife and children may be left to serve one's country.

Dembun wa jikken ni shikazu: "Better than hearsay is actual observation." English parallel: Sight goes before hearsay.

Doku wo motte doku wo seisu: "Control poison with poison." This proverb is from Chinese sources. English parallel: Poison drives out poison.

Eyasuku mono wa ushinai yasushi: "Things easily gotten are easily lost." English parallel: Lightly come, lightly go.

Fuchi ni nozomite uo wo urayamu wa shirizoite ami wo musubi ni shikazu: "It is better to go home and make your net, than to gaze longingly at the fish in the deep pool." That is, prepare for rather than dream of success.

Fukuro no naka no mono wo sagasu yō: "Like searching for a thing in a bag." This expression is used to describe the ease of searching out a thing or person in a limited area.

Gan wa happyaku, ya wa sammon: "A wild goose is worth eight hundred (mon), but an arrow is only three mon." It is wise to venture a small loss for a great gain. English parallel: You may lose a fly to catch a trout.

Gei wa mi wo tasukeru hodo no fushiawase: "Unfortunate is she who is forced to live by accomplishments which give pleasure." This proverb may have reference to *geisha* and others in the entertainment world.

Gei wa mi no ada: "An accomplishment is one's enemy." This is especially true when a person is so unfortunate as to be compelled to live by that accomplishment.

Gei wa mi wo tasukeru: "Accomplishments will save a person." An accomplishment will often be very useful to the one who possesses it. For example, a person who has failed to earn a living in a trade or business may still support himself through some hobby or accomplishment.

Gei wa mi ni tsuku: "An accomplishment sticks to a person." An art or hobby is generally part of the nature of a person and will remain with him long after he has lost his material possessions. English parallel: Art holds fast when all else is lost.

Gei wa michi ni yorite kashikoshi: "A person becomes clever in any accomplishment which he (or she) pursues." English parallel: Every man for his own trade.

Goetsu dōshū: "Bitter enemies in the same boat." (Lit., "Men of Wu and Yueh in the same boat.") These two people of old China were always at war; but when individuals of these peoples are in the same boat, they must share the same fate in case of any danger or calamity. English parallel: Those who are in the same boat should row together.

Gusha mo ittoku: "Even a dunce has one merit." That is, he may help in one thing. English parallel: A fool may give a wise man counsel.

Hajime areba owari ari: "If there's a beginning there's an end." All things must have their ends. This is true, whether meeting with success or adversity.

Hambun demo nai yori mashi: "Even a half is better than nothing." This is a Japanese translation of the English proverb "Half a loaf is better than none."

Hana yori dango: "Dumplings are better than flowers." Substance rather than show. English parallel: Bread is better than song of birds.

Hara mo mi no uchi: "The abdomen also is part of the body." If you wish to be in good health you should take care of the digestive organs.

Hashi naki kawa wa watararezu: "A river that has no bridge cannot be crossed." For any purpose a means is necessary.

Haya-meshi no hito wa shigoto ga hayai: "The quick eater does quick work." The Japanese admire fast eaters. The above proverb is the Japanese translation of the English saying, "Quick at meal, quick at work."

Higashi ni chikakereba nishi ni tōshi: "If you are near the east you are farther from the west." Two advantages cannot be enjoyed at the same time. For example, a rich man is often unlettered, and a scholar frequently lives in poverty.

Hikaru mono kanarazushimo ōgon narazu: "What shines is not necessarily gold." This proverb is taken from the English "All that glitters is not gold."

Himojii toki mazui mono nashi: "When you're hungry nothing is tasteless." English parallel: Hunger is the best sauce.

Hin no nusumi, koi no uta: "Poverty forces people to steal; sexual passion causes persons to compose songs." (Lit., "The stealing of poverty, the poetry of sexual love.")

Hin sureba, don suru: "Poverty makes a man dull witted." English parallel: An empty purse fills the face with wrinkles.

Hito no furi mite waga furi naose: "Look at the manners of others and mend your manners." English parallels: By others' faults wise men correct their own. One man's fault is another's lesson.

Hito wo tsukō wa ku wo tsukō: "To employ people is to employ trouble." It is troublesome to have people in your service or under your control. English parallel: Masters are mostly the greatest servants in the house.

Hito wo tsukō wa tsukawareru: "To employ a person is to be employed."

Hitsuyō wa hatsumei no haha: "Necessity is the mother of invention." This is a direct translation into Japanese of the well-known English proverb.

Hitsuyō wa hō wo shirazu: "Necessity knows no law." This, too, is a Japanese translation of the English proverb.

Hyakubun ikken ni shikazu: "One seeing is better than one hundred hearings." English parallel: Seeing is believing.

I wo motte i wo seizuru: "Control barbarians with barbarians." This Chinese proverb was the frequent strategy employed by them in the feudal period, and has been and still is used by people of all races. English parallels: Fight fire with fire. Play both ends towards the middle.

Ichi koe; ni fushi: "First, the voice; second, the tone." These are the two requisites for a good singer.

Ichinen no kei wa gantan ni ari, ichinichi no kei wa sochō ni ari: "Make a year's plan on New Year's Day, a day's plan in the early morning." English parallel: Monday is the key of the week.

Ichi yōjō; ni kusuri: "First, care of health; second, medicine." This is the Japanese recipe for living healthily and long.

Ichi ni kambyō, ni ni kusuri: "Nursing first, medicine second." Note that this proverb states that good nursing is the first and most important requisite for a patient.

Isha yori yōjō: "Better than a physician is the care of health."

Ichimotsu no taka mo hanatazareba torazu: "Even a superb hawk will not catch game unless it is loosed." English parallel: A hooded falcon cannot strike the quarry.

Inochi atte no mono-dane: "Life is the source of all things." English parallel: Where there is life there is hope.

Isseki ni chō: "One stone, two birds." This is a direct translation into Japanese of the English proverb "To kill two birds with one stone."

Juzu bakari de oshō wa dekinu: "One cannot become a priest just by having a rosary."

Kan wo ōte koto sadamaru: "After a man dies the world's opinion of him is settled." (Lit., "After he is laid in his coffin the matter is settled.")

Kani wa kōra ni nisete ana wo horu: "The crab digs a hole according to its shell." English parallel: Cut your coat according to your cloth.

Kōsan nakereba kōshin nashi: "Without fixed (real) property there is no real purpose." Ownership of real estate has a steadying effect on a person.

Kusuri yori yōjō: "Better than medicine is care of the health." English parallel: Prevention is better than cure.

Magareru eda ni magareru kage ari: "A crooked branch has a crooked shadow." An evil man's deeds are naturally evil. English parallel: Ill sowers make ill harvest.

Mago ni mo ishō: "Even a packhorse driver looks well in fine clothes." English parallel: Clothes make the man.

Makanu tane wa haenu: "Unsown seeds will not sprout." That is, there must be preparation for success. English parallel: Of nothing comes nothing.

Mayowanu mono ni satori nashi: "To one who does not wander there is no enlightenment." According to Buddhist teaching, religious enlightenment or salvation *(satori)* can only come after considerable wandering in search of life's truth.

Mie haru yori hō-bare: "Better than to display a good appearance is to have stuffed cheeks." That is, food is more important than a pose. This is the practical viewpoint of the commoner, but that of the warrior is exactly the reverse. See the proverb *"Bushi wa kuwanedo taka yōji."* ("Though a warrior may not eat, he holds his toothpick high.")

Mochi wa mochiya: "For rice cake go to the rice-cake dealer." English parallel: Every man to his trade.

Mukashi no koto wa mizu ni nagase: "Let the things of long ago drift away on the water." That is, do not hold tenaciously to ways and ideas that are no further use. English parallel: Let bygones be bygones.

Mukashi wa mukashi, ima wa ima da: "Old times are old times, the present is the present." English parallel: Let the dead past bury its dead.

Mukashi no senri mo ima ichiri: "Though a thousand *ri* in olden times, it is only one *ri* now." This is certainly true because the speed of transportation and communication has increased tremendously all over the world and particularly in Japan in the past one hundred years.

Mukashi no tsurugi wa ima no nagatana: "The sword of ancient times is now for kitchen use." This proverb looks back with nostalgia to feudal days when the sword was the pride and symbol of the warrior. In these modern days the proverb might be interpreted as the decline of warfare and the advance of peace.

Nai sode wa furenu: "You cannot give help to a person when you yourself have nothing." (Lit., "You cannot swing long sleeves you do not have.")

Nigeru ga kachi: "To flee is to be victorious." English parallel: Discretion is the better part of valor.

Nomi to iwaba tsuchi: "If I ask for a chisel, bring also a mallet." English parallel: Bread and butter must go together.

Nozomu nara mazu sonae yo: "If you desire something, first prepare for it."

Nusubito no ban ni wa nusubito ga yoshi: "A thief makes a good watchman for thieves." English parallel: Set a thief to catch a thief.

Ron yori shōko: "Proof rather than argument." English parallel: The proof of the pudding is in the eating.

Ryōshin wo shiwan ni unyō suru koto: "To do things that your conscience disapproves." (Lit., "It is a matter of employing your conscience in a miserly way.")

Sanjū-rokkei niguru ni shikazu: "Discretion is the better part of valor." (Lit., "Of the thirty-six plans, flight is the best.") This saying is of Chinese origin. English parallel: He who fights and runs away will live to fight another day.

Saru ni mo ishō: "Do not judge by appearances." (Lit., "Even a monkey may appear to advantage when dressed up.") English parallel: Fine feathers make fine birds.

Se ni hara wa kaerarenu: "There is no time to plan, so we must make the best of it." (Lit., "The back cannot be substituted for the belly.") Food is the first consideration for existence. The above proverb is often quoted to justify a deed that may be termed selfish, on the excuse that life itself has priority over justice and fair play. English parallel: Necessity knows no law.

Senkin no ko wa tōzoku no shi sezu: "He who has a thousand gold pieces will not be murdered by a robber." Because he escapes death by offering money which he values less than life.

Sewashii toki wa yamai nashi: "When you are busy you have no illness." When a man is working vigorously he will not get sick.

Shi wo tsukuru yori ta wo tsukure: "Cultivate rice fields rather than make poetry." Good advice to second-rate poets. Even such poetic people as the Japanese recognize that food is of more practical use than verse.

Shigoto wa dōgu ni ari: "Work depends on tools." For the opposite idea see *"Heta no dōgu shirabe."* ("An unskillful person inspects his tools.") and *"Kōbō wa fude wo erabazu."* ("Kōbō is not choosy about his writing brush.")

Shineba subete chō-keshi: "On death all accounts are cancelled." English parallel: Death quits all scores.

Shō wo in to seba mazu uma wo iyo: "If you would shoot a general shoot first his horse." Begin with lesser things to obtain the greater. English parallel: He who would the daughter win, must with the mother first begin.

Shō no mushi koroshite dai no mushi ikasu: "Kill a small insect to let live a big one." We should save many at the expense of a few.

Shōbai shōbai: "Every man according to his trade." (Lit., "Business is business.") English parallel: Every man does his own business best.

Shōbai wa kadokado: "He is experienced in his own trade." (Lit., "Business is gate by gate.") A dealer knows his own trade best.

Shōchi wa bodai no samatage: "A little knowledge is a hindrance to spiritual awakening." English parallel: A little knowledge is a dangerous thing.

Shōgi wo sasu yori boro wo sase: "Better to sew rags than to play Japanese chess." *Shōgi* is Japanese chess whose enthusiasts often play all day long, forgetting to eat, sleep, or attend to their business.

Shumme mo oite wa doba ni shikazu: "Better than an aged, gallant horse is a hack." English parallel: A live dog is better than a dead lion.

Sumeba miyako: "If you live there, it is the capital." Where you live will become the capital in your eyes and the best of all possible places. English parallel: An Englishman's home is his castle.

Taigei wa mugei: "Many accomplishments are no accomplishments." If you have too many hobbies you will be master of none. English parallel: Jack of all trades and master of none.

Takai mono wa yasui mono: "Expensive articles are cheap articles." That is, it is often cheaper in the long run to buy articles that are expensive rather than the cheaper ones.

Tattoi tera wa mon kara: "An exalted temple is known by its gateway." Beautiful and elaborate gates are often donated to famous temples by satisfied worshipers.

Tetsu wa atsui toki ni ute: "While the iron is hot strike it." A direct Japanese translation of the English proverb: Strike while the iron is hot.

Tsubo no naka de wa hi wo moenu: "Fire does not burn in a jar." That is, a man cannot adequately use his powers in a limited space.

Tsukō mono wa tsukawareru: "The employer is employed." The master of a shop or factory often has trouble getting his employees to do just what he wants. In these modern days of strikes and labor demands, the workers often have more voice in factory management and greater power than the owner of the plant. English parallel: Masters are mostly the greatest servants in the house.

Uma ni wa notte miyo, hito ni wa sotte miyo: "Test a horse by riding him and a person by accompanying him." By attaching yourself to a person you can get to know his character and habits. English parallel: The proof of the pudding is in the eating.

Umi no koto wa gyofu ni toe: "Ask a person about the things he knows best." (Lit., "About sea matters, ask a fisherman.") English parallel: Every man has his forte.

Uri wo futatsu ni watta yō: "Two things that closely resemble each other." (Lit., "Like two parts of a halved melon.") English parallel: Like two peas in a pod.

Urimono ni hana wo kazare: "Make attractive the thing you wish to sell." (Lit., "Decorate with flowers an article for sale.")

Uo-gokoro areba mizu-gokoro ari: "He will do by you as you do by him." (Lit., "If the fish has a heart, the water has a heart.") That is, as the fish wishes so does the water yield. English parallel: Scratch my back and I'll scratch yours.

Uranaishi onoga minoue shirazu: "The fortuneteller does not know his own future." A person who specializes in helping others often cannot help himself.

Ware hito ni tsurakereba hito mo mata ware ni tsurashi: "If I am hard on other people, other people will be hard on me." English parallel: What is sauce for the goose is sauce for the gander.

Yamai wa kuchi kara: "Illness starts with the mouth." Many people get sick from overeating or eating indigestible foods or comestibles that have not been fully cleaned and prepared.

Yo wa nana sagari nana agari: "There are many failures and successes in life." (Lit., "Life has seven downs and seven ups.") Here the word *"nana"* (seven) has the meaning of "many." English parallel: Life has many ups and downs.

Yoi mono ni yasui mono nashi: "Good things are never cheap." (Lit., "Among good things there are no cheap ones.")

Yu ni hairu toki kata (chichi) kara saki ni nurasu to kaze wo hikanu: "When you enter a hot bath, wet your shoulders (breast) first and you'll not take cold." This is good, practical advice. In taking a Japanese bath, the body is first thoroughly washed and the soap suds rinsed off before stepping into the pool or tub.

Yumi wa hikite de ataru: "Whether the arrow will hit the mark or not depends upon the archer." (Lit., "The bow will hit the target, depending on the bowman.")

Yūshō reppai: "The survival of the fittest." (Lit., "The superior prevails, the inferior breaks.")

Zensha no kutsugaeru wa kōsha no imashime: "The overturning of the preceding cart is a warning to the cart following." That is, man learns to be wise by the folly and mistakes of others.

PRIDE

LIKE THE PEOPLE of nearly all other nations the Japanese are not lacking in self-esteem. They are proud of their country, their history, their race, and their accomplishments. They have a strong sense of mission which throughout their history has been characterized by aggressive wars. The individual's sense of rank, prestige, and self-importance is generally concealed under a cloak of humility. The

Japanese language is full of deprecatory phrases which common usage dictates, but their use does not necessarily betoken a humble or modest person.

Donguri no sei kurabe: "Competition among mediocre people." (Lit., "Acorns compare their height with each other.") This is done since there is nothing about which to boast.

Hora wo fuku: "To talk big; to exaggerate." (Lit., "To blow a conch-trumpet.") In old Japan a conch-trumpet was used in battle or a hunt. English parallel: To blow your own horn.

Itachi naki ma no ten hokori: "The marten is proud where there is no weasel." English parallel: Where there are no dogs the fox is king.

Jiman kōman, baka no uchi: "The first chapter of fools is to esteem themselves wise." (Lit., "The boaster and the proud person are fools.") English parallel: Self-praise is no recommendation.

Jiman no kuso wa inu made mo kuwanu: "Not even a dog will eat the stool of a braggart."

Jiman wa chie no yuki-domari: "Boasting begins where wisdom stops."

Keigun no ikkaku: "A crane in a flock of fowls." This expression describes a man or woman who stands pre-eminent for his or her physical beauty or intellectual superiority. English parallel: A jewel on a dunghill.

Keikō to naru mo gyūbi to naru nakare: "Better be the cock's bill than an ox's tail." English parallel: Better be the head of an ass than the tail of a horse.

Kojiki wa tenka banashi: "Unimportant people love to talk big and seem important." (Lit., "Beggars talk of the whole world.") English parallel: Small people love to talk of great people.

Kotoba ōi no shina sukunashi: "Many words indicate shallow character." (Lit., "Numerous words show scanty wares.") English parallel: Empty vessels make the most noise.

Monzen no yase-inu: "A lean dog before the gate." Just as a lean and cowardly dog appears very brave when he is before his master's gate, so many a person of no consequence gives himself airs when supported by a powerful or influential master or patron.

Nishiki wa zōkin ni narazu: "Silk brocade does not make a good mop." Persons of wealth and breeding do not do well in menial positions.

Ōburoshiki wo hirogeru: "A bombastic talker." (Lit., "To spread a big wrapping cloth.") The *furoshiki* is a handy square of gaily-colored cloth in which articles are wrapped and carried. *"Ō-buroshiki"* is a large *furoshiki* or wrapping cloth in which many articles may be carried, hence the word is used figuratively for a pompous, inflated talker.

Ogoru mono hisashikarazu: "The haughty do not last long." Proud people will soon be humbled. English parallel: Pride goes before a fall.

Ogoru Heike hisashikarazu: "The haughty Heike will not prosper long." The proud and haughty Heike family of twelfth century Japan were finally overcome by their rivals the Genji family, who set up in Kamakura a military dictatorship or shogunate. During the Allied Occupation of Japan following the surrender on September 2, 1945, General MacArthur was frequently referred to by the Japanese as "the white Shōgun."

Ryōyū narabi tatazu: "A great man cannot brook a rival." (Lit., "Two great men cannot stand side by side.") English parallel: Two cocks in one yard do not agree.

Ryūkō ai utsu: "Two valorous men quarrel violently." (Lit., "The dragon and the tiger fight each other.") English parallel: Diamond cuts diamond.

Shikaku naru: "To become serious and severe." (Lit., "To become square.")

Shinshō-bōdai ni iu: "To exaggerate." (Lit., "To talk of a small needle as if it were a large club.") English parallel: To make a mountain out of a molehill.

Taikai wa sairyū wo erabazu: "The ocean is not choosy about a small stream." That is, small men and things can contribute to large ones. English parallel: The sea refuses no river.

Taisei wa riji ni irazu: "A great voice does not enter into vulgar ears." Thoughts that are very lofty are not easily understood by the common people.

Temae miso wo ageru: "Self-praise; self-glorification." (Lit., "To praise one's own bean paste.") English parallel: To blow one's own trumpet.

Tora no i wo karu kitsune: "A fox who borrows the tiger's prestige." An official or warrior who assumes an arrogant manner because of his lord's influence. English parallel: An ass in a lion's skin.

Umi ni sennen, yama ni sennen: "A thousand years in the sea and a thousand years in the mountains." This expression is often contracted to *"Umi sen, yama sen"* ("Sea thousand, mountain thousand"), and describes a person who has known the ins and outs of life and has become impudently bold.

Unubore to kasake no nai mono wa nai: "All people have their shortcomings." (Lit., "No person is free from vanity and syphilitic taint.") English parallel: Every ass loves to hear himself bray.

Waga katana de waga kubi kiru: "To suffer because of one's own foolish or bad actions." (Lit., "To cut off one's own head with one's own sword.")

PUNCTUALITY

The average Japanese is not very conscious of the value of time and is often unpunctual in keeping appointments. Invite a friend to dinner and he may turn up half an hour to an hour after the appointed time. This lack of promptness is especially true of people living in rural areas. Urban dwellers, however, through contact with Americans and Europeans, are rapidly learning the value of time and the necessity of being prompt in business engagements. Although in the cities there is much hurrying and rushing about, in rural areas life is more leisurely. However, the Japanese farmer is by no means lazy. He rises early in the morning and spends many hard hours of toil in the field, often returning home long after sundown. Most of the proverbs in this section teach the importance of being on time and the evils of wasting it.

Abura wo uru: "To loaf along." (Lit., "To sell oil.") This has reference to the oil vendor, who leisurely goes from house to house selling the amount of oil demanded by the good wife, often stopping to gossip with her. Hence, the above saying is used to describe a person who loafs on the road while on an errand. English parallel: To spin street yarns.

Ikkoku senkin: "Time is valuable." (Lit., "One instant, a thousand pieces of gold.") The word *"ikkoku"* may be translated "one moment" or "one instant," or sometimes "one minute." The above expression is taken from an ancient Chinese poem, one verse of which reads: "One moment of a spring eve is worth a thousand talents of gold." English parallel: Time is money.

Kisha no hassha de matta nashi: "The train waits for no one." In a land where people are proverbially late, the trains are so prompt that watches can be set by them. In the United States, where promptness is much emphasized, trains are often late. About thirty years ago when an Imperial train arrived late at its destination because of an accident farther up the line, the engineer and the station master, accepting responsibility for the delay, committed suicide!

Kōin hito wo matazu: "Time does not wait for man." It is interesting to note that the word *"kōin,"* here translated "time," is written with two Chinese ideographs, "light" and "shadow." That is, the alternate passage of light and shadow indicate time, which operates independently of man. English parallel: Time and tide wait for no man.

Kōin ya no gotoshi, hitotabi satte mata kaerazu: "Time (light and shadow) flies like an arrow, once gone it does not return."

Kōya (Konya) no asatte: "Habitual delay." (Lit., "The day-after-tomorrow of dyers.") The promise of dyers to complete a piece of work on "the day after tomorrow" has become a proverbial phrase for "habitual delay." English parallel: Jam tomorrow and never jam today.

Matararuru mi ni naru tomo, matsu mi ni naru na: "Let yourself be waited for, but wait for no one." (Lit., "Even though it is advantageous to be waited for, it is not advantageous to wait.") In Japan it was considered a mark of status and the perogative of superiors to keep an inferior waiting.

Matsu mi no tsurasa: "To wait is painful." This is especially so, since the one kept waiting is thus made conscious of his inferior status. English parallel: A watched pot is long in boiling.

Michi kusa wo kuu: "To waste time while doing an errand." (Lit., "To eat the roadside grass.") The figure here is of a packhorse stopping by the side of the road to crop grass. Errand boys will often furiously pedal along the road, then throw themselves off their bicycles at some shady spot and take a nap for half an hour or so before proceeding on their way. English opposite: Don't let grass grow under your feet.

Mukade ni waraji wo hakaseru yō: "Great tardiness of progress." (Lit., "As if a centipede had been made to bind a straw sandal on each of his legs.") If it takes a man some time to bind a straw sandal on each of his feet before starting a walking trip, how much longer would it take to bind with sandals the hundred feet of a centipede! Thus the proposed journey would be considerably delayed.

Osokarishi Yuranosuke: "To be too late." (Lit., "Yuranosuke was too late.") This retainer failed to arrive in time to say farewell to his lord, Takumi-no-kami, before the latter committed suicide by disembowelment. The above proverbial expression, based on the story of the Forty-seven *Rōnin* (lordless *samurai*), is taken from the famous *kabuki* play *"Chushingura,"* and teaches the importance of being on time. The actual name of the leader of the band is Kuranosuke Ōishi, but in the drama it is altered to Yuranosuke Ōishi.

Osoku tomo, nasazaru ni masaru: "Even though late it is better to do it than not to do it." English parallel: Better late than never.

Toki hito wo matazu: "Time does not wait for man." English parallel: Time and tide wait for no man.

Toki wa kane nari: "Time is money." This proverb is taken from the English one and came into use about a hundred years ago when American and British people began coming to Japan.

REALISM

NEARLY ALL JAPANESE are realists. They have no absolute philosophic or moral ideal. There is no absolute right or wrong. Abstract ideas are not appreciated. Metaphysical and psychological problems do not interest them. Much emphasis is put on doing or saying the right thing at the right time or place. Hence, forms, ceremonial, and ritual are deemed most important.

Ami donshū no uo wo morasu: "A great scoundrel goes free." (Lit., "The net misses the fish that could swallow a boat.") *"Donshū no uo"* ("A boat-swallowing fish") is the idiom for a notorious man, a scoundrel. English parallel: Laws catch flies but let hornets go free.

Amida no hikari mo kane shidai: "Amitabha's light rays are in proportion to the amount of gold offered." This proverb may be interpreted literally, since the image of the Buddhist deity is often covered with gold gilt; or figuratively, that the blessings of Amitabha are according to the amount contributed to the temple. English parallel: No penny, no paternoster.

Amida mo zeni hodo hikaru: "Even Amitabha shines according to the money given." This is a variation of the preceding proverb.

Ano yo no sennichi yori kono yo no ichinichi: "Better than a thousand days in the next world is one day in this."

Bōzu no fu-mimochi: "The profligacy of priests." The licentiousness of many Buddhist priests is proverbial in Japan. English parallel: It is a good divine who follows his own instructions.

Bōzu no fu-shinjin: "The priest's unbelief." It often happens that a priest instead of acting in a manner befitting his calling acts in a discreditable way.

Dokuja no kuchi wo nogareta yō: "As if one had escaped the mouth of a poisonous snake." This may be said of one who has made a narrow escape out of mortal danger, or from the hands of a villain.

Eda wo tamen to shite ne wo korosu: "In trying to straighten the branches you destroy the roots." You may fail to reform a person if you pay too much attention to his small faults. English parallel: Burn not your house to frighten away the mice.

Gabei wa ue ni mitazu: "The picture of a rice cake does not satisfy hunger." Reasoning is useless to a hungry man. Here it is interesting to note that the Japanese word for "failure" or "nothingness" is "gabei," which literally means "pictured rice cake."

Hotoke no hikari yori kane no hikari: "Money is more important than religion." (Lit., "The shine of gold coins rather than the shine of Buddha.") Money takes the precedence in the settlement of all mundane affairs. English parallel: Money is the god of the world.

Inoru yori ḳasege: "Toil rather than pray." It is wiser to work than to pray for good luck.

Isshō ḳō nari banḳotsu ḳaru: "Thousands die to raise one hero to fame." (Lit., "For one general to succeed, the bones of ten thousand soldiers lie drying.")

Issun saḳi wa yami no yo: "One inch ahead and the world is pitch darkness." It is useless to talk of the future for unforeseen evils frequently happen. English parallels: The future is a sealed book. The unexpected always happens.

Jigoḳu no sata mo ḳane shidai: "Even orders in hell are controlled by money." Not only in this world but even in hell money is a powerful influence. English parallel: Money opens all doors.

Jū-nin tō-iro: "Many men, many tastes." (Lit., "Ten men, ten colors.") English parallel: So many men, so many minds.

Jū-nin tō-hara: "Many men, many minds." (Lit., "Ten men, ten abdomens.") In ancient Japan the belly or abdomen was considered the seat of the intellect as well as the emotions. Hence, for the warrior class, the approved form of suicide was *"seppuḳu"* ("disembowelment"), more vulgarly called *"haraḳiri"* ("belly-cutting"), in which the abdomen is ripped open and the spirit imprisoned therein is allowed to escape. Both of the two preceding proverbs teach that there are great varieties of customs and tastes in individuals.

Kami wa mitōshi: "The gods see through everything." You can't fool the gods even though you may sometimes deceive men. English parallel: The eyes of God sleep not.

Kōshi mo toki ni awazu: "Even Confucius had his misfortunes." If such a great man had tribulations, ordinary mortals should not complain when misfortune comes to them.

Kuruwa no yuḳi: "Snow on licensed (prostitute) quarters." This saying was printed on a fan together with a painting of the licensed quarters in winter, to indicate that while cooling oneself with a fan, one can enjoy beautiful women. The average Japanese does not regard as evil association with prostitutes and *geisha*. In fact, important political or business arrangements are often begun or carried out in *geisha* houses.

Kyoḳu ni ataru mono wa madō: "Those in charge are puzzled."

Frequently those who are responsible for a decision are perplexed as to what they should do. No one is wise in his own affairs. Hence, the wisdom of consulting others. English parallel: Lookers-on see more than players.

Makereba zoku: "If defeated, you're a traitor." Those who are beaten become rebels. English parallel: The conquered are wrong.

Marui mono ni kakubuta: "For a round thing, a square lid." This saying describes two persons who are associated, but because they are so different by temperament they cannot get along. English parallel: A square peg in a round hole.

Meiba ni kuse ari: "Absolute perfection is not to be found anywhere." (Lit., "The famous horse has a fault.")

Meido no michi ni ō nashi: "On the road to the other world no one is king." English parallel: Death is the great leveler.

Meigetsu no tama mo kizu atawazu: "Even a full-moon-like jewel cannot be flawless." There is no such thing as perfection. English parallel: The best wine has its lees.

Meijin no ko ni meijin nashi: "An expert's child is not an expert." The skill of an artist or of an expert can not generally be handed down through heredity. Hence, in old Japan, some talented disciple was often adopted to carry on the skill and the family name.

Meikyō mo ura wo terasazu: "Even a stainless (clear) mirror does not reflect the reverse side." Even the most scholarly man does not know everything.

Mizu kiyokereba uo sumazu: "If the water is clear fish will not live in it." Most fish prefer muddy water to a clear stream, so men generally avoid associating with a person who is too strict in his habits and manners. Upright men cannot go along with bad people.

Moetsuita kara hi no kitō: "Something that is done too late." (Lit., "Praying to have the fire stopped after it is well ablaze.")

Mono wa hazumi: "You cannot be sure of anything." (Lit., "Things are by chance.") English parallel: Opportunity makes the thief.

Muyō no chōbutsu: "A useless thing." (Lit., "A useless long article.") English parallel: A white elephant.

Ni-no-ya ga tsugarenu: "The enemy is not to be assailed." (Lit., "The second arrow cannot be fitted to the string.")

Ningen banji kane no yo no naka: "Money commands people and all things in the world." English parallel: Money makes the mare go.

Ōta ko ni oshierarete asase wo wataru: "Directed by the child on his back, he crosses the ford." That is, even weaklings and inferiors can sometimes prove useful. English parallel: The chickens give advice to the hen.

Owari yokereba subete yoshi: "The end justifies the means." (Lit., "If the end is good everything is good.") English parallel: All's well that ends well.

Rikutsu to kōyaku wa doko e demo tsuku: "Reason and adhesive plaster will stick anywhere."

Ryō-i no mon ni byōnin ōshi: "There are many seeking help from competent people." (Lit., "At the gate of a good physician there are many ill persons.")

Rongo yomi no rongo shirazu: "A learned fool." (Lit., "He reads the Analects of Confucius but does not understand them.") The moral actions of many Japanese have been and to a certain extent still are based on the "Lun-yu" or Analects of Confucius. So a person may read these important teachings but still fail to understand and practice them. English parallel: Folly and learning often dwell together.

Sawaranu kami ni tatari nashi: "Keep away from anything that might cause you harm." (Lit., "From gods that are left alone, there is no curse.") Don't meddle with something that is not your concern. English parallel: Let sleeping dogs lie.

Shaka ni seppō: "It's no use giving lessons to a great scholar or an expert." (Lit., "Preaching to Sakyamuni.") Sakyamuni, an Indian prince who lived some 2,500 years ago, renounced his family and throne to meditate and preach, eventually becoming the founder of Buddhism. English parallel: Don't teach your grandmother to suck eggs.

Saru ni ki noboru wo oshieru: "To do something that is abso-

lutely unnecessary." (Lit., "To teach a monkey to climb a tree.")
English parallel: It is not necessary to teach a fish to swim.

Subete tsurugi wo toru mono wa tsurugi ni te horobu nari: "All
that take the sword will be destroyed by the sword." This utterance
of Jesus Christ, as recorded in Matthew 26:52, has become a proverb
in every language into which the Bible has been translated.

Suteru kami areba tasukeru kami ari: "If there are gods who
forsake you, there are also gods who assist you." That is, one need
not lose hope when beset with many difficulties and misfortunes.
English parallel: When one door closes another opens.

Ta kara yuku mo aze kara yuku mo onaji: "It is the same whether
you go from the rice field or from the footpath." Their ways may be
different but in fact they agree. Though means may differ, they are
led to the same end.

Takami ni tsuchi wo moru: "Piling up earth in a high place."
That is, to do something that is unnecessary. English parallel: Hard
by the river he digs a well.

Tera no monzen ni oni ga sumu: "Devils live in front of temple
gates." Evil people are to be found even in the vicinity of holy places.
Close beside many of the leading temples and shrines of Japan are
prostitute quarters and teahouses of assignation to cater to the sexual
appetites of worshipers and tourists.

Tera no tonari ni oni go sumu: "Next door to the temple live
devils." This proverb is a slightly different version of the one above.
Bad people are found everywhere, even in the close neighborhood of
a holy place. English parallel: The devil lurks behind the cross.

Tonari no kaji ni sawaganu mono nashi: "There is no one who
fails to get excited when the neighbor's house is on fire." Distant
troubles do not interest most people, but when they come nearer
home we are more willing to do something. English parallel: When
next door is on fire it is high time to look to your own.

Toranu tanuki no kawa sanyō suru: "To calculate the value of
badgers' skins before they are caught." A very risky and foolish thing
to do. English parallel: Sell not the bear's skin before you have caught
him.

Tsuno wo tamete ushi wo korosu: "In trying to straighten the horns you kill the ox." That is, in attempting to make improvements you sometimes ruin the whole project. English parallel: Wanting to make right the eyebrow, he pulled out his eye.

Un wa ten ni ari, botamochi wa tana ni ari: "Our destiny is in heaven's hands, rice dumplings are on shelves." That is, we must not be overanxious about the future but go about our daily duties trusting that some good will eventually come. English parallel: Trust in Providence.

Ushi wa mizu wo nonde chichi to shi, hebi wa mizu wo nonde doku to su: "The cow drinks water and it turns to milk, the snake drinks water and it turns to poison." The same thing used by different animals produces different results. So men, using the same materials, can produce good or evil things. English parallel: One man's meat is another man's poison.

Waga Hotoke wa tōtoshi: "Each person deems his own things best." (Lit., "One's own Buddha is exalted.") English parallel: The crow thinks her own young fairest.

Waga ya no Hotoke tattoshi: "The Buddha in one's own house is the most esteemed." Each person thinks his own religion the best. This is a slightly different version of the proverb given above.

Yorokobi areba kanashimi ari: "Where there is joy there is also sorrow." No man has one or the other all the time. Life with its sweets and bitters must be accepted. English parallel: No joy without alloy.

Zai wo nusumu mono wa nusubito nari, kuni wo nusumu mono wa shokō to naru: "He who steals a man's wealth becomes a robber, he who steals a country becomes a feudal lord." English parallel: One murder makes a criminal, a million a hero.

Zeni aru toki wa oni o mo tsukau: "When a man has money he can employ even a devil." English parallel: Money makes the mare go.

RESPECT

RESPECT FOR SUPERIORS is a very important characteristic in Japanese hierarchical society where each person has his place, be it higher or lower. The Japanese word *"makoto,"* translated "sincerity" in Japanese-English dictionaries, actually means "showing proper respect" or "complete dedication." This complete dedication or the showing of proper respect should be rendered to those superior in age, authority, social position, or learning. Parents, grandparents, elderly people, government or office superiors, teachers and professors, eminent writers and scholars, social and economic superiors, the Imperial family, etc., are all entitled to respect and receive it in due measure. Hence, every Japanese constantly asks himself: "Have I shown proper respect to so-and-so?" or "Has such-and-such a person paid the respect due me?" That being the case, the Japanese language abounds in honorifics, polite expressions, and terms employed by inferiors to superiors, as well as words used by superiors to inferiors. In modern Japan, and especially among youth, there is less concern for this, a fact that is deplored by the more elderly and cultured elements of the nation. Yet enough of it remains to mark the Japanese as being the world's most polite people. However, as we shall see later, this does not prevent them from being at times extremely discourteous and impolite.

Ato-ashi de suna: "To kick sand with the hind legs." This saying, which probably originated from observing the earth-kicking of a dog after he has defecated, is used to describe an ungrateful person who does some evil or shows lack of respect to some old master or benefactor, when he finds that he will get no further assistance from him. English parallel: A runaway monk never praises his cloister.

Bansotsu wa eyasuku, isshō wa egatashi: "Superior people are rare and hard to find." (Lit., "It is easy to get ten thousand soldiers but difficult to find one general.") English parallel: Workmen are easier found than masters.

Bun wa bu yori tsuyoshi: "Literature is stronger than military arts." English parallel: The pen is mightier than the sword.

Chishiki wa tomi no eikyū no izumi: "Knowledge is the eternal spring of wealth." This is the Japanese rendition of the English proverb: Knowledge is the perennial spring of wealth.

Eiyū ai-shiru: "Heroes know each other." Great people easily recognize each other. English parallel: Like knows like.

Eiyū wo shiru mono wa eiyū nari: "He who understands a hero is himself a hero." That is, a man must be a hero to understand a hero. The Japanese word *"eiyū"* may be translated either "hero" or "great man."

Eiyū iro wo konomu: "Heroes (great men) are fond of sensual pleasures." It is interesting to note that the lives of many great men the world over are checkered with love affairs.

Eiyū narabi tatazu: "A great man cannot brook a rival." (Lit., "Heroes cannot stand side by side.") This is probably because neither is willing to acknowledge the other as superior. English parallel: Two of a trade seldom agree.

Eiyū no matsuro wa toki ni awaremu beshi: "The end of heroes is sometimes to be pitied." The last days of great men are frequently quite miserable. Their popularity having waned, they are deserted by friend and foe alike.

Enjaku nanzo kōkō no kokorozashi wo shiran ya? "How can swallows and sparrows know the thoughts (ambitions) of a great swan?" This saying is attributed to an ancient Chinese statesman while he was still a country bumpkin. The interpretation is that mean-spirited persons can not understand the greatness of superior minds.

Fude ni wa ken ni masaru chikara ari: "The brush-pen has a power stronger than the sword." With the brush-pen, drawings, black and white paintings, and literary works are produced. Hence, it is a far more potent weapon than the sword. English parallel: The pen is mightier than the sword.

Furukawa ni mizu taezu: "There is always water in an old river." Old customs persist long in a society or nation. They are not easily replaced by new ones. English parallel: An old establishment never wants customers.

Isha to bōzu wa toshiyori ga ii: "Physicians and Buddhist priests are better if old." They are perhaps more welcome because they have the wisdom and experience of age and are thus more reliable.

Kame no kō yori toshi no kō: "Better than the tortoise shell is the efficacy of old age." Here there is a pun on the word *"kō,"* which according to the Chinese ideograph used, may mean either "a tortoise shell" or "efficacy" ("benefit"). In ancient Japan, and even to a certain extent today, people consulted diviners who heated a tortoise shell and interpreted the future according to the cracks that appeared. (In some other countries the shoulder blade of a deer or sheep was so used.) The above proverb states that the advice of wise, elderly people is much better and more dependable than tortoise-shell divination.

Kangen wa mimi ni sakarō: "Good advice is harsh to the ears." (Lit., "Remonstrance is opposed to the ears.") No matter how good the advice may be, it is often unpleasant.

Kateba kangun, makereba zokugun: "If victorious, a government army; if defeated, traitors." Success legalizes and gives sanction to the cause of the opposition. English parallel: Successful crime is called virtue.

Nagare wo kunde minamoto wo shiru: "The source is important." (Lit., "By drawing water from a stream we learn its source.") English parallel: A tree is known by its fruit.

O-hige no chiri wo harau: "To curry favor with a person." (Lit., "To shake off the dust from a man's beard.") To pay court to a great personage. Flattery and excessive adulation were used in old Japan just as much as they are today. *Geisha,* actresses, and politicians are especially skilled in such practices.

Oi no ki nobori: "An old man climbing a tree." This expression is used to remind an old person not to do something beyond his power.

Oi-ki wa magaranu: "Don't try to make old people conform to new ways." (Lit., "Aged trees cannot be bent.") English parallel: You can't teach an old dog new tricks.

Oitaru uma wa michi wo wasurezu: "An old horse does not forget his path." English parallel: Experience teaches fools, and he is a great one that will not learn by it.

Oite futatabi ko to naru: "In old age one again becomes a child." English parallel: To enter one's second childhood.

Oite masumasu sakan nari: "In old age he becomes increasingly vigorous." English parallel: To enjoy a green old age.

Oite wa ko ni shitagae: "When old, obey your child." In the Japanese family system, the above saying enjoins the old parents who have retired to follow the wishes of their son who is now master of the household.

Oite wa yo ni shitagae-gatashi: "It is hard for old people to follow the changing times." (Lit., "When old, one finds it difficult to follow the world.") This is because the old are less flexible in their ways and in their thinking than the young.

Oji ga oi no kusa wo karu: "The uncle cuts grass for the nephew." This is the opposite of what is generally done, but life has often been topsy-turvy.

Ryōyaku kuchi ni nigashi: "Good medicine is bitter to the mouth." This proverb of Chinese origin teaches that good advice is often distasteful to the person to whom it is given. English parallel: Bitter pills may have wholesome effects.

Shichijū no mitsugo: "At seventy a three-year-old child." This saying is used to denote second childhood or senility.

Shijin wa umaru, tsukuru-bekarazu: "A poet is born, he cannot be made." English parallel: A poet is born, not made.

Sennichi no kingaku yori ichi nichi no meishō: "Better than a thousand days of diligent study is one day with a great teacher." The Japanese have the greatest respect for excellent teachers and eminent scholars. One is reminded of a saying current in America some years ago, that a college is a student on one end of a log with Mark Hopkins on the other.

Shichi (Nana) shaku satte shi no kage wo fumazu: "Keep seven feet behind, lest you tread on the master's shadow." In feudal Japan this practice was actually observed, in order to make pupils show high respect to their teachers or masters.

Sōdan wa toshiyori, kenka wa wakamono: "Old men for consultation, young men for quarrels." The old are more willing to settle matters by mutual negotiation and discussion, while the young are more likely to turn to fighting in the settlement of differences. English parallel: Old men for counsel, young men for war.

Suzume no sengoe yori tsuru no hitogoe: "Better one cry of a crane than a thousand chirpings of sparrows." One word from a wise man is far better than a thousand words from a fool.

Taiki bansei: "Great talents mature slowly." (Lit., "Large utensil evening finish.") That is, great genius often takes a long time to mature. English parallels: Late fruit keeps well. Rome was not built in a day. A slow fire makes sweet meat.

Toshiyori no hiyamizu: "Something imprudent for old persons." (Lit., "Cold water for an old man.") To bathe in cold water is all right for a young man, but for an old man to do so is both unseemly and imprudent. The old should not try to imitate the young.

Toshiyori no iu koto to uma no shirigai wa hazuresō de hazurenu: "You can rely on the advice of old men." (Lit., "The sayings of the aged and a horse crupper look to slip off, but they do not.") English parallel: An old man's sayings are seldom untrue.

Toshiyori no mono wasure, wakai mono no mono shirazu: "An old person forgets things, the young person does not know things." (Lit., "The forgetfulness of an old person, the ignorance of a young person.") English parallel: The old forgets, the young does not know.

Toshiyori no mukashi-banashi: "The aged tell tales of long ago." They live in the past, but many of their tales contain important lessons for today. Hence, they should be heard with great respect.

Toshi yoreba yoku fukashi: "As one advances in age one becomes more avaricious." This cannot be said of all old people, for many become increasingly unselfish and sweet tempered as they grow older.

Toshi wa kusuri: "Old age serves as medicine." That is, medicine to cool and check hot-tempered youth and to give healing to wounded feelings and misunderstandings. English parallel: Older and wiser.

Uwate ni wa uwate ari: "Even a superior person has his superior." (Lit., "To the upper hand there is an upper hand.") It is well to remember that even experts have others who are better.

Wase no meshi ni dojō-jiru: "A stew of loaches over rice from the first crop." A delicious but inexpensive meal for the hard-working farmer. Even such a meal is superior in flavor and nourishing qualities to many of the more elaborate meals of city folks. The expression *"wase no kodomo"* (lit., "the early rice plant's child") is the idiom for "a precocious child."

Yoki fumbetsu wa rōjin ni toe: "For good judgment ask old persons." Because they have long experience and will give you good advice. The counsel of the old is invaluable to the young. Because the Japanese are respectful to the old many young people are helped by the sage advice of their elders.

Zukan soku-netsu wa chōju no in: "A cool head and warm feet are the cause of long life." English parallel: A cool mouth and warm feet live long.

RESPONSIBILITY

THE JAPANESE have a strong sense of responsibility. By punishment of the guilty, the Japanese mean punishment of the responsible man, the man higher up and not his subordinate who is but a tool. Thus, in determining war guilt following the end of World War II, the Japanese cabinet that started and continued the war was held responsible. "Tōjo and his associates are responsible for bringing our country into the war with its disastrous consequences. Hence, he and his ilk should be punished and made to pay the supreme penalty!" That statement I heard made early in October 1945 by a Japanese orator on the corner of a wide street in Tokyo while hundreds of his fellow-countrymen listened approvingly. When the war leaders were brought to trial and sentenced, the Japanese felt that justice had been meted out to the responsible parties.

Chōchin-mochi wa saki ni tate: "The lantern-bearer should go ahead." He who bears the light, whether material, intellectual, or spiritual, should lead the way. English parallel: The candle that goes before gives the best light.

Daikō idezumba sōsei wo ikan sen? "If I don't come forward, what will become of the masses?" In other words, what will happen to the people if I don't do my share by governing them? This saying is an excellent illustration of a ruler's high sense of responsibility.

Gimu wa mottomo chikai mono yori hajime yo: "As to your duty, start with what is nearest to you." That is, you are responsible to carry out your nearest duty. English parallel: Do the duty that lies nearest thee.

Kami wo narō shimo: "The lower orders of society learning from the upper." This saying is a warning to the ruling or upper classes of society that they are responsible for setting a good example.

Kanjō atte zeni tarazu: "The account is correct, but money is short." Some one is responsible to explain or make up the deficit. A fool always comes short of his reckoning. English parallel: The account is correct but not a sixpence appears.

Kanjō wa kanjō: "An account is an account." It is all down in black and white, so you are responsible to make the payment. English parallel: Business is business.

Karigi wa mi ni awanu: "Borrowed garments do not fit well." That is, you are responsible to make use of your own talents in the conduct of life.

Karigi yori araigi: "Rather than borrowed clothes, use washed ones." It is better to wear your own clothes, washed clean, than fine clothes borrowed from others. This is an exhortation to each person to accept his responsibilities to stand on his own two feet.

Kenka ryō-seibai: "In a quarrel both parties are to blame." Generally both sides have done some wrong and are answerable. English parallel: When two quarrel, both are in the wrong.

Koromo bakari do oshō wa dekinu: "A bonze (Buddhist monk) is not made of a priestly robe only." There must also be real learning and sanctity. English parallel: It is not the coat that makes the gentleman.

Maita tane wo karaneba naranu: "You must reap the harvest from the seeds you have sown." Since you undertook to sow the seeds you are responsible for the harvest be it good or bad. English parallel: As you sow, so shall you reap.

Sekinin wo nogareru: "To evade one's responsibility; to be freed of one's responsibility." *"Sekinin,"* the Japanese word for "responsibility" is written with two Chinese ideographs meaning "to endure an ordeal." The sense of responsibility weighs heavily on the Japanese of all classes. Hence the desire to evade as much of it as possible.

Shu ga shu nara, kerai mo kerai: "As masters are, so servants are." (Lit., "If masters are masters, servants are servants.") That is, if the ruling classes carry out faithfully their responsibilities, the lower classes can be counted on to do their duty.

Takara no mochi-kusare: "A treasure decaying in one's hands." The person who has money or talents is responsible for putting them to good use; else they will rot away.

Ue ni mi-narau: "The lower classes follow the example of the upper." (Lit., "Learning by seeing the upper.") It is the responsibility of superior people to be an example to those less gifted. English parallel: Like master, like men.

Usagi no mimi yori hito no mimi: "Better than a hare's ears are a man's." That is, a person should depend on his own senses, and is responsible for their full use.

RUDENESS

THOUGH COURTEOUS TO EQUALS and superiors, the Japanese can be and frequently are rude to strangers and those they consider inferior to themselves. It is considered by some to be the mark of "a great man" to be rude and overbearing to subordinates and those in a lower social class. Often when two Japanese gentlemen quarrel they become painfully polite and the use of honorifics increases. They will smile and use extra polite language, though secretly they would enjoy cutting each other's throats.

In the spring of 1940 I was traveling with my wife and four children on a through express from Pusan at the southern tip of Korea to Peking, China. The train was very crowded, but in our reserved compartment we were not too uncomfortable. At the first stop after crossing over the border into Manchuria, four Japanese men boarded the train, came to our compartment, made peremptory motions for my family to move over, and sat down on our reserved seats. They evidently took us for American tourists, for after seating themselves they made rude remarks about the "selfishness and uncouthness of foreigners," all in Japanese, which they did not know I understood. After a few minutes, I addressed them in their language, told them that I lived in Kyoto, and asked them what part of Japan they were from before they moved to Manchuria. They became quite friendly, apologized for their previous rudeness, and at the next train stop, two of them purchased some fruit and cake which they gave to our children. Thus, the first rudeness of these four to us as strangers and hated Americans was changed to courteous consideration when they came to know us and found that we loved Japan and the Japanese people.

Bata-kusai: "An alien smell." Hence something that is foreign and contemptible. (Lit., "Stinks of butter.") This saying originated long before modern refrigeration or the making of butter in Japan, when it had to be imported from abroad in cans and often arrived in a rancid condition.

Chōnai de shiranu mono wa teishu bakari nari: "In the whole neighborhood it is only the husband who does not know what is going on." This expression is often derisively applied to a cuckold who is ignorant of his wife's unfaithfulness. It is also applied to a man who does not know something descreditable to him about which his neighbors are talking. English parallel: The goodman is the last to know what is amiss at home.

Isha no genkan: "A big front." (Lit., "A doctor's vestibule.") In times past, the vestibule or entrance to a physician's office or private hospital was constructed in an imposing way, with a view to making a good impression on the visitors. When the entrance way of a house or other building is disproportionately large, it is ridiculed as "the doctor's vestibule."

Jibun no atama no hai wo oe: "Attend to your own affairs." (Lit., "Brush away the flies from your own head.") This rude expression is frequently used at the beginning of a quarrel. English parallel: Mind your own business.

Jimbei San no yōkō: "Foolish gossip; or something of no great value." (Lit., "Mr. Jimbei's foreign travel.") *"Jimbei"* is the general term used for "a backwoodsman" or "an uneducated nobody." When such a person goes abroad it is of no value to him or to anyone else.

Ken-en no naka: "On bad terms." (Lit., "Relations between dog and monkey.") The dog and monkey are proverbially on bad terms with each other; hence, people who cannot get along together are said to be on "dog-monkey terms." English parallel: To lead a dog-and-cat life.

Ki de hana wo kukutta yō na aisatsu suru: "To give a blunt answer." (Lit., "To give a greeting as though one's nose was tied by a piece of wood.") This common expression for "a brusque reply" is frequently heard.

Meshi no ue no hai no yō: "A persistent annoyance." (Lit., "Like flies on boiled rice.") Flies persist in swarming upon boiled rice, however often we may drive them away. Hence, something or some one who insistently comes back to annoy us is thus picturesquely described.

Mizu-kusaku suru: "To be reserved." (Lit., "To be water-stinking.") This offensive and rude expression is used to describe a person who is lacking in frankness, or one who insists on treating a friend as a stranger.

Noroi wa waga mi ni kaeru: "Curses come back to yourself." That is, they rebound on the person saying them.

Onoga atama no hai wo oe: "Take care of your own business." (Lit., "Drive off the flies from your own head.") This rude saying is a slightly different version of *"Jibun no atama no hai wo oe,"* q.v.

Ototoi oide: "Never come again." (Lit., "Come the day before yesterday.") In picturesque language the person is saying "Never darken my door in the future." English parallel: Come when we have two Sundays in a week.

Sao no saki ni suzu: "A person who talks long and loudly." (Lit., "A bell on the end of a pole.") A man or woman who incessantly chatters with little of value being said is likened to a jangling bell on the end of a long pole. As a rule, the Japanese have more respect for the man of few words but ready action than for a talkative person whose accomplishments are few. Hence to liken a man to a bell on the end of a pole is to highly insult him.

Tori naki sato no kōmori: "A second-rate person in a third-rate environment." (Lit., "A bat in a birdless village.") Even a person of mediocre attainments is important among those of less intelligence. English parallel: In the land of the blind, the one-eyed is king.

Tōzai wo wakimaezu: "Complete ignorance." (Lit., "Not to know east from west.") This phrase describes an infantile state of simplicity and ignorance. A rude question when addressed to an adult is: *"Tōzai wo wakimaenu ka?"* "Don't you know east from west?"

Ura wo iu: "To speak ironically." (Lit., "To say the reverse.") Such speaking is quite common in Japan and is in accord with the tendency of many to speak enigmatically. The expression *"kotoba no ura"* (Lit., "The reverse side of the words") means "the hidden meaning of words." Also the saying, *"Hanashi no ura omote"* (Lit., "the back and front of a talk") means "the two sides of a story."

SELFISHNESS

MOST JAPANESE ARE NOT SELFISH. In fact, stingy people are greatly despised and the object of much ridicule. Because of their custom of exchanging gifts, the Japanese are said to be very generous. However, this giving of presents may sometimes be based on the selfish motive of getting something back that is better. The custom of giving and returning presents often becomes very burdensome. See also the section on GENEROSITY AND HOSPITALITY and the section on OBLIGATIONS.

Abu hachi torazu: "To fail by being too grasping." (Lit., "To catch neither the horsefly nor the wasp.") Especially true if you try to swat both insects at the same time. English parallels: He that grasps too much, holds fast nothing.

Bō hodo negatte hari hodo kanau: "Though we ask for much, only a little is granted." (Lit., "One asks for a club and is given only a needle.") English parallel: Ask for an ell and you get an inch.

Daiyoku wa muyoku ni nitari: "Greed resembles generosity." Sometimes great selfishness looks like unselfishness. English parallel: Avarice overreaches itself.

Erande kasu wo tsukamu: "Having chosen, you grasp the refuse." That is, too much careful thought about what is best to choose will result in a worse state than no consideration at all. English parallel: Go farther and fare worse.

Fū-un ni jōzuru: "To avail oneself of public troubles." (Lit., "To take advantage of wind and clouds.") A descriptive phrase of a mean and selfish person who advances himself at the expense of others.

Gaden insui: "To be selfish." (Lit., "My rice field, draw water.") The greatest need in Japanese rice cultivation is water. The farmer who draws from some common source more than his share is despised as supremely selfish.

Hisashi wo kashite omoya wo torareru: "To lose the whole by lending a part." (Lit., "To lend the eaves and lose the main house.") This saying reminds us of Aesop's fable of the camel driver who was ousted from his tent by the camel which he allowed to step in little by little. English parallel: Who lets another sit on his shoulder will soon have him on his head.

Hitokuchi mono ni hō wo yaku: "To take more than one can manage." (Lit., "To burn the cheeks by one mouthful.") The selfish person will fill his mouth with more hot food than he can readily chew and suffers the consequences. English parallel: To bite off more than one can chew.

Hito no hana wa akai: "To desire the things of others." (Lit., "The flowers of others are red.") Not satisfied with the flowers in his own yard, he deems those of his neighbor more beautiful and longs for them. English parallel: Better is the neighbor's hen than mine.

Hito no issun, waga isshaku: "One inch of others' (faults) and one foot of mine (seem the same)." The point of view of a thoroughly selfish and prejudiced man.

Hito no mono yori jibun no mono: "The things of my own seem better." (Lit., "Rather than the things of other people, my own things.") English parallel: The laundress washeth her own smock first.

Hito no chōchin de akari: "To use the property of another person for one's own benefit." (Lit., "Light from the lantern of another.")

Hito no fundoshi (mawashi) de sumō wo toru: "To be generous at another's expense." (Lit., "To wrestle in another man's loincloth.")

Hito no gobō de hōji suru: "To reap one's own profit by using the property of another man." (Lit., "To give a memorial feast by using another man's burdock.") At the feast, following a Buddhist memorial service for the dead, it is customary to serve, among other dishes, some cooked burdock. The point of this proverb is to reap one's own profit by taking advantage of another man's effects.

Hito no itai no wa sannen demo gaman (shimbō) suru: "Selfish unconcern about the suffering of others." (Lit., "We can bear even for three years the pains of another person.")

Hyaku ryō no kata ni amigasa ikkai (hitotsu): "A wattle hat for a debt of one hundred *ryō.*" In old Japan a *ryō* was a standard gold coin weighing nearly ten ounces. One hundred *ryō* represent a sum of more than $17,000. Hence, the above saying is an illustration of how a debtor offers to put in mortgage an almost worthless article for a loan of a great sum.

Ichi mon oshimi no hyaku son (shirazu): "Sparing in the use of one *mon* and careless of a hundred." The *mon* went out of use about one hundred years ago, but at that time its value was one tenth of a *rin,* which in turn was one tenth of a *"sen"* or one-thousandth of a *yen.* Like the *mon,* the *rin* and *sen* are no longer in use in Japan. English parallel: Penny wise and pound foolish.

Ikkaku senkin: "Making a fortune at one stroke." (Lit., "One grasp, a thousand gold pieces.") That is, an adventurous and risky undertaking.

Jūbako no sumi wo yōji de hojikuru yō: "To be too careful of details." (Lit., "He scrapes with his toothpick every corner of his piled-up lunch box.") English parallel: To split hairs.

Kan wo katsugu mono wa toshi no ekisen koto wo hossu: "Coffin carriers desire the year of the plague." Because they will have more employment, they selfishly wish evil on others.

Kashita mono wa wasurezu, karita mono wa wasureru: "He forgets not what he has lent, but forgets what he has borrowed." Often a man will remember the obligations of others to him and forget what he owes to others.

Kau wa morau ni masaru: "It is better to buy than to receive." What is bought is cheaper than a gift. Because, according to Japanese custom, a gift must always be returned with a gift just as expensive or more costly than the one received.

Kawa mukō no kenka: "A fight on the other side of the river." That is, something on which a person can look with selfish unconcern.

Koronde mo, tada wa okinu: "Even though he tumbles, he won't just get up." That is, he will rise with something in his hand. This is a description of an avaricious person who makes even an accident yield him something.

Kusuri ku-sōbai: "A druggist charges nine times the cost." (Lit., "Medicine ninefold profit.") This proverbial expression describes the popular feeling in Japan towards the high cost of medicine.

Na wo toru yori toku wo tore: "Rather than get a name, get profit." This saying expressed the viewpoint of the merchant class in old Japan. The warrior class took exactly the opposite position. English parallel: Money first, fame last.

Nata wo kashite yama wo kirareru: "To be injured by someone to whom you have done a favor." (Lit., "To lend your hatchet and get your forest cut down.")

Onore no ta ni mizu wo hiku: "He draws water over his own rice field." Selfishly, he sees to it that his paddy field has enough water, with no thought for the needs of his neighbors. See *Gaden insui,* p. 204.

Rō wo ete Shoku wo nozomu: "Having won Lung *(Ro)* he yearns for Shu *(Shoku).*" This statement from the Confucian classics means that there are no limits to a man's selfishness. The more he gets the more he desires.

Sengoku wo toreba, mangoku wo uramu: "He who takes a thousand *koku* from his land envies another who takes ten thousand. The *"koku"* is the standard unit by which rice and other grain are measured. It is roughly equal to five bushels. In feudal days a person's income was measured by the number of *koku* of rice his land produced.

Shiwambō no kaki no tane: "The persimmon seeds of a skinflint." A miserly person will save even such a common thing as persimmon seeds.

Tsume de hi wo tobosu: "To make a light with fingernails." This expression means to "be very stingy" or "very poor." A miser is said to burn his fingernail parings in order to save oil for lighting.

Waga ta ni mizu wo hiku: "To draw water over my own rice field." A description of an extremely selfish man who is indifferent to the needs of others. See *Onore no ta ni mizu wo hiku,* above; and, *Gaden insui,* p. 204.

Yasumono kai no zeni ushinai: "In buying cheap articles money is lost." It is often more economical to purchase good articles at a higher cost, for they will last longer and give more satisfaction. English parallel: Buy cheap and waste your money.

Yasumono kōte hana otosu: "You lose your status when you buy cheap articles." (Lit., "If you buy cheap things you drop your nose.") The expression, *"hana otosu"* ("drop your nose") means to lose your standing in the presence of others, or in other words to be put to shame, to be publicly humiliated. Such a situation is to be avoided at all cost by every self-respecting Japanese.

Yoko-guruma wo osu: (Lit., "To push a cart sideways.") This saying describes a person who argues or acts unreasonably, also, one who selfishly insists on having his own way.

Yoku ni wa itadaki nashi: "Cupidity has no peak." That is, the heights of avarice are immeasurable. English parallel: A miser's bag is never full.

Yoku ni wa kagiri nashi: "There are no limits to avarice." The Japanese word *"yoku"* may be translated "avarice," "cupidity," "covetousness," or "selfish desire," as well as in a number of other synonymous terms. English parallel: Avarice knows no bounds.

Yoku no fukuro ni soko nashi: "The bag of cupidity has no bottom." That is, the more we possess the more we covet.

Yoku no fukai taka wa tsume wo nukeru: "The avaricious hawk (falcon) loses its talons." It swoops down and fastens its talons on game too large to carry away, and in its struggles to release itself it often loses its claws. So also the avaricious person will often seize something far larger than he can manage and thus come to grief.

Yoku no nai mono ni kuji ga ataru: "The unselfish person will draw a prize." Those who have no particular wish to draw a good lot will frequently win the prize.

SENSITIVITY

As A RACE, the Japanese—especially the Kumaso or aristocratic type— are refined and sensitive in their appreciation of beauty and nature in her various moods. The people are also more intuitive than logical. They can be extremely touchy, for they are very sensitive to the opinion of others. Rather than attack a problem directly they prefer to do it in what Westerners would term a roundabout approach. Thus, if there is any failure, no one is culpable, and no one is put to shame.

Ichi wo kiite jū wo shiru: "To be mentally acute." (Lit., "To know ten from hearing one.") Many intelligent people can infer the whole from a part. English parallel: A word to the wise is sufficient.

Ichiji ga banji: "One thing suggests all the rest." (Lit., "From one thing, ten thousand things.") In this and many other proverbs the words *"ban"* or *"man,"* literally "ten thousand," means "all" or "many."

Ie wo michibata ni tsukureba sannen narazu: "If you build a house by the side of the road, it will not be completed in three years." For every passer-by will offer advice, with the result that the plan is changed, and the house will not be quickly built. Thus, one who only listens to the opinion of others and does not have his own will never be successful in anything he does.

Issun no mushi ni mo gobu no tamashii: "Even a one-inch insect has a five-tenths-of-an-inch soul." Therefore, one should treat fairly even the humblest person. English parallel: Tread on a worm and it will turn.

Kajin wa inagara ni shite meishō wo shiru: "Poets without traveling know places of note." They are able to do this through their intuition and power of imagination. People who boast of their unusual reasoning power quote this proverb.

Kajin wa tōtokarazu-shite kōi ni majiwaru: "Even poets of no rank mingle with people of high rank." Poets, because of their talent and ability are highly respected and thus may associate with people of high social standing. A good example is the New Year poetry contest, in which people of all grades of society participate.

Kokoro no oni ga mi wo semeru: "The pangs of conscience." (Lit., "The devil in one's heart accuses oneself.") English parallel: A guilty conscience needs no accuser.

Kyo wa ki wo utsu: "Man is the creature of his environment." (Lit., "Your place of abode directs your spirit.") In the above proverb, the word *"kyo"* is an abbreviation for *"kyosho"* (dwelling place) or *"jūkyo"* (residence). The proverb teaches that man is often affected by the condition of his surroundings.

Muri ga tōreba dōri hikkomu: "When unreasonableness passes along reason draws back." The two cannot exist together. English parallel: Where might is master, justice is servant.

Nikkō wo minu uchi wa kekkō to iu na: "Don't say 'magnificent' (*kekkō*) until you have seen Nikkō." In the town of Nikkō, about ninety miles northwest of Tokyo, is the famous and pompously beautiful shrine sacred to the spirit of Tokugawa Ieyasu, the first military dictator or *"shōgun"* of the powerful Tokugawa family that controlled Japan for some two hundred and fifty years prior to the opening of that country to Western nations. The numerous buildings of the shrine are lavishly ornate with the wood carvings, paintings, and sculpture of famous artists of that day. Hence, the origin of the proverb: "If you have not seen Nikkō, don't use the word *'kekkō.'*" The word *"kekkō"* may be variously translated "magnificent," "excellent," or "superb." English parallel: See Naples and die.

Saigetsu hito wo matazu: "Years and months do not wait for man." Hence, do the best you can each day. English parallel: Time and tide wait for no man. The Japanese proverb is probably taken from the English one.

Saigetsu nagaruru ga gotoshi: "Time flies swiftly." (Lit., "Years and months are like a flowing stream.") They go by so silently and swiftly one hardly realizes their passing. English parallel: Time passes like the wind.

Sendan wa futaba yori kanbashii (kōbashii): "Talent displays itself even in early childhood." (Lit., "The sandalwood tree is fragrant from the time it puts forth its first two young leaves.") Where there is genius it is early recognizable.

Shihyaku-shi no byō yori hin no byō: "The disease of poverty is the worst of all maladies." (Lit., "Worse than the four hundred and four illnesses is the disease of poverty.") The hard and rigorous life of the poverty stricken is bitterly resented by the Japanese, who are very sensitive to conditions around them.

Sumajiki mono wa miya-zukae: "The position of a government official is really an unenviable one." (Lit., "Imperial Court service is not to be envied.") Because it is time consuming and full of cares in spite of its exalted position. English parallel: Far from court, far from care.

Tōtoi tera wa mon kara shireru: "A person's worth may be known by his looks and speech." (Lit., "An exalted temple is known by its gate.") This is the same proverb as *"Tattoi tera wa mon kara,"* discussed on p. 181. English parallel: A tree is known by its fruit.

Uta ni shishō nashi: "In composing poetry you need no teacher." Since the art of poetry is the product of genius you either have the gift or do not have it, so instruction is of little use. English parallel: A poet is born, not made.

Uta wa tenchi wo ugokasu: "Poetry has tremendous power." (Lit., "Poetry moves heaven and earth.") Truth and sincerity, set forth in beautiful language, is all powerful.

Zatō mo Kyō e noboru: "Even a blind man goes up to Kyoto." This cultural and religious capital of Japan offers so many attractions to rural people in the way of sight-seeing that even a blind man is tempted to go up there. Note that in Japan, you always "go up" to the capital, irrespective of the elevation of your domicile or its compass direction from Kyoto or Tokyo. As the seat of government and the residence of the Emperor, the capital is always above every other city and town in Japan.

SHAME

THERE ARE PERHAPS no more shame-conscious people in the world than the Japanese. They are extremely sensitive to reprimand or ridicule. This has been inculcated from early childhood. The threat to a Japanese child, "If you do or don't do that, people will laugh at you," is a greater deterrent than the American mother's threat, "If you are not good, I'll call the cop!" Most Japanese are very self-conscious. They think the whole world is watching them, and they try to act in such a way that society will commend them. Their whole ethical system is built on the approval or disapproval of society. They are unusually sensitive to criticism and fear more than anything else being made the butt of a joke or the subject for censure, for then they would "lose face." This self-esteem or face, which is so important to all Japanese has been defined as "a confidence that the character which the world sees in one, conforms more or less to the character that one wishes to display."

Early in the 1880's, Mr. James M. Gardiner, who was a member of the Episcopal Mission in Japan and teacher of English in the St. Paul's High School (now St. Paul's University) in Tokyo, had occasion to correct one of his students for misbehaviour in class. The student, Kobayashi Hikigoro, became furiously angry but hid his feelings until an appropriate time when revenge could be had on the American teacher who had put him to shame and caused loss of face before the whole class. Such an occasion presented itself in 1885 when the entire school gave a farewell party in a restaurant to Mr. and Mrs. Gardiner, who were returning on furlough to the United States. After a delicious Japanese dinner had been served and various farewell speeches made, there came the time for entertainmnt. Young Kobayashi, who was an expert swordsman and the possessor of a fine ancestral blade, volunteered to do a sword dance. With blood-curdling yells and terrifying leaps, the student with bared blade advanced towards Mr. Gardiner, who was seated on the floor in the place of honor, slashing to pieces the matting directly in front and on either side of the teacher and missing his face and head by mere fractions of an inch. Fascinated by the whole performance, the American sat perfectly still, nor did he flinch when the sword flashed perilously close. Fifteen years later, Mr. Kobayashi, who had in the meantime become a prominent churchman and a faithful friend of the Gardiners, gave that same sword to his beloved teacher and told him that he, Kobayashi, had intended to kill him in the course of the dance that night, after which he would immediately commit suicide, but since Mr. Gardiner had not dodged or shown any sign of fear, he could not bring himself to carry out his design. Although in his student days Kobayashi Hikigoro was an obstreperous gang leader in the school, he later became one of the finest clergymen in the Japanese Episcopal Church, and from 1902 until his death in 1942, the beloved principal of St. Margaret's School for Girls in Tokyo. Thus, did the wild young student who had "lost face" gain great face years later, and was held in high esteem by Japanese and Americans alike.

Atama ḳara mizu wo ḳaḳerareta yō: "As if one had been doused with cold water from his head (to his feet)!" This expression describes the feelings of a person who has been reprimanded and thus put to shame.

Atama ni hi ga tsuita yō: "As if one's head were set on fire." This is a figurative phrase for confusion and consternation.

Furuḳizu wa itami yasui: "Old wounds easily become painful." That is, people are sensitive about past failures.

Gojippo wo motte hyappo wo warō: "It's all the same whether it be fifty or a hundred steps." (Lit., "To run fifty paces and laugh at him who runs a hundred.") This proverb, which is often quoted in the abbreviated form *"Gojippo hyappo"* ("Fifty steps, one hundred steps") is believed to have come from a remark of the Chinese sage, Mencius, who told of how a soldier who had fled fifty steps laughed at another who had fled only a short distance farther. This saying may be applied to one who laughs at another in ridiculous circumstances, though he himself is in a position almost equally ridiculous. English parallels: The pot calls the kettle black. Six of one and half a dozen of the other.

Haḳuhyō wo fumu ga gotoshi: "To be fearful and undecided what to do." (Lit., "As if walking on thin ice.")

Haḳuhyō wo fumu ḳoḳochi ga suru: "To feel as if treading on thin ice." This proverb is a slightly different version of the preceding one. It may have originated from the well-known English proverb: To walk on thin ice.

Hiḳare-mono no ḳo-uta: "A false show of courage." (Lit., "The dragged-off person's little song.") The mere bravado of a convict who sings or hums a popular air as he is being dragged off to execution. By showing that he is not afraid he does not lose face before his fellows.

Homerareru yori soshirareru na: "Rather than be praised, try not to be slandered." This is an exhortation to avoid anything that might bring criticism from other people. As a race the Japanese are extremely critical and also very susceptible to criticism.

Idobata no chawan: "A risky undertaking." (Lit., "A tea cup on the edge of the well.") This popular saying is often used to describe many precarious situations.

Inochi nagakereba haji ōshi: "Life has many disgraces." (Lit., "A long life has many shames.") This proverb of Chinese origin teaches that the longer a man lives the more chance he has to experience shame. English parallel: Long life has many miseries.

Karite kita neko no yō: "Like a borrowed cat." A cat borrowed from its master becomes quiet and inactive when brought under the roof of a man who needs its services. This expression is used to describe a person who keeps very quiet before company; often because he is ashamed to reveal his ignorance for fear that he will be ridiculed or censured.

Katawara ni itai: "To be ashamed (of something)." (Lit., "To feel pain in the side.")

Kiku wa ittoki no haji, kikanu wa isshō no haji: "To ask is a temporary shame, not to ask a life-long shame." In making inquiries a Japanese will often start with the apologetic phrase: *"Shitsurei desu ga . . ."* ("It's very rude of me, but . . .") Having then apologized for his ignorance, he will seek the desired information. English parallel: Be brave to ask so as to learn.

Kiku wa ichiji no haji, kikanu wa matsudai no haji: "To inquire is a temporary shame, not to inquire an eternal shame." To ask a person about what you do not know may make you ashamed for only a moment, but to remain ignorant will make you ashamed for a long time.

Kurushii toki wa mi hitotsu: "When in pain it's best to be alone." So that others will not see your suffering and you be put to shame. Thus, as part of his stoical nature, a Japanese will frequently smile and laugh when he is suffering deeply either physical or emotional pain.

Kurayami no haji wo akarumi ni mochidasu na: "Don't expose to the light shameful things committed in the dark." To bring to public notice a scandal which should be kept secret for the sake of honor and decency, is considered by the Japanese to be very foolish. English parallel: Don't wash your dirty linen in public.

Mi no hodo wo shire: "Know your own limitations." The word *"hodo"* means not only "limitation" but also "one's position" or "one's social status." Hence, the above proverb has the wider meaning of: "Don't get into an embarrassing situation by attempting something that is beyond your ability or social standing."

Naga-iki sureba haji ōshi: "A long life has many shames." This proverb is slightly different in form but identical in meaning to *"Inochi nagakereba haji ōshi,"* above. English parallel: To live long is to outlive much.

Nieyu wo nomaseru: "To betray shamefully somebody's confidence"; or "to make a person suffer a harrowing humiliation." (Lit., "To make a person drink boiling water.") In old Japan such a procedure was sometimes used as a form of torture to obtain a confession from a prisoner or subject.

Okujō oku wo kasu: "To construct a roof over a roof." That is, to do work that has already been done by another person or firm, thus subjecting one to ridicule. English parallel: To paint the lily.

Rengi de hara kiru: "To attempt to do something in an ineffective way." (Lit., "to commit *harakiri* with a pestle.") Naturally, it would be awkward as well as impossible to disembowel oneself with as blunt an instrument as a wooden pestle. To attempt to do so would expose a person to ridicule or censure, than which to a Japanese there is nothing more fearful.

Shirazaru wa ayamareru ni masaru: "It is better to be ignorant than to be mistaken." English parallel: Better untaught than mistaught.

Shiranu ga Hotoke: "Ignorance is bliss." (Lit., "Not to know is Buddha-like.") That is to say, it is sometimes best for a man not to know about a scandalous affair, lest if he did he would be subject to ridicule.

Shiroi ha wo miseru na: "Don't laugh in public." (Lit., "Don't show your white teeth.") This is a warning not to open the mouth in laughter, for people will make light of a risible person. Old-fashioned Japanese, especially women and the well-bred, will cover their mouths with their hands when laughing or picking the teeth. English parallel: A maid that laughs is half taken.

Tabi no haji wo kakizute: "You may scratch away shame committed while on a journey." This well-known proverb states that during a journey or while away from home, discipline can be relaxed and shameful things may be indulged in with impunity. With the relaxation of discipline, Japanese travelers and military men did many shameful things abroad from 1930 to 1945 which they would never do at home. English parallel: Once over the borders one may do anything.

Tou wa ittan no haji, towanu wa isshō no haji: "To inquire is a moment's shame, not to inquire is a life-long shame." English parallel: He that nothing questioneth, nothing learneth.

Tora no o wo fumu ga gotoshi: "A feeling of extreme dread of some danger." (Lit., "Like treading on a tiger's tail").

Umi no mono tomo, yama no mono tomo tsukanai: "The true nature of the thing is not clear." (Lit., "It belongs neither to the sea nor to the mountain.") The above expression applied to a man, means that he is still an unknown entity. It causes a Japanese much embarrassment when he cannot determine what niche in society a man occupies or should occupy. English parallel: It is neither flesh nor fish.

Zashiki e inu wo ageta yō: "Like a dog taken up on the matting floor of the drawing room." This saying describes the stupid look of surprise and embarrassment of a person at finding himself in an unusual situation.

SIMPLICITY

THE JAPANESE ARE ADMIRERS and practicers of the simple life. This can be observed in their art as well as in their daily living conditions. Their love for neatness is seen in their homes, their gardens, and their culture, where simplicity is studiously cultivated. Ostentation is shunned as vulgar, and the display of wealth is considered extremely bad taste. Much admired is the man who in his life and deeds displays Spartan-like self-discipline and will power. Through frugal living the Japanese believe that strong character and robust bodies develop.

Asameshi mae no shigoto: "A task that can be done in a short time." (Lit., "A piece of work before breakfast.") Any job that can be done quickly and easily is spoken of as "a pre-breakfast job."

Hari no ana(mimi) ḳara ten nozoḳu: "To peep at the heaven through the hole (ear) of a needle." This is said of a person who takes a narrow view of things.

Ichi mono areba ichi rui wo sou: "If you have one thing you have one added trouble." Hence, to avoid trouble and care have no possessions at all. English parallel: Much coin, much care.

Ido ni zashite ten wo miru: "To get a limited outlook." (Lit., "To look at the heavens from the bottom of a well.")

Ido no ḳawazu taiḳai wo shirazu: "A frog in the well knows not the ocean." This saying is frequently used when speaking of a man of narrow experience. English parallel: Home-keeping youths have homely wits.

Mandō mizu wo utta yō na shizuḳesa de atta: "The whole hall is as quiet as though sprinkled with water." English parallel: A pin might be heard if dropped.

Meshi-tsubu de tai tsuru: "To make a big gain with a small sacrifice." (Lit., "To catch a sea bream with a grain of boiled rice.")

Mugi-meshi de ḳoi tsuru: "To gain much with small investment." (Lit., "To catch carp with boiled barley.") The Japanese regard the carp as the noblest of fresh-water fish and boiled barley as the cheapest of food. English parallel: To throw a sprat to catch a whale.

Natsu no mushi ḳōri wo shirazu: "The summer insect knows not ice." Thus is described a man who has had few experiences in life, and knows little of the world.

Seijin yume nashi: "Holy men sleep dreamlessly." Because they have no guilty conscience and generally are so poor no thief would enter their homes.

Senjōjiḳi de nete mo tatami ichi mai: "Man's actual needs are small." (Lit., "Though you sleep in a thousand-mat room, you occupy only one mat.") The standard "mat" *(tatami)* by which all Japanese rooms are measured is three feet by six feet. This is considered the sleep area needed for one person. Man's material comforts need not be many in order to live happily.

Shōjin tama wo idaite tsumi ari: "The little man in embracing a jewel has sinned." That is, even insignificant people if they have only one talent should use it. Each person should make use of his opportunities, no matter how small or seemingly insignificant. English parallel: No sweat, no sweet.

Taiken wa taigu ni nitari: "A great sage is often taken for a great fool." Because of his simple tastes and ways of speech, a person of great intelligence often outwardly resembles a fool.

Yoshi no zui kara tenjō nozoku: "To judge things from a narrow and limited experience." (Lit., "To look at the heavens through the tube of a reed.")

Yoso no gochisō yori uchi no chazuke: "Better than a feast elsewhere is a meal at home of tea and rice." English parallel: Dry bread at home is better than roast meat abroad.

SUBMISSIVENESS

IT HAS ALREADY BEEN POINTED OUT that the Japanese are natural collectivists, and gregarious in their activities. Their willingness to be regimented is shown in their unquestioning obedience to superiors and their acceptance of those in authority. For many generations the Japanese have placed much emphasis on conformity, and individualism has been discouraged. This has led to the development of a submissive people. This trait made the work of the Allied occupation forces comparatively easy, once General MacArthur and his staff were recognized as responsible authority for the development of a new Japan. With the withdrawal of the occupation forces and the increasing emphasis upon individualism and freedom, many of the younger generation have gone to the extreme of mistaking liberty for license, thus leading to a plethora of strikes, demonstrations, and other social disturbances. University students have been especially active in such unsocial behaviour, but the majority of the people are law-abiding and submissive.

Atama wo sageru: "To be submissive; to bow." (Lit., "To lower the head.") This submissiveness does not necessarily imply politeness.

Ayamatte aratamuru ni habakaru nakare: "Don't hesitate to acknowledge a mistake and correct it." This proverb is taken from the Analects of Confucius. English parallel: It is never too late to mend.

Chikara wa seigi: This is the Japanese version of the English proverb "Might is right."

Chimmoku wa shōdaku no uchi: "Silence is part of consent." This is taken from the English proverb "Silence gives consent."

Deshi wa shi ni masarazu: "The disciple does not surpass his teacher." This proverb denies the possibility of any disciple ever excelling his master, which if true would prevent any improvement or advance in the world. English parallel: The stream can never rise above its source.

Haritsumeta yumi wa itsuka yurumu: "The tightly strung bow will relax in time." This teaches that a state of tension cannot be endured for a long time. English parallel: A bow long bent at last waxeth weak.

Hinata no kōri: "Ice in the sunshine." This expression is used to indicate a case or conditions where things gradually get dissolved. Problems when left alone may slowly be solved.

Jiko no hombun wo mamore: "You yourself do your duty." That is, watch yourself that you always do your duty to superiors and those in authority. English parallel: Let the cobbler stick to his last.

Jū yoku gō wo seisu: "Yielding (lit., gentleness) well controls stiffness." This truth, taken from Chinese writings, is well exemplified in *jūdō (jūjitsu),* the art of self-defense, in which the stiff strength of a more powerful antagonist is used to defeat him. It has also many examples in Japanese history, not the least of which was the attitude of the Japanese people and government during the Occupation by the American military government. English parallels: A soft answer turns away wrath. She stoops to conquer.

Kasei wa tora yori mo takeshii: "A tyrannical government is fiercer than a tiger." A despotic ruler is more to be feared than the most terrible wild beast.

Kussezareba nobizu: "Without bending, there is no growth." There is no extension or progress without yielding. The Japanese by carrying out this precept after their surrender in World War II have made great advances socially, politically, and economically.

Makeru ga kachi: "To lose is to gain." By yielding he conquers. Anyone who can patiently endure the shame of defeat can manage finally to obtain victory. This is well exemplified in the progress of Japan since her surrender in the war twenty years ago.

Minoru ine wa ho wo tareru: "Ripening rice plants hang down their heads." That is, a man of great learning or character acts and speaks modestly. He is submissive to authority, though he may be superior to those over him. English parallel: The boughs that bear most hang lowest.

Nagai mono ni wa makareyo: "Let a long object wrap around you." That is, submit meekly even to an injustice, if done by a person who has greater power or influence than you. This proverb still has a strong hold upon Japanese thinking. It partially explains why the people and government meekly submitted to the Occupation by the Allied forces, and even co-operated with them. English parallel: Kings have long arms.

Oriru yori nabike: "Better to bend than to break." The bamboo and the willow are both bending plants, much admired and used by the Japanese.

Ryōba hito-muchi: "A word to the wise is sufficient." (Lit., "A fine horse, one whip.") An intelligent man will carry out the instructions of his superior, even though the orders are brief.

Ryōba wa ben-ei wo mite yuku: "A fine horse runs on by observing the shadows of the whip." A wise man works satisfactorily with only general instructions from his superior or employer.

Ringen ase no gotoshi: "The Emperor's word is like sweat." It is final and cannot be recalled. Hence, submission is the only alternative.

Tenshi nigon nashi: "The Sovereign (lit., 'Child of Heaven') has no two words." The ruler's word when once uttered cannot be altered. Thus, when in August, 1945, the Emperor's orders to surrender to the Allied Powers were broadcast over the radio and published in the newspapers, the Japanese promptly obeyed, although some in the armed forces wished to continue the fight.

SUPERSTITION

THOUGH THE JAPANESE are a highly educated and literate people, superstitious beliefs and practices have long been dominant and to a certain extent still prevail, as indicated by the proverbs and sayings in this section, which follow under appropriate headings.

ANIMALS:

Asa no kumo wa kataki to omotte mo korosu na: "Don't kill a spider in the morning even though you may think it is the enemy on whom you have sworn vengeance." This is because a spider in the morning portends good luck. According to the Buddhist doctrine of the transmigration of the soul, a spider or any other animal might contain the soul that in a previous existence was a man or woman. For example, in many rural areas snakes living in the rafters of a farmer's home are not molested, in the belief that they may contain the spirits of some deceased member of the family.

Ashita no koto wo iu to tenjō no nezumi ga warau: "If you talk about tomorrow's matters, the rats above the ceiling will laugh." Here, again, the spirits of ancestors who know more about the future than mere humans, and may be embodied in the rats of the ceiling, will mock the people of the house who talk too much about plans for the morrow.

Baishaku sezareba shi-shite namekuji to naru: "If you do not take the part of a 'go-between' you will turn into a slug after death." This saying emphasizes the Japanese belief that a man must arrange another man's marriage at least once in a lifetime. Here we have also the Buddhist idea of the transmigration of the soul. The role of a go-between or matchmaker *(baishaku-nin)* is so tiring and also so important, that if a person shirks that responsibility, his soul at death will be reborn in the body of one of the lowest and laziest of creatures —a slug.

Ie no naka ni tori haireba fuku kitaru: "A bird flying into the house brings good luck." This belief is based on the homonym *"tori,"* which may mean either *"bird"* or *"to take,"* depending on the written Chinese ideograph used.

Itachi ni michi wo kirareta toki, ishi wo nagenu to bakasareru: "When a weasel cuts across your path, he will bewitch you if you don't throw a stone at him." It is believed that by throwing a stone at weasels, foxes, and badgers, the evil influences which such animals exert on man can be overcome.

Iwashi no atama mo shinjin kara: "Better have faith in something, even though it be the head of a sardine." That is, you may worship anything you wish, so long as you have faith in it. A sardine's head is often nailed over the lintel of the front door in the belief that it will drive away evil influences.

Karasu ga naku to kyōji ga aru: "The cawing of a crow presages some calamity." It is interesting to note that in both the East as well as the West the cries of a raven or crow are believed by the superstitious to be a portent of evil.

Kitsune ni tsumamareta yō: "As if possessed (bewitched) by a fox." This phrase is used when a person seems quite at a loss what to do. For a full discussion of fox bewitchment see the author's book, *Inari: Its Origin, Development and Nature,* in Transactions of the Asiatic Society of Japan, Second Series, Vol. XII, pp. 49–54.

Kitsune no yome-iri: "The wedding procession of the fox-bride." This expression is used to describe a shower when the sun is shining. English parallel: The devil is beating his wife.

Mayu ni tsuba wo nureba kitsune ni bakasarenu: "If you put spittle on your eyebrows, the fox will not bewitch you." In many countries, including Japan, there is the belief that spittle has magic or medicinal value. Hence, the wetting of the eyebrows with saliva would strengthen the eyes and enable the person to see the fox better and thus not be bewitched by him. See the Bible (Mark 7:33 and 8:23) for instances where Jesus Christ used spittle in healing blind men.

Neko ga kao wo arau to ame ga furu: "When a cat washes her face rain will fall." From long years of observation, men have noticed that just before a rain, cats will wash their faces and birds preen their feathers.

Neko wo koroseba shichidai tataru: "If you kill a cat it will haunt you and your family for seven generations." The cat is believed by the Japanese to be a most vindictive creature.

Oya wo niramu to karei ni naru: "If you scowl at your parents you will turn into a sole." As the sole has eyes on one side only, so a disrespectful glare by children on their parents makes the former liable to turn into that fish. This superstitious belief is a warning to children always to show proper respect to their elders.

Rainen no koto wo iu to oni ga warau: "If you talk of next year the devils will laugh." English parallel: Next year is the devil's joke.

Shakutori-mushi ni shaku wo torareru to shinu: "If you are measured by the looper-worm (measuring-worm) you will die." This belief is still held in many rural areas.

Suzume kaichū ni itte hamaguri to naru: "Sparrows dropping into the sea turn into clams." This is a popular and widely-held superstition.

Tokage wo yubi-sasu to yubi ga kusaru: "If you point at a lizard, your finger will rot." This saying is quite current among Japanese children.

Tori-kage ga shōji ni sasu to kyaku ga kuru: "When the shadow of a bird falls upon the sliding paper door, guests will come." This saying probably originated from the double meaning of *"tori,"* which according to the way it is written may mean "bird" or "take, receive, or get." A guest always brings a gift with him for someone in the home. Hence, the words "to receive," "a gift," and "guest" are closely associated in the Japanese mind. Thus the shadow of a bird on the translucent white paper of a sliding door would clearly indicate the coming of a guest. This, to Westerners a far-fetched idea, is quite understandable and logical to Japanese. See the explanation of *"Ie no naka ni tori haireba fuku kitaru,"* p. 221.

Tsubame ga su kuwanu toshi wa kaji ni au: "In the year when swallows do not return to their old nest, there will be a fire in that house." This saying is widely believed in Japan, where in rural areas swallows frequently nest under the eaves of the house.

Yoru kuchibue wo fuku to hebi ga deru: "If you whistle at night, snakes will come forth."

Yoru no kumo wa oya to omotte mo korose: "Kill any spider you find at night, even if you think it is your parent." A night spider is considered bad luck. In this and other proverbs we have the idea of transmigration of the soul taught in Buddhism. See *"Asa no kumo wa kataki to omotte mo korosu na,"* p. 221.

BAD LUCK OMENS:

Cha wo kakete asameshi wo kū to shusse shinai: "If you pour tea on hot rice at breakfast, you will never advance in the world." This superstition probably originated because it was considered unseemly to slight heaven's gift—a hot meal of rice—by pouring tea on it.

Hanao no kireru wa fukitsu no chō: "When a sandal strap (clog thong) breaks it is an evil omen." The snapping of a clog thong or sandal strap is believed to foretell an evil accident. Hence the thongs or straps are frequently examined and carefully replaced before they break. No doubt in times past serious accidents have resulted from the sudden breaking of a clog or sandal thong.

Hōki de butareru to sannen ikinai: "If a man is beaten by a broomstick he will not live three more years." Probably he will die of shame and fright.

Hōki (Hashi) ga oreru to engi ga warui: "When a broomstick (chopstick) breaks it is a bad omen."

Hon wo fumu to bachi ga ataru: "If you tread on a book you will receive divine retribution." This saying probably originated to inculcate respect for learning and scholarship.

Ichi zen meshi wo kuwanu mono: "A person must not eat only one bowl of rice." For to do so would recall disagreeable associations with death; since one bowl of rice is always placed for the dead, at the family Buddhist altar.

Kiri hitoha: "One leaf of paulownia." The leaves of this tree fall early in autumn and thus announce the end of the hot and the beginning of the cold season. Hence, the fall of a single leaf of the paulownia may signify the coming of some evil or ill luck.

Kushi wo hiroeba ku wo hirō: "To pick up a comb is to pick up affliction." To pick up a comb from the ground or floor is believed by the Japanese to bring bad luck. This thought probably originated from sound of the syllables for *"kushi"* (comb) when pronounced separately, *"ku"* means "suffering," and *"shi"* means "death." Hence, to pick up a comb *("kushi")* may also involve picking up "suffering and death." Thus, through a play on words, a comb becomes a fearsome thing.

Kushi wo hirō nara, funde kara hiroe: "If you pick up a comb, pick it up after you have stepped on it." This act is believed to drive out the evil spirit in a comb, thus making its retrieval safe.

Tera no ji-nai de korobu to sannen no uchi ni shinu: "The person who falls down in the grounds of a temple will die within three years." Because of this widely-held belief, people walking within the precincts of a temple do so with extreme care.

Yoru shitsunai wo haku to bimbō suru: "If you sweep your room at night you will become poor." This proverb was probably invented to make people clean their rooms in the morning. However, on New Year's Eve the rooms are swept and prepared for the following day's celebration.

Yume wa yoru katarazu: "Don't talk of dreams at night." This superstitious taboo is perhaps based on the fact that talking of dreams at night is conducive to having more dreams and nightmares when you go to sleep that evening.

BODY PARTS:

Asa tsume wo kireba hi ni haji wo kaku: "If you trim your nails in the morning you will be put to shame that day." This saying may have been started to serve as a warning against the impropriety of so doing.

Ashi no ura ga kayui no wa ii zenchō: "When the bottom of your foot itches it is a good omen."

Atama no ōkii hito wa un ga ii: "A man with a big head has a good destiny."

Ena to issho ni ōgi wo uzumereba, sono ko shusse suru: "A child whose placenta is buried with a folding fan will advance in the world." This popular superstition may have started from the fact that in ancient Japan the folding fan was often the symbol of leisure and authority.

Ha no nuketa yume wa fukitsu: "It is a bad omen to dream that your tooth falls out."

Hitai no hiroi mono wa un ga ii: "A person with a broad forehead will have good luck."

Kebukai mono wa iro-bukai: "A hairy person is sexy."

Kami no ke wo moyasu to kichigai ni naru: "If you burn the hair of your head you will become insane." This superstition may have arisen from the belief in ancient Japan that the hair symbolizes the sexual or adorned life. See the preceding proverb.

Kuchibue wo fuku to bimbō suru: "If you whistle you will become poor." This is a warning against the habit of whistling, which is considered flippant. During my thirty-five years of residence in Japan I have heard very little whistling.

Mimi ga kayui to ii koto ga aru: "When your ear itches good things will come."

Mimitabo no ōkii hito wa un ga ii: "People with big ear lobes are lucky." It is interesting to note that the pictorial representations of the Seven Gods of Luck show them to have large ear lobes.

Mune ni te wo atete neruto unasareru: "If you sleep with your hands upon your breast you will have bad dreams."

Tsuki-akari de hari-ana wo tōsu to meshō (shiryoku) ga yoku naru: "If you thread a needle in the moonlight your eyesight will improve."

Tsume wo moyasu to kichigai ni naru: "If you burn your nail parings you will become insane."

Uso wo tsukeba Emma ni shita wo nukareru: "If you tell a lie you will have your tongue plucked out by Yama." Yama is the Sanskrit name of the presiding judge in hell, which in Japanese is pronounced *"Emma."* The above proverb is often quoted to children to warn them against lying.

Yoru mimi no ana ga kayui to yokujitsu moraimono ga aru: "If your earholes itch at night you will receive a gift the next day."

DISEASES:

Akai mono wo tsukaeba hōsō karoshi: "A person who makes use of red things will have a light case only of smallpox." This proverb originated before vaccination was practiced and smallpox was quite prevalent. Red suggests blood, the principle of life and health, warmth and cheerfulness. It is a very dynamogenous color; hence, it was believed in ancient times to counteract the effects of severe disease. In old Japan, infants and aged persons wore red to give them added protection and strength at such critical times of their lives.

Budō wo ueru to byōnin ga taenai: "If you plant a grapevine (about your house) there will never be an end of sick people." This saying may have come from the fact that a large and heavy vine on the house is likely to make the building too shady, dark and damp; this giving rise to unhealthy occupants.

Netsubyō ni kakattara yotsu-suji ni wara-ningyō wo sutero: "If you are taken with a fever throw away at the crossroad a straw effigy (of yourself)." This belief and practice is still found in rural areas, for I have often at crossroads found such effigies. The belief in contagious magic is quite common among primitive people in many other parts of the world.

THE FAMILY:

Akago yonaki suru toki niwatori no e wo toguchi ni hareba naki yamu: "When an infant cries at night, paste on the door the picture of a barnyard fowl, and he will stop crying." I have frequently seen such pictures pasted on doorways, especially in rural sections of Japan.

Akai ishi wo hirō to oya ni hanareru: "If you pick up a red stone you will part from your parents." The Japanese word for "stone" *(ishi)* may also mean "will" or "volition," depending on the Chinese ideographs used to write it. Red being a dynamogenous color, as previously explained, the child who picks up such a stone would probably have his will power strengthened, assert his independence, and leave for parts where he would no longer be under parental control.

Hi itazura suru to ko wa ne-shōben wo suru: "A child who plays with fire will wet the bed while sleeping." This is a severe warning to children against playing with fire. Because of early and rigorous toilet training of children, bed wetting is considered a matter of shame by parents.

Masu no soko wo tatakeba maigo ga mitsukaru: "If you strike the bottom of a measure, the missing child will be discovered." The *"masu"* is a square boxlike measure of capacity, whose pronunciation forms the last part or abbreviation of the verbs *"orimasu" ("irimasu")* —"he is here"—and *"arimasu"*—"we have him." Thus through sympathetic magic and the play on words, it is believed that the child who has wandered off can be located.

Mutsuki wo soto ni yoboshi suru to, ko ga yonaki suru: "If diapers are left hanging out to dry overnight, the child will cry that evening." This saying is quoted to discourage mothers from leaving diapers overnight on the line. It probably originated from an early belief that the cold night air on the diapers would make the sleeping child so uncomfortable that he would cry out. This may also be termed sympathetic magic.

Nagai no kyaku wa hōki wo tateru to kaeru: "The long-staying-guest will leave if you stand a broom upside down." This practice is still indulged in by many Japanese, but chiefly by those in rural areas.

Nagai no kyaku wa geta ni kyū wo sueru to kaeru: "The long-staying guest will leave if you apply moxa to his clogs." If you cauterize the footware of the guest who overstays his welcome, it is believed that through sympathetic magic you will also burn the soles of his feet, and he will "hot foot it" for home. This popular proverb and superstition is still widely practiced.

Naku ko wa sodatsu: "A crying child thrives." Probably because it is good exercise for the child, though hard on the ears of others in the home.

Otoko no ko ni onna no na wo tsuke, onna no ko ni otoko no na wo tsukeru to, jōbu ni sodatsu: "If you give female names to boys and male names to girls, they will grow up in good health." This practice is still followed in some rural areas, to mislead the demons of disease and bad luck.

Oya ni ninu ko wa onikko: "Children who do not resemble their parents are 'devils' children.' " The word *"onikko"* (devils' children) is also used to indicate children who are unworthy of their parents.

Oya wo tataku to te ga magaru: "If you beat your parents, your arm will grow crooked." This is a warning against showing disrespect to parents.

Tabi haite neru to oya no shinime ni aenu: "If you sleep with your socks on you will miss your parent's deathbed." The word *"shinime"* translated "deathbed" is literally "death-eyes" and has reference to the duty of the children to close the eyes of their dead parent. Not to be present when your parent breathes his last is considered lacking in filial piety and a dire calamity. The proverb quoted above may have originated to discourage the wearing of socks in bed for fear of soiling the bedding. Another possible explanation is the Japanese word for socks, *"tabi,"* which may also mean "trip" or "journey," according to the Chinese ideograph used for writing it. Hence, if a man persists in keeping on his *"tabi"* both night and day, he may find himself on a trip and away from home when he should be there by his dying parent.

Yūkoku kodomo ga sawagu to ame ga furu: "When children romp in the evening, it will rain."

FOOD AND DRINK:

Asa cha-bashira ga tatsu to engi ga ii: "A tea leaf floating upright in the cup in the morning means good fortune." It may also indicate the coming of a visitor. A similar English superstition is current.

Cha wo nomu to iro ga kuroku naru: "If you drink tea you will have a dark complexion." This is a very common belief. Hence, Japanese women who esteem a fair complexion drink far less and generally weaker tea than men.

Doyō no ushi no hi ni unagi wo kū to kusuri: "Eels eaten on ox's day during the dog days are medicine." This is a well-known and widely practiced superstition. On such days sea-food restaurants do a thriving business in grilled eels. The ox is the second of the signs in the Chinese zodiac, which are each assigned to every recurrent series of twelve days as well as twelve years. The signs are: rat, ox, tiger, hare, dragon, snake, horse, ram, monkey, cock, dog, and boar.

Kiji wo kueba sannen no furu kizu mo deru: "If you eat pheasant's flesh, three-year-old wounds will open." Since the pheasant has a very fierce temper, eating the flesh of the bird is thought to irritate the old scars of the eater.

Kutte sugu ni neru to ushi ni naru: "If you lie down right after eating you will turn into an ox." This saying is probably based on observation of cows and oxen who, right after eating, lie down and chew the cud.

Namekuji wo nomu to koe ga yoku naru: "If you swallow a slug your voice will become fine." This proverb is sometimes carried into effect by singers and vocalists in Japan, especially by those who practice or recite lyrical dramas known as *"utai,"* which are taken from *Nō* plays.

Shishi kutta mukui: "To pay dearly for one's follies." (Lit., "The retribution for having eaten wild boar's flesh.") According to popular thought, those who eat wild boar's meat will have pimples on their skin. Most likely the pimples are the result of eating such rich and indigestible food.

Tanin no nomikoshi no cha wo nomu to toshi ga yoru: "To drink tea left in the cup of another person will cause you to become old." This proverb encourages sanitary practices.

GOOD LUCK OMENS:

Koromo wo kaeshite nereba omō hito wo yumemu: "If you sleep with your robe turned inside out, you will dream of your loved one."

Kuwa no ki no sakazuki wo tsukau to chūki senu: "If you use a wine cup made of mulberry wood, you will not be stricken with paralysis."

Mukae sōrei wa kitsu: "It is good luck to meet a funeral procession coming towards you." However, to have such a procession overtake you is held to be very bad luck.

Nokorimono ni fuku ga ari: "There is luck in what remains." I have often had my Japanese host insist on giving me the last helping of food or cake saying: "It is lucky to take the remainder." English parallel: There is luck in the last helping.

Suisho no tama wa mayoke: "A crystal gem will drive away the devil." In medieval Europe there was a similar belief in the power of gems to keep away evil influences.

TIMES AND SEASONS:

Ganjitsu no asa wa shitsunai wo hakanu mono: "Do not sweep the interior of a house on New Year's morning." It is believed that to do so would remove from the house all good fortune.

Higan no chūnichi ni tsutta haze wo kū to chūki senu: "If a person eats gobies caught by angling on the middle day of the spring equinox, he will not get paralysis."

Hiru umareru ko wa chichi ni niru, yoru umareru ko wa haha ni niru: "The child born in the daytime resembles its father, the child born at night resembles the mother."

Nido aru koto wa sando aru: "What has taken place twice will do so thrice." English parallel: Misfortunes never come singly.

O-hyaku-do wo fumu: "To worship a hundred times at a shrine by walking or running back and forth from a given point." (Lit., "To step a hundred times.") It can also mean to call on another person repeatedly to solicit a favor. Even as late as the first quarter of the twentieth century there was so much "red tape" in Japanese government that it was necessary to go many times to village, city, or county offices for such simple matters as the registration of persons, business, land, or other property. There is a famous shrine in the city of Kyoto which is especially patronized by students and scholars. In the ninth century a renowned scholar, Sugawara Michizane, lived in that metropolis, which was then the capital of Japan. He became the favored advisor of two emperors, but his enemies whispered calumnies into the ear of the ruler, who ordered the scholar banished to the island of Tsukushi, the ancient name for Kyushu. Despite this grossly unfair punishment, Sugawara Michizane remained until his death two years later, loyal to his imperial master. Twenty years after his death he was restored to all his honors and given the highest titles. Later, he was deified as the god of learning, and a shrine to his memory was built in northwest Kyoto. To this day, before and during examination periods of schools and colleges, numerous students can be seen running one hundred times around the shrine precincts, in the belief that they will then be successful in their studies.

Women:

Araigami de benjo e yuku to kichigai ni naru: "Women who go to the privy with unarranged washed hair will become insane." (Lit., "With newly-washed hair going to the privy makes you insane.") This superstition is also a maxim to enjoin order and decency in women's habits.

Asa onna (bōzu) ni akinai sureba sono hi rieki ōshi: "If you make a sale to a woman (or priest) in the morning you will profit greatly that day." Many tradespeople go by this saying.

Chijirege no onna wa iro-bukai: "A curly-haired woman is amorous." Prior to World War II straight hair was admired and sought after by most Japanese women, but fashions have changed, and now many women, especially those in large urban areas, go to their hairdressers for *"pamanento"* (permanents).

Hōki wo matagu to nanzan suru: "The woman who steps over a broomstick will have difficult childbirth." This very common superstition may have come from an early warning to keep such articles as broomsticks carefully put away, and not lying on the floor where people may stumble over them.

Rinki onna ni tsuno ga haeru: "Horns will grow on the head of a jealous woman." This saying is based on an earlier superstition that held that a jealous woman would become a demon. Thus, the white paper hood worn by the bride at a Shinto wedding ceremony is called *"Tsuno-kakushi"* (horn-concealer).

Setsuin wo kirei ni sōji suru to osan ga karui: "The woman who keeps the privy clean will have an easy delivery."

Setsuin wo kirei ni sōji suru to utsukushii ko wo umu: "The woman who keeps the privy clean will bear a beautiful child." The two proverbs given above, though based upon superstition, are encouragements to be sanitary.

Toishi wa onna ga matagu to wareru: "When a woman steps over a whetstone it will split." This saying probably originated with the belief in the sacredness of swords which are sharpened on a whetstone, and the periodical uncleanness of women.

SUSPICION

OMNISCIENT ESPIONAGE from 1600 on has kept all Japanese suspicious of every one, even of his own family. There is a general tendency to regard strangers as enemies. Three centuries of dictatorship have made the Japanese compulsive personalities. The Tokugawa police state and to a greater extent the "thought-control police" of modern Japan prior to World War II, had complete information on and control of every person in Japan. Every loyal Japanese was expected to report to the authorities any and everything suspicious that another person said or did, and especially so if that person were a foreigner.

Complete records were kept by the police on every man, woman, and child in Japan. The guardians of the law were extremely busy interrogating people and writing down in their record books the statements made. Thus, there arose a complicated network of spying and counterspying, in the center of which the police held tremendous power. Hence, it is no wonder that the Japanese became an exceedingly suspicious race. One of the first acts of the Allied Occupation officers was to break the throttle-hold of the police and grant freedom of thought, speech, and publication to the people under the new constitution. The younger generation of Japanese are much less suspicious than their elders, but still less free and outgoing than the young people of the United States or Western Europe.

Amari umasugiru (yōsugiru) kara hontō de nai deshō to omoimashita: "Since it was much too good they (he) thought it could not be true." English parallel: Too good to believe.

Ashi ni kizu mochya sasahara hashiru: "A man with a guilty conscience will flee through a plain of bamboo grass." (Lit., "A man with a wound in his foot will run across a bamboo-grass plain.") He will do this even when there is no need to run away. The expressions *"ashi ni kizu motsu"* (lit., "to have a wound in the foot") and *"sune ni kizu motsu"* (lit. "to have a wound in the leg") both have the meaning, "to have a guilty conscience." English parallel: He who is guilty believes that all men speak ill of him.

Asu wa ame, hito wa dorobō: "Expect rain for tomorrow, suspect robbers in other people." That is, don't be too sure about any thing or any person.

Ataru mo hakke, ataranu mo hakke: "It may hit or it may miss —the prediction." It all depends on chance as to whether the divination is accurate or not. Although thousands of Japanese consult diviners, they are rather suspicious of the predictions.

Atsumono ni korite, namasu wo fuku: "Having learned his lesson with hot soup, he blows cold fish salad." English parallels: A scalded cat dreads cold water. A burnt child fears the fire.

Bōzu damaseba shichidai tataru: "If you deceive a Buddhist priest you will be cursed for seven generations." This is because a priest is considered a holy man. Some people say that this proverb depicts the vengeful nature of the priest, who can never forgive treachery on the part of his paramour or anyone else.

Bōzu maru-mōke: "The Buddhist priest makes a complete profit." The priest makes money without investing any capital, using only his round shaven head and his prayers which cost him nothing. The word *"maru"* literally means "round" but should here be translated "entire," "complete," or "whole"; but at the same time the word jocularly suggests the priests shaven "round" head.

Chi ni ite ran wo wasurezu: "In peace do not forget war." As a nation, be suspicious of other peoples and be prepared for war, is the maxim Japan has followed, as shown in their history. English parallel: In fair weather prepare for foul.

Danji ie wo izureba shichi nin no teki ari: "As soon as a man sets out from his house he has seven enemies." A man's home is his castle. As soon as he leaves it, he must be prepared to face innumerable enemies and fight for his very survival. Soldiers also should be ready to face death anywhere and at any time.

Dorobō no tojimari: "Even a robber fastens his door." Everyone tries to secure his own possessions since no one can be trusted.

Fune ni korite koshi wo imu: "Having learned your lesson in a boat, you dislike a palanquin." Both sway and may make a person sick.

Gishin anki wo shōzu (umu): "Suspicion generates dark devils." English parallel: Fear peoples the darkness with monsters.

Hakarigoto wa mitsunaru wo tattobu: "In strategy secrecy is esteemed." It is the highest strategy not to let the enemy know of your plans.

Hanashi hambun ni kike: "Listen to only half of a person's talk." That is, believe only half of what you hear, be it good or evil.

Hashi ni mo bō ni mo kakaranu: "He is not to be caught by bribes or threats." (Lit., "Not to be caught with chopsticks or a club.")

Hebi ni kamarete kusare-nawa ni ojiru: "He who has been bitten by a snake fears a decayed rope." A rotten rope in the grass may often resemble a snake.

Hikui tokoro ni mizu tamaru: "Water collects in a low place."

When any crime is committed, suspicion is often cast on some person of low character.

Hi no nai tokoro ni kemuri wa tatanu: "Where there is no fire, no smoke will rise." This is the Japanese translation of the well-known English proverb: No smoke without fire.

Hito wa mikake ni yoranu mono: "A person is not always what he appears to be." English parallel: Appearances are deceptive.

Hito wo mitara oni to omoe. "When you see a person regard him as a devil." Suspect a devil in any one you meet. One should not be too ready to trust a stranger.

Hito wo mitara dorobō to omoe: "When you see a person, regard him as a robber." Suspect a robber in anyone you meet. It is wise to be suspicious of strangers.

Hiru ni wa me ari, yoru ni wa mimi ari: "Day has its eyes, night has its ears." That is, be careful all the time.

Hitotsu ana no mujina (kitsune): "Badgers (foxes) of the same hole." That is, accomplices of the same plot. This phrase is used when two or more suspicious characters are seen together. English parallel: Birds of a feather flock together.

Homeru hito ni yudan suru na: "Don't be careless of the man who praises you." That is, a flatterer will sometimes take you at a disadvantage.

Ie ni nusubito wo yashinau: "To support thieves in one's own house." Even in your own home there may be dishonest persons, so watch out. English parallel: So many servants, so many thieves.

Ie ni wa nezumi, kuni ni wa nusubito: "Rats in houses, robbers in countries." Be suspicious, for dishonesty is widespread. English parallel: Every mountain has its wolves.

Ja no michi wa hebi: "Snakes follow the way of serpents." Both *"ja"* and *"hebi"* may be translated "snake" or "serpent," for the same Chinese ideograph is used. However, "ja" has also the meaning of a *large* serpent or snake. The significance of the above proverb is that people of the same occupation know each other, especially if it is a dishonest one. English parallel: One devil knows another.

Kabe ni mimi ari, shōji ni me ari: "Walls have ears, paper sliding doors have eyes." Japanese houses are so slightly constructed that often one can easily hear through the wall what is going on in the next room, or peep through a crack or hole in the paper sliding doors that divide one room from another. Because there is so little privacy, one must be very careful of what ones says or does, lest it be reported. The very structure of houses in Japan has contributed to spying and the suspiciousness of the people. English parallel: Walls have ears.

Kabe ni mimi ari, tokuri ni kuchi ari: "Walls have ears, wine bottles have mouths." By plying the wine bottle men have been made to reveal secrets otherwise inaccessible. English parallel: Pitchers have ears.

Kaden ni kutsu wo irezu: "Avoid a compromising situation." (Lit., "Don't put your shoe into a melon patch.") Don't behave in a suspicious way. This proverb is of Chinese origin.

Kane-uke suru tomo, hito-uke su na: "Though you stand surety for a loan, don't do it for a person." Since there is no trusting a person's character, it is safer to secure a loan for someone on your own responsibility.

Kemuri wo mite hi aru wo shiru: "Seeing the smoke you know there is a fire." This is the Japanese translation of the English proverb; "Where there's smoke there's a fire."

Kiite gokuraku, mite jigoku: "It sounds good but in fact looks very bad." (Lit., "Sounds like paradise, looks like hell.") In other words, there is a great deal of difference between a hearsay and a truth.

Kiku to miru to wa ōki no sōi: "There is a big difference between what one hears and sees." English parallel: Fancy surpasses beauty.

Kitsune wa kawa no tame ni korosaru: "Be eternally vigilant." (Lit., "Foxes are killed for their skins.") Even very intelligent persons may be destroyed because someone wants something they have. Hence, one should be unceasingly careful and suspicious of others. English parallel: Foxes are killed for their skins. The English and the Japanese proverbs apparently were independently coined.

Nagaruru mizu wa kusarenu: "Running water does not get stale." This proverb may be metaphorically interpreted in a number of ways, of which one is: "Go about your work in a clear and above board manner, and people will not suspect you to be an evil person."

Naoki ni magaru eda: "Crooked branches on straight trees." An honest man may have dishonest children and other dependents. English parallel: Straight trees have crooked roots.

Oni ni koromo wo kiseta yō: "He looks like a devil who has put on a priest's robe." This proverb also appears in its shortened form: *"Oni ni koromo,"* "the devil in the priest's robe." English parallel: A wolf in sheep's clothing.

Osato ga shireru: "To betray one's origin." (Lit., "One's village is revealed.") In ancient Japan peasants were forbidden to travel, so villages and communities were much isolated and developed their own customs and ways of speech. Hence, a person who slipped off and came to another place could easily be detected. Even in these modern times, breeding and character are revealed in speech and action.

Rika ni kammuri wo tadasazu: "Don't behave in a suspicious manner." (Lit., "Under peach trees adjust not your diadem.") This dictum of Chinese origin teaches that it is wise to avoid any action that may be suspicious to others.

Rusu mimai wa ma-dōi ni seyo: "When the master is away make calls at remote intervals." This is to prevent any suspicion that the caller has designs on the chastity of the wife.

Sandome no (wa) shōjiki: "The third time is the truth." One is more likely to accept as true a statement made three times by as many people and on separate occasions.

Shōteki to mite anadoru bekarazu, taiteki to mite osoru bekarazu: "Always be alert in the presence of any enemy." (Lit., "Don't despise your enemy though you take him to be small, nor fear your enemy though you take him to be great.")

Soko ni wa soko ga aru: "There's a reason underlying the given reason." (Lit., "There's a bottom to the bottom.") The real reason or ulterior motive is sometimes hidden and undiscernable to outsiders.

Tsumbo no haya mimi: "The quick ears of a deaf man." He is eager to hear and frequently hears or thinks he hears things that were not said.

Tsumbo no me ga hayakute utagai-bukai: "Deaf persons are quick-eyed and very suspicious."

Tsuno wo dasu: "To show jealousy or anger." (Lit., "To extend the horns.") The allusion is especially to the cross face of a jealous woman.

Tsue ni sugaru to mo, hito ni sugaru na: "Though you depend on a staff, do not depend on men." This proverb is an exhortation to be distrustful of people. It may also be interpreted as an encouragement to be independent.

Ura ni wa ura ga aru: "The reverse side has its reverse side." Life is an intricate matter, so look at it closely from all sides. English parallel: The reverse side of the shield.

Uwasa wo sureba kage ga sasu: "Gossip about a person and his shadow will appear." In other words, be careful about what you say behind a person's back. English parallel: Talk of the devil and he will appear.

Warō mono wa hakaru-bekarazu: "A laughing person cannot be estimated." Beware of laughing people, for they may laugh while watching and meditating some evil upon you.

Yodomizu ni gomi tamaru: "Trash accumulates in stagnant water." That is, in disagreeable surroundings you will find unpleasant and evil people.

Yoku iu mono yoku okonawazu: "He who talks well does not act well." Beware of persons who take out in talk what they should accomplish in deeds.

Yume wa saka-yume: "Dreams go by contraries." Though this saying is frequently quoted, sometimes dreams do come true.

Yūrei no hama-kaze: "A spectre in the wind on the seashore." That is, something that soon disappears and about which we need not worry.

Zemmon ni tora wo fusegi, kōmon ni ōkami wo susumu: "To check a tiger at the front gate and let in a wolf at the rear gate." This saying describes a person who is not suspicious enough. Hence, it is most important to be suspicious of everyone until the person proves himself trustworthy.

THRIFT

LIKE SCOTLAND, the poor natural resources of Japan have forced the people to be thrifty. Again like the Scottish people, the thrift of the Japanese is not stinginess. Careful not to waste, the Japanese people could live on what Americans throw away and squander. A stingy or miserly person is much despised and laughed at in Japan. So also is the man who makes a show of his wealth. In feudal Japan, and to a certain extent today, carefulness and frugality are virtues.

Amai mono ni ari: "What may bring profits attracts people." (Lit., "To sweet things, ants.") Like ants, the Japanese are constantly watching for anything that may add to their food or welfare. English parallel: Ants never bend their course to an empty granary.

Ari wa tsune ni amaki wo tsuku: "Ants are always attracted to sweets." This is a slightly different wording of the foregoing proverb.

Dokkoi sō wa ton'ya de orosanu: "Assent cannot so easily be had." (Lit., "Yo-heave-ho! wholesale dealers would not sell at that price.") That is, a price must be given that is agreeable to both the buyer and the seller. English parallel: You are reckoning without your host.

Ebi de tai wo tsuru: "To make a profitable exchange." (Lit., "To catch a sea bream with a shrimp.") That is, to get something valuable in return for something small. English parallel: A little bait catches a big fish.

Eiyō ni mochi no kawa wo muku: "To be too much of a spendthrift." (Lit., "To luxuriously peel the skin of a rice cake.") The rice cake is always eaten in its entirety; to peel it would be foolish and unthrifty.

Fujiyū wo tsune to omoeba fusoku nashi: "It pays to be thrifty." (Lit., "You will lack nothing if you think privation is always with you.") This proverb is attributed to Ieyasu, the founder of the Tokugawa shogunate that ruled Japan from 1603 to 1867.

Ii mono wa yasui: "Good things are cheap." This saying teaches that really good things are worthwhile and cheap, even though you may have paid quite a price for them. English parallel: The best is best cheap.

Ikigake (Yukigake) no dachin: "The pack-horse driver's fee for carrying a package on the way he is traveling." In olden days when roads were bad and there was no vehicular travel on them, merchandise and other articles were sent from one place to another by pack horse. When known to be going in a certain direction, the pack-horse driver would sometimes be asked to take a package for a nominal fee, which he would pocket as an addition to his wages. Hence, the above is often used in the sense of "taking the same opportunity to do more than one thing at a time," or "carrying off something into the bargain."

Kane ga kane umu: "Money gives birth to money." There is an identical English proverb, but with no evidence of borrowing.

Kane ga kataki: "Money is an enemy." For many people money has been their downfall. English parallel: A man's wealth is his enemy.

Kane wa tenka no mawarimochi: "Money changes hands." (Lit., "Money is that which goes round in the world.") Hence, when it comes to us it should be used with care. English parallel: Money is the great traveler in the world.

Kasegu ni oitsuku bimbō nashi: "There is no poverty that can overtake toil."

Kasegu ni bimbō oitsukazu: "Toil cannot be overtaken by poverty." This is a slightly different version of the preceding proverb. English parallel: Diligence is the mother of good fortune.

Mono ni sutari nashi: "Everything has its use." (Lit., "There is nothing to be thrown away.") English parallel: Everything is good in its place.

Muda nakereba fusoku nashi: "Unless there is wastefulness there is no deficiency." English parallel: Waste not, want not.

Saikensha wa saimusha yori kioku yoshi: "Creditors have better memories than debtors." This is taken from the original English proverb.

Shihyaku-shi byō yori hin no yamai: "Worse than all diseases is poverty." This is perhaps because the sick man can sleep when the debtor cannot. The Japanese word *"shihyaku-shi,"* translated "all," is literally "four hundred and four."

Sui wa mi wo kū: "Fashion is ruin to some people." There are some people who use up their fortune by overindulgence in some hobby or elegance, such as the collection of paintings by great masters, ceremonial tea implements, many of which are very old and expensive, dwarf-tree cultivation, etc. These elegancies and others, while most interesting, can prove quite expensive.

Tatte iru mono wa oya demo tsukae: "Make use of those who stand around, even though they are your parents." When you are busy you are justified in putting to work any who are idly standing by.

Uetaru inu wa bō wo osorezu: "The starving dog fears not the stick." This means that extreme need will drive a person to desperate measures, even though he knows that punishment will ensue. English parallel: Hunger will break through stone walls.

Yugami hachi koku, sugu ku koku: "Leaning bears eight *koku,* straight nine *koku.*" It would appear that the leaning rice would bear more heavily than the straight plants, but such is not agriculturally the case. Just as straight growing rice produces more than the plants that lean over, so men who are upright in character are more fruitful than those who stoop to evil practices. A *"koku"* is a unit of measure of about five bushels. A farmer's or landowner's income was estimated on the number of *koku* of rice his land produced. In the feudal period each fief differed according to the number of *koku* of rice grown on it. Hence, there were some very rich lords as well as a number of poor ones. The capacity of merchant vessels was also measured by the number of *koku* the ship would hold.

Yuki wa hōnen no chō (kizashi): "Snow is an indication of a bountiful harvest." The words *"chō"* and *"kizashi"* both mean "omen" or "indication." From long observation and experience, Japanese farmers know that heavy snowfalls in winter will produce the much-needed extra moisture in the ground which will result in good rice crops. English parallels: A snow year, a rich year. Snow is the poor man's fertilizer.

Zeni aru toki wa zeni naki hi wo omoe: "When you have money, think of the time when you had none." Thus, you will be careful in spending it and live thriftily. English parallel: In fair weather prepare for foul.

TOLERANCE

Through centuries of living in a small thickly populated country in flimsily built houses which in urban and even in many rural areas are closely packed together, thus giving little privacy, the Japanese have learned to be tolerant. In matters of religion, though often there was fierce disagreement by the priests of the different Buddhist sects, the average layman showed a tolerance that almost amounted to indifference. Although quite suspicious of chance acquaintances and strangers, the average Japanese is quite tolerant towards those he knows and feels he can trust.

Atarashii tatami demo tatakeba gomi ga deru: "If you beat even new floor mats dirt will come out." That is, if you inquire too fully into the private lives of others, unpleasant matters will come out. Hence, it is best not to be too exhaustive in your inquiries.

Atarazu to iedomo tōkarazu: "You are nearly right in your conjectures." (Lit., "Though not hitting the mark you are not far from it.") This expression stems from an ancient Chinese saying.

Ayamachi no nai hito wa nai: "There is no person without a fault." English parallel: To err is human.

Chawan wo wata de ukeru: "To turn aside or be oblivious to a slight or insult." (Lit., "To accept a teacup with cotton.") English parallel: A soft answer turns away wrath.

Chi narazu rō narazareba kō taru ni atawazu: "Unless a man be foolish and deaf he cannot be a lord." That is, he must appear not to know or to hear certain things, if he is to be a successful ruler. English parallel: he who would rule must hear and be deaf, see and be blind.

Chikakute mienu wa matsuge: "One can very easily find another's faults but not one's own." (Lit., "Eyelashes though near are not seen.") English parallel: We see not what sits on one's shoulder.

Chōben bafuku ni oyobazu: "Too long is as bad as too short." (Lit., "A whip that is too long reaches beyond the horse's flank.")

Chisha ni mo senryo no isshitsu ari: "Even a wise man makes one error in a thousand considerations." English parallel: No one is wise at all times.

Chūgen mimi ni sakarō: "Good advice sounds harsh to the ear." (Lit., "Faithful words are opposed to the ear.") Though unpleasant, we should be tolerant enough to follow good advice, for it will later prove most helpful.

Demono haremono tokoro kirawazu: "Boils and tumors are not averse to appearing anywhere." This proverb is often quoted to describe people who are tactless in speech.

Doku ni mo kusuri ni mo naranu: "It serves neither for poison or medicine." This is said of a person who is neither bad nor good.

Dokuyaku henjite kusuri to naru: "A poisonous drug changes and becomes medicine." Just as poison sometimes serves the purpose of medicine, so a bad man may sometimes be reformed and become a good and useful person.

Gyoku-seki konkō: "To mix together the good and the bad." (Lit., "A mixture of jewels and common stones.") In the world we find both. *"Konkō"* is the word for "mixture." *"Shimbutsu konkō,"* often called *"Ryōbu Shintō,"* is a mixture of Shinto and Buddhism and is found in many places of worship in Japan.

Haremono ni sawaru na: "Don't touch a boil." That is, be careful how you treat certain moody and fickle persons. English parallel: Let sleeping dogs lie.

Heta ga aru no de jōzu ga shiru: "Because there are the unskillful, we know the skillful." If there were not men of inferior skill, the superior skill of some artists would not be so striking. Hence, even the unskillful are useful and have their place.

Hito-goto iwan yori waga hachi harae: "Instead of talking about other people's affairs, let me drive off my own wasps."

Hito manabazareba chi nashi: "If a person does not learn, he lacks intelligence." English parallel: Learn not and know not.

Hito ni hito kuse: "Every man has (at least) one fault." Hence, we should be generous and understanding in judging others. English parallel: Every man has his hobby horse.

Hito no konomi wa jūnin toiro: "The tastes of ten people differ as ten colors." Since this is so, we should be tolerant.

Hito no shinan to suru toki sono gen ya yoshi: "When a man is about to die his words are good." Even a wicked man will make a truthful confession when he is on the point of death.

Hito ono-ono chōtan ari: "Each person has strong and weak points." Perfection cannot be expected from anyone.

Hito wa bambutsu no reichō nari: "Man is the spiritual head of all creation." This observation is often quoted to impress on a person the necessity of behaving reasonably and nobly.

Hito wa hito, ware wa ware: "People are people, I am I." This is an exhortation for a spirit of independence and tolerance in one's thoughts and actions. That is, let others take their own ways and I mine. English parallel: Live and let live.

Hito wa boku-seki ni arazu: "Man is neither wood nor stone." He is made of flesh and blood and hence has his frailties as well as strong points.

Hito (Nin) wo mite hō toke: "Look at the person and expound the (Buddhist) law." This is advice to teach people according to their nature and capacity. English parallel: Cleave the log according to the grain.

Ichi mai no kami ni mo ura omote: "Even a sheet of paper has the back and front sides." That is, one must look carefully into the nature of anything before forming an opinion. English parallel: There are two sides to every question.

Ichi ri ichi gai: "One benefit has one detriment." There is always an advantage and a disadvantage to everything. English parallel: No garden without its weeds.

Ittoku isshitsu: "One gain one loss." People and things have strong and weak points. English parallel: Where light is there is shadow.

Ii ato wa warui, warui ato wa ii: "Evil follows good, good follows evil." From experience we learn how good fortune is frequently followed by evil fortune, and bad luck by good luck.

Iiyō kiki-yō: "How you speak, how you hear." In Japan much emphasis is placed in social intercourse on the manner of speaking, as well as on the mental attitude in hearing a person's speech.

Iwanu wa iu ni masaru: "Silence surpasses speech." To hold one's peace before company is often better than to speak. English parallel: Silence is more eloquent than words.

Jibun no koto wa jibun de seyo: "The things that concern you, you should do." English parallel: Let every tub stand on its own bottom.

Jū yoku gō wo seisu: "Gentleness skillfully subdues wrath." English parallel: A soft answer turns away wrath.

Katatsumuri no tsuno arasoi: "The snails lock horns." That is, a petty quarrel about trifles.

Kei-ei ai awaremu: "The folly of self-pity." (Lit., "The figure and its shadow are pitying each other.") This saying describes the sad state of a person in which his figure and its shadow are sympathizing with each other.

Kōbō mo fude no ayamari: "Even Kōbō makes mistakes with his brush." Kōbō Daishi, also known as Kukai, was the founder of the Shingon sect of Buddhism, and the most learned priest of the ninth century. He is reputed to have invented the written syllabary called *"hiragana"* and was equally famous as a scholar, sculptor, painter, and penman. English parallel: Even Homer nods.

Koboshita chawan wa tsuide miru: "To try to put together a dropped teacup." That is, to regret a matter that cannot be changed. English parallel: Don't cry over spilt milk.

Kokoro wa mochi yō: "Everything depends on one's way of thinking." In being tolerant we should remember that a person's mental attitude is of great importance. English parallel: The mind can make a heaven of hell, and a hell of heaven.

Kusatte mo tai: "Even though rotten, it is a sea bream." Things of intrinsic value should be retained and used regardless of age. The sea bream is highly esteemed in Japan and called the king of fishes because its flesh is dainty and the fish has a dignified look. English parallel: An old eagle is better than a sparrow (young crow).

Marui tamago mo kiri yō de shikaku, mono mo ii yō de kado ga tatsu: "Even a round egg can be made square in the way you cut it, words can be sharp in the way you speak them." Kind words and tolerance can go a long way in winning the love of other people.

Mono mo ii yō de kado ga tatsu: "Things sound pointed according to the way of speaking." This proverb is the last half of the one given above. English parallel: Smooth words make smooth ways.

Manzoku wa shizen no tomi nari: "Contentment is natural wealth." This proverb, which is widely quoted in Japan, is taken directly from the English one.

Meimei no hachi harae: "Let each person drive away his own wasps." If each person tended to his own problems he would not have time to criticize others. English parallel: Sweep before your own door.

Mekura sennin, meaki sennin: "A thousand blind, a thousand who see." That is, a thousand illiterates against a thousand literates. The world's opinion is so evenly balanced, that there is nothing to be gained in striving after unusual and often unappreciated excellence. Against this pessemistic interpretation we can say, that it is worthwhile to attain excellence so as to help the half of the world who do not appreciate it.

Minu ga hana: "Not to see is a flower." It is more tolerant sometimes not to see certain things than to be on a constant watch for error.

Mono ieba kuchibiru samushi aki no kaze: "It is better to leave many things unsaid." (Lit., "If a thing is said, the lips become very cold, like the autumn wind.") The above wise saying is a *"haiku"* or seventeen-syllable poem by Bashō, the well-known versifier who lived and wrote about three hundred years ago. Note that my literal English translation also has just seventeen syllables. The meaning of the proverb-poem is that there are times when it is wise to maintain silence. English parallel: Speech is silver, silence is golden.

Mono ni wa hodo ga aru: "There is a limit to things." This proverb enjoins us to be tolerant and moderate in doing anything.

Mono ni wa hyōri ari: "Everything has its front and back sides." We should remember that there are two sides to everything.

Morai mono ni kujō wo iu na: "Don't make complaints against a gift." English parallel: Don't look a gift horse in the mouth.

Morau mono wa natsu mo kosode: "If it is a gift, even a *kosode* in summer is welcome." A *"kosode"* is a wadded silk garment used for winter wear.

Mukashi wa mukashi, ima wa ima: "Judge and act by present standards." (Lit., "Old times are old times, the present is present.") English parallel: Let bygones be bygones.

Nakute nana kuse, atte shijūhachi kuse: "A faultless person has seven faults, a faulty person forty-eight faults." The word *"kuse,"* here translated "fault," has also the meaning of "habit" or "peculiarity." Bearing the above in mind, it behooves us to be tolerant. English parallel: Every man has his faults.

Nigeru sakana wo Ebisu ni mairasu: "Take philosophically your loss and don't complain." (Lit., "Present to Ebisu the fleeing fish.") Ebisu is the god of fishermen and one of the seven gods of luck.

Nusubito ni mo sambu no ri ari: "Even a robber has a 30 per cent justification." We should bear in mind that even criminals have some reasons for their misdeeds. English parallel: Give the devil his due.

Ōgon-jidai to wa ōgon no hakkutsu-zarishi jidai nari: "The Golden Age was the age in which gold was not dug out." This proverb is the Japanese version of the English: The Golden Age was the age in which gold did not reign.

Okame hachi-moku: "A bystander sees eight moves ahead." The reference is to the Japanese chess games of *go* and *shōgi*. Bystanders see more than players, or think they do.

Okame ni mienu mi no kurō: "Lookers-on do not see a person's own troubles." Hence, they should be tolerant. English parallel: None but the wearer knows where the shoe pinches.

Onore ni hossezaru tokoro wo hito ni hodokosu nakare: "What you do not wish done to you, do not to others." This Confucian maxim is the negative form of the Golden Rule uttered by Jesus Christ five centuries later: "Whatever you wish that men would do to you, do so to them." (Matthew 7:12).

Onore wo motte hito wo hakaru: "Judge others by yourself." (Lit., "Bearing in mind yourself, weigh others.") That is, be aware of your own shortcomings, and don't be too hard on others.

Rakugaki ni meihitsu nashi: "For scribbling there is no excellent handwriting." No matter how excellent a handwriting a person may have, he should not scribble on the wall. English parallel: A white wall is a fool's paper.

Ryūme no tsumazuki: "The best of persons sometimes make mistakes." (Lit., "The stumbling of a fabulous horse.")

Ruri wa moroshi: "Emeralds are easily broken." Precious things, such as our dealing with other people, should be handled with care.

Saru mo ki kara ochiru: "Even a monkey will fall from a tree." Since skillful people sometimes make mistakes, we should be tolerant of all. English parallel: A good marksman may miss.

Seken wa seken sa: "Let the world go as it may." (Lit., "The world is the world, you know.") English parallel: Let people talk and dogs bark.

Senryo-no isshitsu: "One mistake in a thousand thoughts." That is, an oversight. There is no one so wise that he does not sometimes make a slip. English parallel: Even Homer nods.

Shisha wo uramazu: "Be tolerant of the dead." (Lit., "Don't bear a grudge against the dead.") English parallel: Death pays all debts.

Sonso no aida ni kessuru: "To negotiate"; "to use diplomacy." (Lit., "To arrive at a decision while giving a public dinner.") In Japan, important matters, whether business or political, are often discussed and decided at public dinners or *geisha* parties.

Sugitaru wa oyobazaru ni shikazu: "Too much is worse than too little." (Lit., "It is best not to attain than to exceed.") English parallel: Too much spoileth, too little is nothing.

Tade kū mushi mo sukizuki: "There is no disputing taste in a person." (Lit., "There are even worms that eat smartweed as a matter of taste.") The smartweed *("tade")* has a very pungent flavor, but some worms feed on it. Latin parallel: De gustibus non est disputandum.

Tateyama-jita no goshō wo negawazu: "Those who are at the foot of Tateyama do not seek after the future life." Since Tateyama is a sacred mountain, those living at its base are not so concerned about future existence. Those who live farther away are much more earnest believers. Nearness to some great opportunity makes for indifference, while distance lends enchantment.

Tendō hito wo korosazu: "The Way of Heaven does not kill men." The phrase *"Tendō"*—"Way of Heaven"—is a Confucian term for the supreme moral rule or order in the world. The above proverb teaches that this moral order is merciful to the just who suffer from injustice. English parallel: God tempers the wind to the shorn lamb.

Tendō wa ze ka hi ka? "I have lost my faith in Providence." (Lit., "Are the ways of heaven righteous or evil?") This may be the despairing cry of a person who suffers from some unjust treatment.

Tōdai moto kurashi: "The beacon does not shine on its own base." (Lit., "The base of a lighthouse is dark.") For example, while abroad one sometimes learns things about his own country that he did not know at home. English parallel: One has to go abroad for news at home.

Tobu tori mo ochiru: "A flying bird will sometimes fall." Skillful persons sometimes fail; so we should be tolerant.

Tokoro kawareba shina kawaru: "With change of locality there is change of articles." Every place has different customs and things. English parallel: So many countries, so many customs.

Tōku no bōsan arigatai: "A Buddhist priest from far off is welcome." Distance makes the object of one's adoration more worthy.

Tsumbo ni teppō, mekura ni battō: "Those lacking physical senses are fearless." (Lit., "To a deaf man the discharge of a gun, to a blind man a drawn sword.") Such may be fearless but not brave.

Uetaru mono ni soshoku nashi: "For a hungry person there is no coarse food." English parallel: Hunger is the best sauce.

Uetaru mono wa shoku wo erabazu: "The famished person is not choosy about his food."

Uete wa sōkō wo itowazu: "The starved person is not disgusted with refuse and bran." English parallel: Hunger makes raw beans relish well.

Umi ni sennen, kawa ni sennen to iu shiromono: "A know-it-all person." (Lit., "He is the sort of person who has lived a thousand years by the sea and a thousand years by the river.") Such an old-timer is not to be caught with chaff. The above long proverb is frequently used in the contracted form, *"Umi sen, kawa sen"* ("Sea thousand, river thousand").

Ushi ni hikarete Zenkōji mairi: "To make a virtue of necessity." (Lit., "Led by an ox she makes a pilgrimage to Zenkōji.") The story goes that a certain irreligious old woman lived near Zenkōji, a famous Buddhist temple in the city of Nagano. A wandering ox, passing by one day, caught on his horns a piece of cloth being bleached in the yard. The old woman chased after him and followed the animal to the temple. So impressed was she by what she saw and heard, that she became a faithful visitor to the holy place.

Ushioi ushi ni owareru: "Things sometimes go by contraries." (Lit., "The cowherd is chased by his cow.") The above proverb is often quoted when some underling dictates the policies of some group or organization. English parallel: To put the cart before the horse.

Waga mi no koto wa hito ni toe: "About matters that concern me ask others." If a man wishes to know about himself, he should ask others to tell him frankly what they think. To do so requires real broad-minded tolerance.

Yabu wo tsutsuite hebi wo dasu: "Let well enough alone." (Lit., "By poking at a bamboo thicket you drive out a snake.") This proverb has been contracted to *"Yabu, hebi"* ("Bamboo-thicket, snake"). That is, in making too much fuss over some affair, one is apt to reveal a fact that is disadvantageous to one's own self.

Yabu hebi wo dasu na: "Don't drive a snake from a bamboo thicket." For the reason given in the preceding proverb, it is sometimes better to be tolerant than insistent. English parallel: Let sleeping dogs lie.

Yanagi ni kaze: "To be conciliatory." ("Winds against the willows.") This refers to the gentle, nonchalant attitude of a person who is attacked or rebuked for something. The advice is to softly elude such attacks, as willows bend to the wind. In Japan willows are greatly admired not only for their beauty but also because they seldom break in the wind or with the weight of snow. Equally admired is a person who can elude a difficult or rude question and thus avoid outright conflict.

Yanagi ni yuki-ore nashi: "Willows are never broken by snow." So a slender man is not necessarily weaker than a stout one, for the former often outlives the latter. Likewise, a conciliatory person will often hold out and gain his ends better than a rugged personality who strongly resists his opponent. This is an excellent proverb for teaching tolerance.

Yuku mono wa owazu, kitaru mono wa kobamazu: "Not to give chase to those who leave, nor refuse those who come." This proverb teaches that it is a waste of effort to try to stop a person who is determined to leave, and a wise procedure to receive those who come.

WILL

THE JAPANESE of feudal and pre-World War II days put much emphasis on mental and spiritual as well as physical discipline for the cultivation of strong will power. When once they are convinced of the action they should take, the Japanese can be and generally are very strong willed and resolute. All during the four years of the tragic conflict with the Allied Powers, the Japanese were told through every medium of their propaganda that although the enemy were greatly superior in material resources, the strong will power their own nation possessed was more than enough to counteract this and thus win the final victory. The decisive defeat of their armed forces and the order to surrender by their beloved Emperor, left the Japanese numb with amazement and shattered their morale. Confused and dazed, their self-confidence overthrown, it was some time before the people realized that all was not lost and that there was still a useful and honorable place for their nation in the world. Having arrived at this truth, the recovery of the Japanese has been amazingly rapid.

Amadare ishi wo ugatsu: "Falling raindrops will wear through a stone." That is, a strong will can overcome any difficulty. English parallel: Constant dripping wears the stone.

Ari no omoi mo ten made todoku: "Even the wishes of an ant reach heaven." Since the wish of even such a small creature as an ant is heard by heaven, determination or will power by humans can accomplish anything.

Ayamachi wa futatabi suru nakare: "Do not commit the same mistake a second time." That is, use your strong will so that you will not make the same error twice.

Daijōbu kane no wakizashi: "As sure as the metal dagger." The *"wakizashi"* is the metal short sword or dagger worn for self-protection by all men of the upper classes prior to the Meiji era. Hence, the above proverb indicates something quite sure and certain.

Doku kuwaba sara made nebure: "If you eat poison lick even the dish." Do thoroughly and with strong will power whatever you undertake, whether it be good or evil. English parallel: Go the whole hog.

Fundoshi shimete kakaru: "To brace oneself for an effort." (Lit., "To tighten one's loincloth.") As a boy in Japan, I have often seen carpenters, jinrikisha men, and other working men tighten their loincloths before making some special effort. English parallel: To gird up one's loins.

Gyūba no gotoku shieki saruru nakare: "Don't be forced to work like oxen and horses." The implication is that humans should use their own will power to drive them to work. English parallel: Be not like dumb driven cattle.

Hi ga futte mo yari ga futte mo: "No matter whether it rains fire or spears." This saying expresses a strong determination to carry on a project or to go out, regardless of inclement weather. English parallel: Though it should rain pitchforks.

Ichinen iwa wo mo tōsu: "A concentrated mind will pierce a rock."

Isshin iwa wo mo tōsu: "Wholeheartedness will pierce a rock." English parallel: Where there's a will there's a way.

Ichinen ten ni tsūzu: "Intense earnestness overcomes all obstacles." (Lit., "An intense zeal prevails upon heaven.") English parallel: Faith will move mountains.

Inochi kara nibamme: "Something very important and valuable." (Lit., "Second only to life.") To carry out or preserve such an important matter requires determination and will power.

Ishi ni tatsu ya no tameshi ari: "There are instances when an arrow will stick into a rock." A figure of speech for intense determination.

Ishibotoke ni mono iwaseru: "To cause a stone Buddha to speak." This phrase is used to describe the determination of a strong-willed person to have his way at any cost.

Issun no shita ni go shaku no mi wo son su: "The tongue is more powerful than the sword." (Lit., "To one inch of tongue five feet of blade loses.")

Ittō ryōdan: "To take drastic action." (Lit., "To cut a thing in two halves with one sword stroke.") English parallel: To cut the Gordian knot.

Iwa wo mo tōsu kuwa no yumi: "A strong will can overcome all obstacles." (Lit., "A mulberry bow will even shoot through a rock.")

Kenzen naru seishin wa kenzen naru shintai ni yadoru: "A healthy mind lives in a healthy body." This proverb is a direct translation of the English saying: A sound mind in a sound body.

Kyūshi ni isshō wo aru: "To narrowly escape from the very jaws of death." (Lit., "To secure one life from nine deaths.") The Japanese phrase *"kyūshi,"* literally "nine deaths," has the meaning of "certain death."

Kyū sureba tsūzu: "When driven to extremity you become proficient." When in a fix you will find your way out. English parallel: When things are at their worst, they will mend.

Omō ichinen iwa wo mo tōsu: "A firm resolve pierces even a rock." English parallel: Where there's a will, there's a way.

Omoi tatta ga kichinichi: "The day in which you make up your mind is the best day in which to do it." (Lit., "The day in which you decide to do it, is your lucky day.") English parallels: "There is no time like the present. Never leave until tomorrow what you can do today.

Seishin ittō nanigoto ka narazaran: "There is nothing that cannot be achieved by firm determination." This popular proverb is from a Chinese source. English parallel: Nothing is hard to a willing mind.

Semman nin to ie domo ware yukan: "I will go forward though ten million oppose me." In this quotation from the great Chinese sage, Mencius, the meaning is that when a person is convinced that his cause is just, he will advance against all odds and fight to the last. This is an abbreviation of the proverb that follows.

Uchi kaerimite yamashii karazareba, semman nin to ie domo ware yukan: "If after looking within myself I find nothing of which to be ashamed, though ten million oppose me I shall go forward." That is, if my memory is free of anything to make me ashamed, nothing can withhold my advance.

Tobu tori wo otosu ikioi: "So powerful as to bring down a flying bird." (Lit., "So vigorous as to cause a flying bird to fall.")

Unda mono wo tsubuse: "Break the boil that has come to a head." That is, deal decisively and in good time with a difficult problem.

Uraba no inu wa iwashi wo kuwanu: "The dog on the sea coast will not eat sardines." That is, one who is used to dainties will not relish coarse food.

Usagi wo mite taka wo hanatsu: "To let fly the falcon (hawk) at the sight of a hare." This means that everything should be done with a definite end in view.

WIT

JUDGED BY THEIR STANDARDS and contrary to the opinion of foreigners, the larger number of whom do not have a good grasp of the language, the Japanese and especially the Edoites are quite witty. The saying, *"kichi wa danwa no yakumi nari"*—"Wit is the spice of conversation"—clearly indicates the importance the Japanese attach to wit. The following are examples of Japanese wit as revealed in their proverbs and sayings.

Ahiru no kaji-mimai: "An ungainly gait." (Lit., "Like a duck on a visit to fire-sufferers.") When a fat woman walks in an awkward and ungainly way, this expression is used.

Aita kuchi ga fusagaranu: "To be openmouthed with amazement." (Lit., "To be unable to close one's open mouth.") This expression is used in reference to the gaping wonder of a person who is amazed at some surprising sight or absurdity. In early days foreigners in Japan were thus gaped at. In November, 1945, I was traveling in a U.S. Army jeep deep in the mountains of Hiroshima prefecture. As we climbed, the road became narrower, steeper, and rougher. Suddenly we came to a dead end. There was no room in which to turn, for to the right was a steep bank, and in front and to the left a sudden drop of more than fifty feet. At this point the road itself was barely the width of the jeep's tracks. On the suggestion of my driver I got out, only too glad to do so. I watched while the young soldier maneuvered the vehicle and backed it up the steep bank on the right until it was almost in a vertical position. Turning the front wheels to the left, he brought the jeep partly down to the narrow road. After repeating this maneuver the third time, the driver succeeded in completely turning the jeep around with all four wheels on the road. The only other witness of this feat of American driving, was an old charcoal-maker, who was gaping with wonder and astonishment at the two white men—perhaps the first he had ever seen—and the singular skill of the driver. As we drove off down the road, I looked back and saw the old fellow with eyes popping and mouth still wide open in utter amazement.

Aita kuchi ni botamochi: "An unexpected windfall." (Lit., "A bean-jam rice cake into the open mouth.")

Ana no mujina wo nedan suru: "To sell without showing." (Lit., "To name the price of the badger in the hole.")

Atama dekkachi shiri tsubome: "An excellent plan with poor results." (Lit., "An enormous head and narrow hips.")

Atama kakushite shiri kakusazu: "To only partly hide one's faults." (Lit., "He hides his head but cannot hide his buttocks.") This statement is made of a man who tries in vain to gloss over his falsehood or knavery.

Bikuni ni kushi wo saseru yō: "Attempting an absurdity." (Lit., "Like trying to put a comb upon the nun's head.") Buddhist nuns in Japan have shaven heads, hence it is impossible and useless to get combs to stay on them.

Dai wa shō wo kaneru, shikashi shakushi wa mimikaki ni naranu: "The large serves also for the small, yet a dipper will not do for an earpick." In Japan, earpicks *("mimikake")* are often made in the shape of a small ladle or dipper.

Edokko wa satsuki no koi no fukinagashi: "The Edo man is but a windbag." (Lit., "The Edo man is like the May carp floating in the breeze.") That is, he is full of wind and lazy. By "May carp" is meant the carp-shaped cloth or paper streamers which float from a flagstaff on Boys' Day—May 5—in the yards of homes that have boys in the family, one fish for each boy.

En no shita no chikara mochi: "Wasted effort; thankless labor."

(Lit., "A strong man under the veranda.") This expression is applied to the thankless task of a person who tries to help some project or cause but gets no appreciation.

En no shita no mai: "A thankless task." (Lit., "To dance under the veranda.") This saying means to "make a vain effort" or "to do something without being known or thanked."

En no shita no sōji: "A vain effort." (Lit., "To clean up under the veranda.") This is similar in meaning to the preceding proverb.

Fune wo kogu: "To nod in sleep while sitting up." (Lit., "To row a boat.") Japanese small boats are propelled by an oar in the stern. The rower makes a motion which closely resembles the nodding of a seated person who is half asleep.

Hajime choro-choro, naka kakka, oya wo shinuru mo futa toru na: "First a slow fire, next a blazing hot fire, then don't remove the lid even though your parents die." This is a humorous recipe for cooking rice.

Hato ga mame-deppō wo kutta yō: "To wear a look of stupid surprise." (Lit., "Like a pigeon that has swallowed a peashooter.") English parallel: To look like a duck in a thunderstorm.

Hanage wo yomu: "To make a fool of a man." (Lit., "To count the hairs in his nostrils.") Pretty women are said to have done this. English parallel: To lead a man by his nose.

Hana no shita yori hana no shita: "Below the nose rather than under flowers." This is a good example of a Japanese pun, their favorite form of wit. The word *"hana"* may mean either "nose" or "flower," depending on the Chinese ideograph used, and the phrase "below the nose" is a familiar way of referring to the mouth. Hence, the above proverb can be taken to mean, "It is preferable to have something to eat rather than sit beneath beautiful flowers." In cherry-blossom-viewing parties, food, drink, and pretty women are taken along so both the gourmand and the aesthete can be well satisfied.

Hyōtan kara koma ga deru: "An unexpected surprise." (Lit., "A pony emerges from the wine gourd.") the gourd *("hyōtan")* when dried and polished is used as a receptacle for rice wine *("saké").* Should a pony instead of *saké* suddenly come out of the gourd, it would be an incredible miracle. The above saying is often used to indicate that a joke has turned into an actuality, or a sudden good fortune has befallen someone. English parallel: Unexpected things often happen.

Imo-gara de ashi tsukū: "A useless and foolish effort." (Lit., "To spear the feet with dried taro stems.") The stems of the taro are so soft it would be impossible to spear the feet with them.

Ishi-usu ni kimono wo kiseta yō: "Like a millstone dressed in a kimono." This is a humorous expression to describe an exceedingly short and fat person waddling around in an ungainly manner.

Itoya no jishin: "Great confusion." (Lit., "An earthquake in a thread shop.") This figurative expression is used to describe any condition of great entanglement and confusion.

Ja ga ka wo nonda yō: "Like a serpent that has swallowed a mosquito." This expression is used to describe the stolid face of an impassive person, or one who remains unsatisfied even after he has partaken heartily of food and drink. English parallel: Like the cat that has swallowed the canary.

Jitabata iu temo, niwatori wa hadashi: "You can't cover up your faults with many words." (Lit., "However much you may struggle in your speech, a chicken is barefoot.")

Jōdan kara homma (makoto) ga deru: "Truth often comes out of a joke." English parallel: Many an earnest word is spoken in jest.

Ka no namida: "Anything very small." (Lit., "The tears of a mosquito.") See also *"Suzume no namida"*—A sparrow's tears, p. 261.

Karasu no gyōzui: "Just a dip." (Lit., "A crow's bath.") This saying is applied to a person who comes out too soon from his or her bath.

Kusai mono ni futa wo suru: "To attempt to hush up a disgraceful affair." (Lit., "To cover up a stinking thing.") A person involved in a scandal will seek to hush up the affair so as not to affect his business or political standing.

Makkura de hana wo tsumamarete mo wakarimasen: "Pitch black." (Lit., "So dark that even if your nose were pinched you would not know who did it.")

Masamune de daikon wo kiru: "The employment of needless great means." (Lit., "To cut a radish with a *Masamune* blade.")

Masamune blades forged by the fourteenth-century swordsmith of that name, are considered among the finest made and to this day are greatly prized. To use one as a kitchen knife would be considered a desecration.

Mato naki ni ya wo hanatsu: "An aimless procedure." (Lit., "To shoot an arrow where there is no target.")

Matsu no ki ni semi: "An ill-matched couple." (Lit., "A cicada clinging to a pine tree.") This phrase is used in describing a couple who are quite different in height and build.

Mawata de kubi wo shimeru: "To admonish gently." (Lit., "To strangle a person with floss-silk.")

Me ga kuitaku, mo tsume-komenu: "Though the eyes want to eat, no more can be stuffed in." English parallel: Your eyes are bigger than your stomach.

Mekura ni chōchin: "An unnecessary article." (Lit., "A lantern for a blind man.")

Mekura ni kagami wo uru na: "Don't make a sale useless to the purchaser." (Lit., "Don't sell a mirror to a blind person.")

Mekura ni michi wo osowaru na: "Don't be taught the right road by a blind person." That is, it is useless to ask a blind man about the right way when he himself cannot see it. Likewise, it is useless to ask something of a person who is least likely to be able to enlighten you.

Mekura ni mekiki: "An unreliable criticism." (Lit., "The criticism of a blind man.") A blind man cannot possibly be a judge of artistic curios. Thus, the above expression is applied to a person who cannot rightly judge of something, though he may presume to be a connoisseur.

Mekura no mekura tebiki: "A blind man leading a blind man." That is, absolutely unreliable and dangerous guidance. English parallel: "If the blind lead the blind, both shall fall into the ditch." Matthew 15:14.

Mekura no kagami, hōshi no kushi: "Useless articles." (Lit., "A blind man's mirror, a priest's comb.") Since the blind man cannot see himself in the mirror, and the Buddhist priest with his smooth shaven head cannot comb his hair, both articles are utterly useless.

Mendori susumete ondori toki wo tsukuru: "Men often get good advice from their wives." (Lit., "Encouraged by the hen the cock tells the hour.") English parallel: A wife often tells her husband what to do.

Mimi wo ōte suzu wo nusumu: "The self-delusion of a misguided person." (Lit., "Covering his ears he steals the bell.") The thief steals a bell after stopping his own ears for fear of others hearing the sound he may cause. English parallel: The cat shuts her eyes while she steals the cream.

Mōki no fuboku ni aeru ga gotoshi: "A lucky and lifesaving experience." (Lit., "Like a blind turtle coming across a piece of driftwood.") English parallel: Like a drowning ant meeting with a leaf.

Neko ni kambukuro wo kabuseta yō: "To be suspicious and afraid." (Lit., "Like a cat with its head covered by a paper bag.") This saying describes a person who recedes step by step without turning around.

Neko ni koban: "An utterly useless article." (Lit., "A gold coin to a cat.") English parallel: Casting pearls before swine.

Neko ni nembutsu, uma ni zeni: "Unavailing efforts." (Lit., "Buddhist invocations to a cat, money to a horse.")

Neko no hitai hodo: "A very small space." (Lit., "As large as a cat's forehead.") This humorous expression is used to describe a very small plot of ground.

Neko yori mashi: "Preferable to a cat." This is a witty saying descriptive of a person who may be welcomed as a handy assistant rather than an inconvenient visitor. Any person who drops in at a busy time is "better than a cat," for he can help with the work at hand.

Nemimi ni mizu: "A great surprise." (Lit., "Water into the ear of a sleeping person.") English parallel: A bolt from the blue.

Nigashita sakana wa ōkii: "The fish that got away was large!" Regret magnifies the loss. Fishermen are the same the world over.

Nikai kara me-gusuri: "A futile or ineffective effort." (Lit., "Putting in eye drops from the second floor.") English parallel: Like fanning the sun with a peacock's feather.

Niwatori wo saku ni gyūtō wo mochiu: "The absurdity of unnecessary effort." (Lit., "To use an ox-butchering knife to split a fowl.") English parallel: To use a musket to kill a butterfly.

Nomi no fūfu: "A little man with a big wife." (Lit., "A flealike couple.") The Japanese early noticed that the female flea was much larger than the male.

Noren ni ude-oshi: "The foolishness of unnecessary effort." (Lit., "Hand wrestling against a hanging curtain.") Small shops such as rice-wine, vermicelli, and rice-cake shops which front the street often have gaily decorated short curtains hanging before the entrance, which the customer pushes aside with no effort as he enters. Obviously, it would be very foolish if he used much muscular effort in shoving aside these flimsy hangings.

Noren to sumō: "Wrestling with a shop curtain." This figure of speech describes a situation in which a man has to work with or against an unresponsive person.

Nuka ni kugi: "To do something that is unavailing." (Lit., "To drive a nail into rice bran.") English parallel: Water on a duck's back.

Nure-te de awa no tsukami-dori: "To gain without work." (Lit., "To grasp millet with wet hands.") This expression is used when a man gets possession of a large fortune unexpectedly and with no special effort. English parallel: To make money with a wet finger.

Obi ni mijikashi, tasuki ni nagashi: "It lacks perfection." (Lit., "Too short for a sash, too long for a sleeve-tie.") Since a perfect thing is rare, we should be content with the best we can get. This expression is frequently used in choosing a wife. English parallel: Too much spoileth, too little is nothing.

O-hige no chiri wo harō: "To flatter or curry favor with a person." (Lit., "To brush the dust off a person's beard.") I have seen *geisha* on a train doing just that to an elderly and wealthy man with whom they were on a trip.

Ryūtō-dabi: "An anticlimax." (Lit., "A dragon's head and a snake's tail.") This expression is applied to a grand beginning and a tame ending. English parallel: To go up like a rocket and come down like a stick.

Sagi wo karasu to ii-kurumeru: "To argue unreasonably." (Lit.,

"To make out a heron to be a crow.") This witty saying describes an unreasonable person's method of arguing just to make a point.

Saru no suiren: "To do something that is unnatural." (Lit., "The swimming of a monkey.") Since the monkey lives in trees it is not fit for him to swim.

Seiten no hekireki: "A sudden surprise." (Lit., "A thunderclap from the blue sky.") This is a direct translation of the English "A bolt from the blue."

Sendō ōku shite fune yama ni noboru: "Too many sailors drive the boat up the mountain." English parallel: Too many cooks spoil the broth.

Shirami no kawa wo yari de sogu yō: "Unnecessary effort for a small result." (Lit., "Like slicing off the skin of a louse with a spear.") English parallel: To kill a fly with a long spear.

Sora no mitsu no rōka: furō-ka, terō-ka, kumorō-ka: "In the sky there are three halls: *("rōka")*—Will it rain? *("furō-ka?")* Will it clear up? *("terō-ka?")* Will it become cloudy? *("kumorō-ka?")* The word *"rōka"* means "a hall," but in the above saying it is used as a pun by forming the ending of three verbs dealing with the weather. Much of Japanese wit consists of a play on words with the same sound but different meanings.

Suppon to o-tsuki sama hodo chigau: "As different as can be." (Lit., "As different as the snapping turtle from the moon.") English parallel: As different as chalk from cheese.

Suzume no namida: "A very small quantity." (Lit., "A sparrow's tears.") See *"Ka no namida,"* "A mosquito's tears," p. 257.

Taka no atta suzume no yō: "Like a sparrow meeting a hawk." This describes a man or an animal meeting and becoming overawed by an enemy of much greater strength.

Taizan meidō-shite nezumi ippiki: "Much fuss with small results." (Lit., "A great mountain rumbles and brings forth only one mouse!") English parallel: Much ado about nothing.

Tana kara botamochi: "An unexpected piece of good luck." (Lit., "A bean-jam rice cake from the shelf!") English parallel: A windfall.

Teki naki ni ya wo hanatsu: "A warlike operation with no objective." (Lit., "To let fly an arrow where there is no enemy.")

Tōfu ni kasugai, nuka ni kugi: "To try to do the impossible." (Lit., "To drive a clamp into bean curd and a nail into rice bran.") This expression is used to describe the futility of attempting to reform a depraved or profligate person. English parallel: Pouring water into a sieve.

Tombi no aburage wo sarawareta yō: "A stupid look of surprise." (Lit., "As if fried bean curd were snatched off by a kite.") The fried bean curd *("aburage")* is a common article of food, and children carrying it home would frequently have it snatched out of their hands by the sudden swoop of a kite, leaving them in openmouthed and empty-handed surprise.

Tora wo egaite neko ni ruisu: "An attempt ending in failure." (Lit., "In drawing a tiger, he comes up with something like a cat.") This saying is used to describe the failure of a poor artist to produce a faithful picture of something.

Tsuri-otoshita uo wa ōkii: "The fish that dropped off the hook was large." Losses are always magnified when told by fishermen everywhere.

Uma wo ushi ni norikaeru: "To make a change for the worse." (Lit., "To transfer from a horse to an ox.") In traveling, a horse is better than an ox. The above saying would be in order if a man took a train after traveling by plane.

Ushi wo uma ni norikaeru: "To make a change for the better." (Lit., "To take a horse after riding an ox.") If a man decided to travel by plane after riding a train, the above proverb would be applicable.

Uo to kyaku wa mikkame ni hana ni tsuku: "Too much of a good thing." (Lit. "Fish and guests stink on the third day.") This proverb is from the English one: "Fish and guests smell at three days old."

Ware-nabe ni toji-buta: "Like to like." (Lit., "To a cracked kettle, a mended lid.") Both husband and wife have faults. English parallel: Every Jack has his Jill.

Wasureneba koso omoidasazu: "It is just because I do not forget that I do not remember." This paradoxial expression indicates that some thought is always on one's mind.

WOMEN

THE DEGREE OF A NATION'S ADVANCEMENT in culture and civilization is revealed in the position of its women. In the early periods of Japanese history women had a high place, but with the advance of Buddhist and Confucian teachings the members of the fair sex were relegated to a subordinate position. With the acceptance of many Christian teachings a generation or two ago, the place of women in Japanese life began to improve. The new Constitution of Japan gives the same rights to women and men. Girls and boys are given equal educational opportunities. In the eyes of the law, there now is no discrimination. Women can vote on equal terms with men. After they attain adulthood they are no longer under the control of their fathers, elder brothers or husbands. They can enter any profession and are eligible for any position, provided they can produce evidence of the needed training and experience. While many modern Japanese women, especially in urban areas, make full use of their new opportunities and freedoms, the power of social pressure is still so strong, notably in rural regions, that relatively few women defy the old customs and practices. Hence, it may be said that the majority of Japanese women are still in an inferior position, though their situation continues to change for the better. Needless to say, most of the proverbs in this section deal with women of pre-World War II Japan.

Aki no ōgi: "A useless article." (Lit., "A fan in autumn.") In autumn, when it is cool, there is no need for a fan. Hence, the above saying is often used in reference to a deserted or divorced woman.

Bi wa hisō nomi: "Beauty is only superficial." (Lit., "Beauty is only the skin.") This is the Japanese version of the English proverb: "Beauty is but skin deep." Nevertheless, Japanese women take great care of their complexions, and when they wish to appear particularly beautiful, will whiten their faces and necks.

Bijin hakumei: "Beautiful women are unfortunate." Their beauty often exposes them to many dangers and temptations.

Bijin ni gujin ōshi: "Among beautiful women there are many fools." English parallel: Beauty and folly are often companions.

Bijin to iu mo kawa hitoe: "Though you speak of a beautiful woman, it is only one layer of skin." English parallel: Beauty is but skin deep.

Bijin wa iwanedo, kakure nashi: "Though a beautiful woman does not say anything, she cannot be hidden." That is, her looks will draw the attention of people. English parallel: A fair face will get its praise though the owner keeps silent.

Bijin wa sei wo tatsu ono: "A beautiful woman is an ax that cuts off life."

Deichū no hasu: "A lotus flower in the mud." This describes a young woman who keeps her chastity in spite of morally unhealthy surroundings. English parallel: A rose amid nettles.

Gaikotsu no ue yosōte hanami kana: "Behold a skeleton is all dressed up and out flower-viewing!" From the Buddhist standpoint even pretty women are nothing but a bag of bones to which they will be eventually reduced.

Gaimen (Gemen) nyo-Bosatsu, naimen nyo-Yasha: "Externally a female Buddha, internally a female devil." *"Bosatsu"* is the Japanese for the Sanskrit *"Bodhisattva,"* which means a "Buddha-elect." *"Yasha"* is the Japanese for the Sanskrit *"Yaksha,"* a demon. Thus the above expression describes a person who has the appearance of an angel and the heart of a she-devil. English parallel: All saint without, all devil within.

Happō-bijin wa hakujō: "One who pleases everybody is cold." (Lit., "An eight-sided beauty is cold hearted.") The term *"happō-bijin"* ("eight-sided beauty"), while originally applied to women, is also used in referring to men who try to please everyone. Politicians may be termed eight- or many-sided when they try to curry favor with all people.

Idobata kaigi: "Gossip around the well." (Lit., "A conference by the wellside.") The village well in every country has always been the favorite place for women to gather and gossip. In these modern times should we not change the saying from *"idobata kaigi"* ("wellside session") to *"denwa kaigi"* ("telephone session")? In Europe and America long and useless chattering is still often heard at Mrs. Grundy's tea party or over the telephone.

Iro no shiroi no wa shichi nan kakusu: "A white complexion hides many defects." Here the term *"shichi nan,"* though literally "seven defects," is best translated "many defects." The Japanese have always admired a white skin, and the above proverb states that the fair complexion of a woman is a redeeming feature in spite of numerous defects which she may otherwise have. It is interesting to note that when Japanese women wish to appear especially beautiful, as when a bride makes up for her wedding or a *geisha* prepares for a party, they always apply to their faces and necks a pure white paste.

Iya to atama wo tate ni furu: "Saying No! she nods her head up and down." Though verbally she declines, she gives assent with her head motions. No wonder the poor Japanese man, just like his brothers all over the world, is confused! English parallel: Maidens say "No" and mean "Yes."

Joshi to shōjin wa yashinai-gatashi: "Women and small (inferior) men are difficult to rear." In this proverb the Chinese philosopher, Confucius, expressed the difficulty of preventing women and servants from being too familiar. The problem is how to show them due love and consideration, while still insisting that they keep at a respectful distance as inferiors.

Kagami kumoreba kokoro ga kumoru: "When the mirror is foggy the heart is cloudy." This saying refers to the belief that female chastity is symbolized in the highly polished face of a mirror. In ancient Japan all mirrors were metal and were highly prized by women as their most important possession.

Kagami to misao wa onna no motsubeki mono: "A mirror and chastity are two things a woman must have."

Kajin hakumei: "A fair woman is unfortunate." Her beauty makes it difficult to keep out of trouble. See *"Bijin hakumei,"* p. 263.

Katami koso ima wa ada nari: "What was indeed a keepsake (of him) is now an empty thing." Love tokens sometimes become meaningless.

Kawari-yasuki wa onna no kokoro: "Easily changed is a woman's heart." English parallel: Woman is fickle.

Miyama no sakura: "A hidden beauty." (Lit., "Cherry blossoms in the recesses of a mountain.") The comparison is to a beautiful woman of whom few know.

Momo kuri sannen, goke ichinen: "Peach and chestnut trees take three years to bear fruit, but a widow remains so for a year only."

Mushi ga tsuku: "To be injured by insects (worms)." This phrase is used to describe a girl whose character has suffered by having a secret lover. On the contrary, a girl carefully watched over by her parents for the sake of her chastity is called "a girl kept in a box" *("hako ire musume,"* q.v.), where worms and insects (i.e., secret lovers) cannot harm her.

Mushi mo korosanu kao wo shite iru: "She is utterly harmless and innocent." (Lit., "She looks as if she would not kill even a worm [insect].") English parallel: She looks as if butter would not melt in her mouth.

Musume zakari: "A flourishing young woman." (Lit., "A young woman in her bloom.") That is, she is in the flower of maidenhood.

Musume nihachi: "Sweet sixteen." (Lit., "A young woman two eights!")

Naku semi yori nakanu hotaru ga mi wo kogasu: "A silent consuming passion." (Lit., "Unlike the singing cicadas, the silent fireflies burn themselves.") This proverb is often applied to a woman deep in love. She is silent, but the flames of desire consume her.

Nikui, nikui wa kawaii no ura: " 'It's hateful, it's hateful' is the other side of, 'It's lovable!' " In Japan, as in all the world over, women often say the opposite of what they mean.

Onna hideri wa nai: "There is no scarcity of women." (Lit., "There is no woman drought.") Since there is no lack of women, men will find plenty who are willing to marry them.

Onna kashikoi shite ushi wo urezu: "The shrewdness of the woman fails to sell the ox." Women are not good at business ventures.

Onna no chie wa hana no saki: "A woman's wisdom is at the end of her nose." The meaning is that a woman is intuitive and impulsive but not very wise.

Onna no fu-wa wa otoko no sensō wo umu: "The disagreements of women give birth to the wars of men."

Onna no kami no ke wa daizo wo tsunagaru: "A hair from the head of a woman can tie a large elephant." That is, a beautiful woman has great fascinating power. English parallel: One hair of a maiden's head pulls harder than ten yoke of oxen.

Onna no kokoro wa neko no me: "A woman's heart is as changeable as the eyes of a cat."

Onna no nenriki wa iwa wo mo tōsu: "A woman's will power will pierce even a rock."

Onna no ichinen iwa wo mo tōsu: "A woman's wholehearted desire will pierce even a rock."

Onna no sarujie: "The monkey wisdom of a woman." This is the abbreviated form of the next proverb.

Onna no chie wa saru-jie: "A woman's wisdom is monkey wisdom." This saying is a slighting reference to a woman's intelligence, which is likened to a cunning but shallow-witted ape.

Onna sannin yoreba kashimashii: "Women are born chatterboxes." (Lit., "Three women together make it noisy.") The Chinese ideograph for woman, when arranged in a group of three, forms the ideograph for "noisy" *("kashimashii")*.

Onna uji nakushite tama no koshi: "A woman without lineage may ride in a jeweled palanquin." That is, a very beautiful low-born woman may sometimes marry a nobleman or acquire a wealthy husband. English parallel: A woman of no birth may marry into the purple.

Onna wa koware-mono: "Women are fragile things." They must be handled with care. English parallel: Daughters are brittle ware.

Onna wa kuchi ga ōi: "Women are talkative." (Lit., "A woman has numerous mouths.") The idiomatic phrase *"kuchi ga ōi"* means "to have many mouths" or "to be talkative." English parallel: One tongue is enough for two women.

Onna wa kuchi-saga-nashi: "Women are gossipy." (Lit., "Women have mouths of no natural quality.") They love to talk scandal and are evil tongued.

Onna wa ma-mono: "Woman is a bewitching creature." (Lit., "Women are devilish things.") Through their evil influence, they have been the ruin of many men.

Onna wa onna dōshi: "Women should associate with women."

(Lit., "Women with fellow-women.") Since women are different
from men in their sentiments and ability, they should form a sep-
arate group. The above proverb was early used as an argument
against coeducation.

Onna was sangai ni ie nashi: "Woman has no home in the three
worlds." This proverb of Chinese origin, indicates that women have
no home of their own except their father's or their husband's home.
The "three worlds" or states of existence in Buddhist lore are: "the
world of desire," "the world of form," and "the world of formless-
ness," roughly corresponding to the worlds of the past, present, and
future. Because of the influence of Buddhism in Japan, women do
not receive the gallantry they do in the West, for they are deemed
creatures whose sinful nature is contemptible.

Onna yamome ni hana ga saku, otoko yamome ni uji ga waku:
"Widows bear flowers, widowers breed maggots." This familiar
proverb points to the fact that widows always keep themselves at-
tractive and remarry very soon, while widowers are often slovenly
and untidy in their habits.

Rinki nashi onna wa hazumi-naki mari: "A woman without
jealousy is like a ball without bounce." A certain amount of jealousy
makes women more interesting and attractive.

Ryōte ni hana: "Flowers in both hands." This expression was
originally applied to men who possessed both learning and talent. In
more recent times the phrase has acquired the meaning of "having
two paramours at the same time," or "being accompanied by two
fair women at the same time."

Sanjū goke wa tachi-nikui: "It is difficult for a widow at thirty
to remain so." The Japanese reason that a woman at thirty, having
reached the full development of her sexual life, cannot generally
remain unmarried when at this age she loses her husband.

Sanjū furisode, shijū shimada: "Long swing sleeves at thirty,
shimada-style coiffure at forty." This saying is a shaft aimed at women
who make themselves ridiculous by dressing and acting much young-
er than their age, since *shimada*-style hairdressing and long sleeves
are only for young girls.

Shichinin no ko wo nasu tomo, onna ni kokoro wo yurusu na:

"Don't give your heart over to a woman, even though she has borne you seven children." This warning against reposing full confidence in a wife is based on the Buddhist doctrine of the lecherous nature of woman.

Sode no hinu no wa onna no mi: "To have a thousand wettings of the sleeves is a woman's lot." When crying, Japanese women generally wiped away their tears with the inside lining of their long sleeves, before the use of handkerchiefs came into vogue. In feudal times women were treated very unkindly by men and were socially in an inferior position.

Tateba shakuyaku, suwareba botan, ayumu sugata wa yuri no hana: "Standing, she is a herbaceous peony; sitting, a tree peony; her manner of walking, like a lily." A radiant beauty is thus described. Both the herbaceous peony and the tree peony are noted in Japan for their exquisite flowers.

Tora yori osoroshii hijirimen: "More fearful than a tiger is scarlet silk-crepe." Scarlet silk-crepe is used in Japan for a woman's undergarments. Hence, to be with a woman who is undressed is a fearful thing for a man who tries to lead a strict moral life.

Yome, tōme, kasa no uchi: "Seen at night, seen at a distance, or under a paper umbrella (make women look to advantage)." Girls and women are thought to appear more beautiful under the above three circumstances.

Yowaki mono yo, nanji no na wa onna nari: "Oh ye weak things, your name is woman." The Japanese is a direct translation of the English proverb: Frailty, thy name is woman.

Yūjo no makoto to tamago no shikaku wa nai: "A harlot with sincerity and a square egg do not exist."

INDEX